Praise for *Predicting Events wi*

"Even astrologers who understand and use the tools of transits and predictions can't always explain it well. Some can, and Celeste Teal is one of them... What is really interesting to me is not so much the simplicity and directness of the explanations and examples, but the fact that the author manages to cover so much ground."

—*American Astrology*

"... Teal presents this complex subject in such clear terms, using poignant examples that can be easily mastered. This is a top-notch how-to manual suitable for anyone interested in making accurate forecasts. Highly readable, easy to grasp and filled with case histories, this book illustrates the best techniques in modern astrology."

—*Dell Horoscope*

"... The author has developed a nice, easy way to guide the reader into some of the finer points of moving the static horoscope forward. Quite a lot of good information is packed into this book."

—*Aspects Magazine*

"Whether you're interested in astrology or not, this book is essential. The pace is like a suspense novel, with chart examples inserted at exactly the right points, with smooth prose that makes for easy reading and accessibility. I learned more from this book than I have from virtually any other book in my astrological library."

—Trish MacGregor, author of *Your Intuitive Moon*

Predicting Events
with Astrology

About the Author

Celeste Teal (Arizona) has been a passionate student of astrology for nearly thirty years. A graduate of the West Coast College of Astrology in Westminster, California, in basic and advanced courses, she attained professional certification in 1986. Teal is a member of the American Federation of Astrologers and the Arizona Society of Astrologers. Besides hosting her popular astrology website, The Moon Valley Astrologer, she writes feature articles for popular astrology magazines, including *Dell Horoscope, American Astrology* (now called *Horoscope Guide*), and *Astrology: Your Daily Horoscope*. Celeste Teal has authored four previous books on astrological techniques: *Predicting Events with Astrology* (1999), *Identifying Planetary Triggers* (2000), *Eclipses* (2006), and *Lunar Nodes* (2008), all published by Llewellyn Publications.

To Write to the Author

If you wish to contact the author or would like more information about this book, please write to the author in care of Llewellyn Worldwide, and we will forward your request. Both the author and publisher appreciate hearing from you and learning of your enjoyment of this book and how it has helped you. Llewellyn Worldwide cannot guarantee that every letter written to the author can be answered, but all will be forwarded. Please write to:

Celeste Teal
℅ Llewellyn Worldwide
2143 Wooddale Drive
Woodbury, MN 55125-2989

Please enclose a self-addressed stamped envelope for reply,
or $1.00 to cover costs. If outside U.S.A., enclose
an international postal reply coupon.

Many of Llewellyn's authors have websites with additional information and resources. For more information, please visit our website at http://www.llewellyn.com.

Predicting Events with Astrology

Revised and Expanded Edition

Celeste Teal

Llewellyn Publications
Woodbury, Minnesota

First Edition
Fourth Printing, 2014

Cover art © Grant Faint/Photographer's Choice/PunchStock
Cover design by Ellen Dahl
Editing by Connie Hill
Llewellyn is a registered trademark of Llewellyn Worldwide Ltd.

Chart wheels were created using Solar Fire Gold by Esoteric Technoligies PTY Ltd, published by Astrolabe, Inc., www.alabe.com.

The material in chapter 1, pp 11–20, was first featured in the August 1997 issue of *Horoscope Magazine*. Copyright Dell Horoscope. The material in chapter 7, pp 140–151, was first published in the September 2007 issue of *Horoscope Magazine*. Copyright Dell Horoscope.

Library of Congress Cataloging-in-Publication Data
Teal, Celeste, 1951–
  Predicting events with astrology / Celeste Teal. — revised and expanded ed.
    p.   cm.
  Includes bibliographical references and index.
  ISBN 978-0-7387-1553-7
  1. Predictive astrology. I. Title.
  BF1720.5.T43   2009
  133.5—c22   2009036583

Llewellyn Publications
A Division of Llewellyn Worldwide Ltd.
2143 Wooddale Drive
Woodbury, Minnesota 55125-2989
www.llewellyn.com

Printed in the United States of America

Other Books by Celeste Teal

Identifying Planetary Triggers

Eclipses

Lunar Nodes

*To Shell: thank you for getting me stirred up
enough against astrology to open a book and find my calling.*

*Also dedicated with love and appreciation to my husband
for his support and faith in me;
and to my sons, Abe and Zack,
whose encouragement has always meant so much.*

Acknowledgments

A special acknowledgment goes to those whose charts are featured in this work. Thanks for allowing me to tell your stories and for taking the time and effort to recall personal experiences with such detail. In many cases this was a difficult task, and the world of astrology is in your debt for what it might learn from your experiences.

Acknowledgment also goes to all of those astrologers—past, present, and future—who have or will contribute to the storehouse of astrological knowledge. That is my intention in this work. Acknowledgment especially goes to the great Evangeline Adams for being a source of inspiration, to her teacher Dr. Heber Smith for his insightful essay on aspects, and to Ronald C. Davison for his masterful teaching.

Contents

Part Two: The Return Charts

Part Three: The Planets & Other Points

Chart Data

Unless otherwise specified, chart data was obtained from the birth certificates of the individuals whose stories appear. While chart information is provided, names have been changed for purposes of privacy except when requested otherwise.

Chapter Five

Chapter Six

Chapter Seven

Introducing the Prediction Techniques

The purpose of this book is to provide some of the most complete and workable methods for predicting events based on the birth chart. Much research and time have gone into the preparation of this work, and technical points are explored in depth and in such a way as to fill a gap in the current available material on the keys to prediction. Many finer points in delineation are illustrated throughout this work and will be appreciated by the serious student of astrology.

Care has been taken in writing this material to ensure that the reader is always aware that the individual has free will, and that the planetary combinations only reflect current conditions. Because the individual tends toward particular strengths and weaknesses, as shown in the birth horoscope, the reoccurring planetary configurations are usually accurate in reflecting a time when the inherent issues surface, as well as the individual's probable response to conditions and circumstances.

The planets are impartial, though of a specific nature and vibration. Because individuals differ, the response to the same type of planetary energies will differ from one person to another. The natal chart is what holds this key, and the astrologer must be aware of this before attempting to make a forecast. For example, if the natal chart shows loss through speculation, then a lucky transit means little in regard to gambling. It is more likely that the individual will feel that she or he can win, takes a risk, and experiences a loss instead. However, in a chart indicating gain through speculation, the same lucky transit could be predictive of a big win. So, the natal horoscope must always be used as a foundation and in conjunction with subsequent charts. Chapters 3 through 9 cover a variety of topics and how to find the potential for love, money, health, and so forth.

Promise & Potential

We are all created as equals in the fact that we are provided with what we need to progress in our own spiritual evolution during the current lifetime. This is shown in the natal chart and each one holds the potential for a lifetime of study. This is the individual map of the heavens, and it is what sets apart each individual from every other. To discard or ignore some of the qualities is to surrender a vital part of one's self. A soul is completed by the combination of a myriad of factors—some are admirable and some are not so admirable. Sometimes, a quirk in the personal nature, revealed by the horoscope configurations, is also the root of special talent. What appears initially to be the greatest liability may later prove to be the finest asset. In order for soul growth to be attained, each part must somehow be integrated and given direction. It is up to the individual to accomplish this task, and astrology shows the way.

Fortunate and unfortunate events occasionally occur that seem to have no connection whatsoever to actions taken by the individual. In these cases, it appears as if the person is either the lucky recipient of a miracle or an unsuspecting victim. These types of events are also reflected in the horoscope, and the timing of them can be found in the charts. In the case of an accident or reversal, it will usually be seen that the planet in the individual's chart that describes the event will be harshly aspected (in difficult relationship to another planet) at the time. The individual might have been repressing or misdirecting some particular energy at the time, inadvertently attracting harm. In the case of miraculous events that benefit the individual, there will undoubtedly be superb aspects (fortunate relationships) involving the Sun, Jupiter, or Venus. In either case, the potential can still be traced to the nativity.

Only when both progressions and transits stimulate a pattern from the nativity will an important event occur. The bigger the event, the more stimulated the patterns in the nativity will be, whether for good or ill. For a major event to take place, it will be clearly evident by the number of repeating planetary links to those found in the nativity. Delineation of several dozen charts illustrates this point.

If the astrologer is adept at forecasting, the information gathered from a study of the aspects can be extremely useful, allowing his or her client to prepare for conditions, to be aware of the potential, and to respond in the wisest and most appropriate way.

Chart Calculation Techniques

For this work, the Tropical Zodiac and the Placidus House systems are used. The natal horoscope is the main point of reference. It is occasionally referred to as the radical chart or the radix. It occupies the inner wheel throughout the illustrations in Part One, unaltered in any way. This natal horoscope should be calculated based on accurate and precise birth data including the time, date, and location of birth. Precision is a must to predict accurately. Even a few minutes off can cause subsequent charts to be unreliable.

Although it is not necessary, for purposes of efficiency, computer calculations are recommended. Time is valuable and several charts may be used in conjunction in some of the following techniques.

Astrological Clock

Since the astrologer is human and can make mistakes in entering data for a computer to calculate, all data should be double-checked before beginning a reading. A slight error among the coordinates can greatly alter subsequent charts. One basic tool helps to check work. The astrological clock system can be used to find the Sun's position at any hour, therefore providing the basis for the rest of the chart. In case of accidentally entering a PM time instead of AM, knowing this system makes the mistake quite apparent. It is also handy for mentally figuring a rough chart when someone gives the birth data.

In this system, two-hour time intervals are assigned to each of the house cusps. The 1st house cusp becomes 6:00 AM (sunrise), the 4th house cusp is 12:00 AM (midnight), the 10th house cusp is 12:00 PM (noon), and the 7th house cusp is 6:00 PM (sunset). Thus, the 2nd house cusp is 4:00 AM, the 3rd house cusp is 2:00 AM, and so on around the wheel.

The Sun will bring its sign to the area of the chart that holds the time of birth. Let's say the given birth time is noon. At noon, the Sun is overhead, so whatever sign the Sun is in will be overhead at noon, on the 10th house cusp.

Secondary Progressions

Secondary Progressions take priority in foretelling events, since they reflect conditions for the individual at any time in question. They describe the unfolding natal potential. While the natal chart shows the influences under which a person is born and themes that will play out over a lifetime, it does not show when a particular influence or set of conditions will come

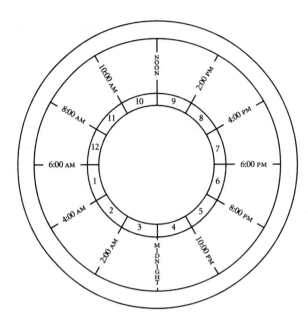

Figure 0a: The Astrological Clock

about. It is the progressions that set the stage for potential events, showing detailed conditions and circumstances for a particular time frame according to the aspects formed between progressed and natal planets or between two progressed planets.

The progressed aspects show the "plot" of a story and lay the foundation for the types of events that will be triggered by the transits. Secondary progressions are known as the day for a year method. The motion of the planets each day after birth is symbolic of their progressed position for an equal number of years of life. This chart is placed around the birth chart to

easily see the aspects. The progressed chart is calculated for the birthplace, or for the current residence. While the relocated progressed chart may yield valuable insights, progressing the chart to the birthplace works very well for all practical purposes. All of the charts presented here show the birthplace progressions for ease in reproducing the charts.

Part One of this work is dedicated to delineation of the progressed chart at times of specific and important events in the lives of various individuals. The illustrations allow students to master this technique.

Transits

Transits refer to the currently transiting planets, first of all, as they energize the house of the natal chart that they are transiting, and secondly as they form aspects to planets and important points in the natal and progressed chart. The transiting planets describe activity related to the matters of the house they are transiting, according to their nature.

The transits are very predictive of events when used in combination with the progressed chart. It is not enough to assume that because a transiting planet forms an aspect to a natal planet that any major event will take place based on the nature of the two. That is why relying only on descriptions of the transits is often inaccurate or overstated. Unless there is a theme presented in the progressions for the transits to stimulate, a simple transit may go by with hardly any notice.

The transits are used in conjunction with the progressions and are presented and detailed as they relate to specific events. They are positioned in the outermost wheel, around the natal and progressed charts. At times of major events, there are frequently two or more exact aspects from outer transiting planets to natal or progressed places.

Solar & Lunar Returns

A Solar Return chart or Solar Revolution is calculated for the precise time the Sun returns to its birth position. Since this represents a major life cycle, the new configurations of that chart take on exceptional meaning, and can be read as indicative of the coming year. The new chart is read in much the same way as a natal chart, except it is only for one year. The Solar Return chart is read with the natal planets inserted since the natal potential must be considered. Alternately, the natal chart wheel is placed around the return.

The Lunar Return is a chart calculated for the moment in time that the Moon returns to its natal position. This occurs approximately every twenty-eight days, and the resulting chart can be used to effectively forecast the next four weeks. It is read very similarly to a natal chart except that it is reflective only of the next four weeks. Return charts are calculated for the current place of residence.

Part Two goes into detail on the returns, where actual events are illustrated. Precessed and non-precessed calculation methods are discussed, as well as direct and converse motion returns.

Eclipses & the Nodes

Eclipses and the transiting nodes of the Moon are extremely valuable for predicting events. If an eclipse occurs very near to a sensitive degree in the natal chart, a process is set into motion that will show related events when the degree is transited by important planets. This may last for several months or even years in some cases. The amount of time depends on the type of eclipse and the length of time the eclipse lasts. The nodes also bring a tremendous emphasis to any planet they are near, whether natal, progressed, or transiting.

Chapter 15 is dedicated to eclipses and the nodes, which are presented and commented on throughout the delineation of charts when active. In addition, a table of eclipses from the year 1900 through 2050 has been carefully tabulated and conveniently located at the end of that chapter.

Horary

Horary is a method used to answer an important and pressing question. The calculation for the chart is based on the time the astrologer receives and understands the question from an individual who has a deep need for the answer. A most rigid type of chart to read, it is usually used to answer yes or no. Rules must be followed perfectly in obtaining the answer, and subjectivity destroys the ability to read the chart. The concept behind the Horary chart is that strong vibrations are present at the time an important question is formed in the mind of the individual. Therefore, the answer to the question also lies in the heavenly configurations at that moment.

Some very basic Horary techniques are used in this work when appropriate. The Ascendant of the current transiting chart is combined with the natal and progressed charts to gain insights. This is called the Horary Ascendant. For instance, if an individual's chart is to be studied for the present configurations, the moment the astrologer first becomes inclined to look into the chart will reveal otherwise overlooked detail when using this method. If answering a question for someone, the time of that question is used, and so on. The first natal planet to rise to this new Horary Ascendant becomes important in establishing the foremost events likely to transpire in the life of the individual. These concepts will be presented and commented on in various delineations throughout this work.

Special Points

Investigation into some finer points, such as the Aries Point, proves it deserving of special notice for predicting events. The zero degree of any cardinal sign is representative of some entanglement with the world at large. The Pleiades, a fixed star group in the last degree of Taurus, is sometimes prominent at the time of misfortune. These special points along with the Vertex, which is a point of fate and destiny, and a condition called Saturn Chasing the Moon, are presented and commented on in delineation throughout this work. These keys to prediction are also given special attention in Part Three.

Terminology

There may be certain instances when wording is used that appears to give the planets power. This is done only in an attempt to more particularly describe the personal signature of that planet. The old classifications of the planets as benefic or malefic, and aspects as good or bad have been rightly discarded when it comes to natal astrology and character analysis. But, when it comes to forecasting events with accuracy, the old classifications apply. Tragedies do not coincide with favorable aspects among the benefic planets, and fortunes do not come from difficult aspects among the malefic planets. The classic literature is replete with terms that invoke very specific images.

For example, the term *benefic* is used to describe Venus and Jupiter because of their beneficial nature. They bring benefits: joy, gains, credit, and praise. They are prominent in the chart and involved in nice aspects when happy occasions come about. On the other hand, Mars and Saturn are described in the classics as *malefic* in nature. They are prominent during bad spells; they coincide with bad spells; they coincide with accidents, suffering, loss, and when upsetting or limiting conditions exist, situations we prefer to avoid.

When two malefic planets come into a harsh aspect with one another, this signifies a critical and trying period. Classic astrologers go so far as to label certain aspect combinations as evil. Mars in square with Saturn or Uranus are among these. The former suggests that willful actions could lead to a reversal, while the latter indicates sudden unexpected developments. These aspects require careful handling to avoid ruin, ridicule, accident, or loss, so such an aspect is otherwise known as an affliction.

Students will learn to identify such features as an "afflicted benefic on an angle," which suggests distress, or "dis-ease." The benefic planet represents ease and harmony so that if it is prominent by being on an angle, the cusp of the 1st, 4th, 7th, or 10th houses, while at the same time receiving harsh aspects, conditions are such that there's an interference to harmony, causing temporary dis-ease, which may come in the form of an actual illness, or through grief or loss.

By calling the aspects for what they represent, one is in an excellent position to judge the chart, to forecast with accuracy, and to find ways for the individual to use his or her free will to solve or step out of the way of encroaching problems. The insights of the astrologer can help an individual access the necessary spirit to navigate life.

PART ONE

Secondary Progressions

chapter one

Preliminary Techniques & Delineation of the Progressed Chart

One of the best methods for predicting trends and events is by utilizing Secondary Progressions. The progressed horoscope is most instrumental in determining the type and time of an event. It shows how the life is progressing according to the planetary aspects in force at any specified time. The planets change position very slowly in progressions, and, therefore, an aspect formed between a progressed planet or point with a planet in the nativity is significant, revealing current conditions. When the influences of the progressions are combined with those of the transiting planets a wealth of information is provided. Transits of the planets are more powerful when they make contacts involving the progressed aspects or points than if they are only contacting natal points. They trigger developments promised in the progressions.

The Secondary Progression method employs the assumption that a day of planetary transits equals one year of life. Simply put, if you wanted to find out the trends that are current in the life of someone who is twenty years old, you would look up the positions of the planets for the twentieth day after birth. This gets more complicated when you want a reading for a point in time that is midway between two birthdays, but it can still be done, and computer programs calculate it easily. Certainly, computer calculations are recommended for the Secondary Progressions in order to accurately calculate the progressed Ascendant and Midheaven.

Obviously, the progressing outer planets will not change position very much over a lifetime. The progressing inner planets move along slowly, and their speed depends on how close they were to a stationary point at the time of birth. The progressing Sun always moves forward at the rate of about a degree a year (a degree per day), and the progressing Moon, which moves the most quickly, still takes two and a half years to progress through one whole sign. It progresses forward approximately one degree per month. The progressed Moon position can only be counted on to give accurate timing information when the exact time of birth is known.

Because of these minute movements, each aspect made by the progressed planets to the birth planets are extremely significant, but for the same reason the orbs must be kept very tight. One degree of orb is recommended in most cases. Major aspects within the one-degree orb describe current influences. For instance, let's say that progressed Mercury is coming up to make a conjunction to the natal Venus. The time period in which Mercury is within one degree approaching Venus until one degree past Venus is the time during which the aspect will manifest an influence. This would be for a period of about two to three years when the individual could expect more social contacts

and an accelerated lifestyle, even if the two were not in aspect at birth.

In respect to an aspect made between two outer planets, the orb may need to be reduced to less than one degree. Especially if one or both planets were near stationary at birth, an aspect might remain within a one-degree orb over a large portion of the life and would need the assistance of several other similar indicators at the same time to produce notable activity. The aspect describes more of a way of life.

The Sun and Moon can be given an orb of about one and a half degrees due to the personal nature of their influences. In the case of the progressing Sun, this means that each contact made is going to be within orb for about three years altogether. For the Moon, which progresses about a degree a month, the influence of its aspects will be felt for about three months. Tracking the motion of the progressed Moon usually reveals that its aspect to natal planets or to other progressed planets acts as a trigger for significant happenings. It also functions as a mood gauge, showing the tempo of daily life.

A factor that should not be overlooked in working with progressions is when the angles of the chart are involved with a planet. This means that either the natal Ascendant or Midheaven forms an aspect with a progressed planet, or that the progressed Midheaven or progressed Ascendant is in aspect to either a natal or progressed planet. These contacts have top priority when interpreting the chart. They show times of change, going in new directions, and life-altering experiences, according to the planet and angle involved.

The indications of an active Midheaven are similar to those of an active Sun, and involve some of the outermost aspects of life. The reputation and status, as well as professional concerns and dealings with authorities, are some of the areas likely to be affected. The Midheaven is active when the public reputation, the vocation, and/or issues involving one's honor are at hand.

The Ascendant indicates more personal and private issues, and in this regard it is similar to the Moon. Domestic and family issues become a focal point during active phases of the Ascendant. Aspects to the progressed Ascendant are most personally significant and should head the list of angular aspects.

To set up the charts from which to make a forecast, I recommend using a three-wheel chart. The natal chart should be in the innermost wheel, with the progressed chart and transiting planets outside of it. Note the degree of the progressed Midheaven and progressed Ascendant and don't overlook the nodes, as you will find later that they also are very important.

First of all, make a list of any contacts involving one of the angles as described previously, since these will have the most noticeable impact. The more aspects involving the angles, the more potential there is for eventful times. The aspects can be interpreted the same way as you would a natal chart, however the effects are more condensed. The effects may be felt more intensely, but for a shorter period of time than someone who has the aspect in their natal chart.

Identify the ruler of the progressed Ascendant sign, and note its aspects. This is the personal planetary ruler and its aspects reveal where a person is going and the kinds of experiences he or she will meet with.

The next list to make is aspects involving the Sun, either natal or progressed. Then list aspects involving the *natal* Moon, and then aspects of each remaining planet; natal and progressed. Any natal planet of prominence should be given extra attention. An angular planet or one that makes many contacts would fall in this group as well as the natal chart ruler and any planet that is part of a stellium. Last, list the aspects the progressed Moon will form in the coming year and when. It moves about a degree per month.

Timing Successful Changes

To illustrate these techniques, I've chosen the chart of Evangeline Adams. She was born February 8, 1868, at 8:30 AM in Jersey City, NJ. In her book, *The Bowl of Heaven*, she says that she chose the middle of March 1899 to move from Boston to New York and make her life there as a professional astrologer. She explains that she chose this time because she had seen in her chart the most favorable conditions coming up that she would have in her life, and that they were especially favorable for her astrology.[1]

In her progressed chart drawn for March 16, 1899, the things she said are only too easy to see. Although Pluto had not yet been discovered and she was not aware of it, her progressed Ascendant is advancing rapidly, nearing her Pluto. It suggests a milestone, a turning point, and the potential to have a very powerful impact on the world through her personality. It is indicative of partings and self-initiated changes. She takes command of her life.

The next series of contacts are magnificent. Her progressed Ascendant is sextile her Jupiter. This raises her ambitions, strengthens her self-confidence, and should bring her some distinction. She can form favorable associations with authorities or those who can help her advance. The Sun and Jupiter, two beneficial planets, have progressed to form a conjunction, and both are approaching the one-degree orb of conjunction to her natal Venus. How could anything go wrong with

these three combined?! Venus is her new ruler, ruling her progressed Ascendant in Taurus. She is well protected and the stars are shining benevolently on Evangeline. Additionally, all three planets are near the natal Ascendant, so that by the time the progressed Sun has moved out of orb of either Jupiter or Venus, it will conjunct the Ascendant. Progressing Jupiter is moving along swiftly and will also reach the Ascendant within a few years. Undoubtedly, Evangeline was eying those aspects involving Jupiter and the Sun as especially favorable.

There are two afflictions in the progressions, including a square of progressed Mars to natal Saturn. This aspect suggests there would be some frustration and setbacks in regard to relocating. It is descriptive of the hostility of the first hotel proprietor who was unfriendly to her astrology. Evangeline describes how the first place she chose to rent a room was unsuccessful due to the proprietor's dislike of astrology practice. Progressed Mars is conjunct progressed South Node, so there are some conflicts or troubles through male associations, even danger of accidents, likely coming through a male association. While these aspects will be seen to manifest in the events that led to her overnight fame, their influences will be negligible when weighed against her favorable aspects. Even the next major aspect the progressed Moon

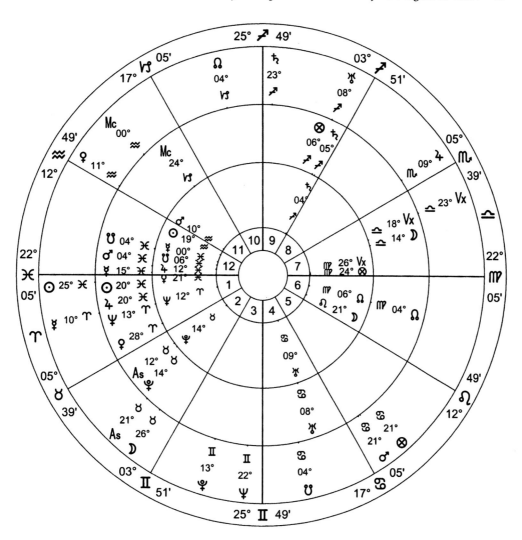

Figure 1a: Evangeline Adams Progressed Chart
Center Wheel: E. Adams Natal Chart: Feb. 8, 1868; 8:30 AM LMT; 74W05, 40N44
Middle Wheel: Progressed Chart; Mar. 16, 1899; 8:30 AM LMT; 74W05, 40N44
Outer Wheel: Transit Chart: Mar. 16, 1899; 8:30 AM EST; 74W05, 40N44

will form is a trine to her natal Sun, excellent for women in business and bringing gains through associations with those of a high or respected position.

Here is a review of Evangeline's major progressed aspects:

- Progressed Ascendant nearing Pluto suggests the desire and ability to improve her circumstances.

- Progressed Ascendant sextile her Jupiter shows a rise in life, financial gain, and social advantages.

- Progressed Midheaven trine natal Part of Fortune suggests professional advancement.

- Progressed Sun conjunct progressed Jupiter denotes success, good fortune, good health, and gains through influential people. It is favorable for new undertakings, for travel, and for making associations.

- Progressed Sun conjunct natal Venus denotes bright prospects, new friends, gratified emotions, blissful feelings, and the pursuit of happiness.

- Progressed Jupiter conjunct natal Venus shows peace, happiness, financial gains, and social success.

- Progressed Mars conjunct South Node suggests danger of accidents.

- Progressed Mars in square to natal Saturn indicates a critical and trying period that necessitates caution and self-control to avoid discord, disputes, or other turbulence.

- Her overall progressed themes lean toward credits and gains.

The next step is to look at the transiting planets. As mentioned earlier, when the transiting planets make a contact to a progressed planet or point or to a natal placement that is also involved in a progressed aspect, the effects are more powerful than if they are only contacting the natal planet. The orbs of the transiting planets can be wider although their aspects will be close at eventful times.

In Evangeline's chart, the transiting Sun has just entered her 1st house near the configuration involving the progressed Sun, progressed Jupiter, and natal Venus on the Ascendant. The Sun is sextile her progressed Midheaven. This may have told her the day to embark on her journey. Mars is transiting in trine to the progressed grouping, providing energy, confidence, assertiveness, and luck; excellent for advancing her interests. Saturn is approaching a conjunction to the natal Midheaven, indicating professional rewards from past hard work and preparations. Saturn is square her natal Ascendant, testing relationships and timing the end of some of them. It is trine her natal Moon though, an excellent time to implement personal or business changes. Neptune is square her natal Ascendant and Venus, introducing some confusion and a transitional phase in her life direction, but its sextile to natal Moon increases her intuitive faculties and helps offset any difficulties of the square. Transiting Uranus in the 9th house is near natal Saturn. By wide orb, it stimulates the square of Saturn to progressed Mars/South Node so there are some accidental conditions present.

With the transiting Sun coming to conjunct such a powerful group, a climax of activity could be expected. On this day, transiting Mars in trine lends power to the configuration, increases potential gains from new ventures and she is highly motivated to initiate them. Transiting Sun in sextile to the progressed Midheaven shows her good choice in timing to further her career. Honor and achievement are indicated. Even the transiting Moon trines her progressed Midheaven on one side and her natal Part of Fortune/Vertex on the other side as she departs from Boston to relocate in New York. She is personally protected, but there is potential to have an unusual or unexpected brush with danger in her travels.

Her chart indicators easily conform to the rule of three similar aspects needed to foretell an event. This rule must be adhered to when interpreting the chart.

Either for good or bad, one aspect is not enough to foretell an event. There will always be several indications of a like nature for an event to transpire.

Ms. Adams used both the progressions and the transits. She saw ahead of time that she could be successful at this time, so she waited and when the time was right, she capitalized on it, becoming an overnight success when she reached New York. Her book tells the whole story of how the second proprietor who rented her a room was fascinated with astrology and had her give him a reading that same evening. She saw so much misfortune coming to him in the immediate future that it frightened her. She warned him and asked about two previous times in his life when he had been under similar conditions. He recalled that there had been minor fires on both occasions. And, it happened again. That night and well into the next day, which was St. Patrick's Day, the Windsor Hotel burned to the ground. Many of the proprietor's family members and friends were killed, including his favorite daughter. Evangeline, being on the first floor, was lucky to escape without injury. The proprietor told the newspaper reporters about Evangeline's astrological reading, and she was on her way to fame, although she wasn't happy about the circumstances that brought it about.

Converse Progressions

There is an additional step that will throw even more light on a reading, and this is by using Converse Progressions. Converse Progressions are identical to the Secondary Progressions, except that they are calculated in reverse to a point in time before birth that is equivalent to the same day after birth. To find the converse positions of the planets for someone aged twenty, you count backward to the twentieth day prior to birth. The better computer programs will do this for you. The same can be done with the transits by subtracting the age in years and days from the date of birth. Even though these converse planetary positions are different than the forward-moving ones, the overall picture shows similar themes.

The two progressed charts can be compared to see what contacts are made between a converse progressed planet and a forward-motion progressed planet or a converse transit that connects with a forward-motion progressed planet. Unless your charts are set up in a very organized manner, this can easily become overwhelming, so I recommend doing them separately first and making the list of aspects before combining the two. For the same reason, the second technique is best used to verify and expand on themes found in the first set of progressions and transits.

For example, in Evangeline's chart, her converse progressed Moon is conjunct the cusp of the natal 4th house, often coinciding with the time of a move. The converse progressed Sun and Mars are within a one and a half degree orb of conjunction, which stresses new enterprises and fresh starts in accordance with the life purpose. This converse conjunction is trine the forward-motion progressed Ascendant/Pluto, showing that her personally motivated actions could further these interests. Transiting Sun favorably stimulates the configuration. Converse progressed Mars is sextile forward-motion progressed Mercury, giving resourcefulness and initiative in handling her affairs. Converse transiting Saturn forms nice aspects to them.

The converse progressed Mercury is opposing natal Uranus, showing the unusual events linked with travel. This aspect may have given more trouble without the multitude of aspects assisting at the time. However, in Evangeline's chart, the fact that natal Uranus and Mercury are friendly, in part showing her brilliance for speaking and writing about astrology, increases the probability that any later contact between the two will work out to her advantage. A close contact of the two is repeated in the converse transiting Uranus

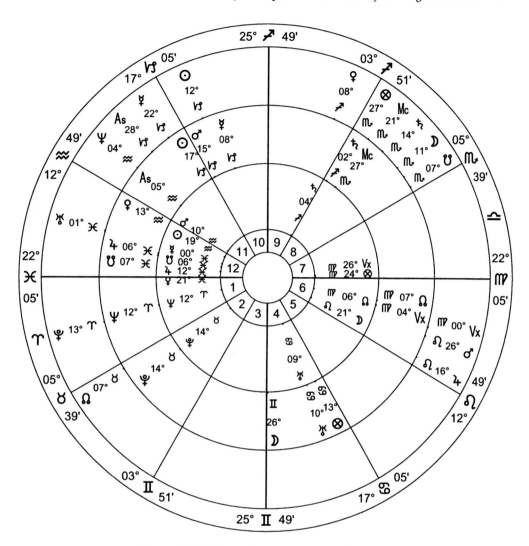

Figure 1b: E. Adams Converse Progressed Chart

Center Wheel: E. Adams Natal Chart: Feb. 8, 1868; 8:30 AM LMT, Jersey City, NJ; 74W05, 40N44

Middle Wheel: Conv. Progressed Chart: Mar. 16, 1899; 8:30 AM LMT, Jersey City, NJ; 74W05, 40N44

Outer Wheel: Conv. Transit Chart: Jan. 2, 1837; 8:30 AM LMT, Jersey City, NJ; 74W05, 40N44

conjunct her natal Mercury. It suggests the connection between her travels and her vocation, as well as her surprising experiences and her name in print as an astrologer. (The contact is repeated in forward motion transiting Mercury in square to her natal Uranus.) These influences added to her restlessness to forge changes.

The converse progressed Ascendant is sextile natal Saturn and forward-motion progressed Saturn, showing steadiness and solid achievement of a permanent nature. This Ascendant in Aquarius signifies Uranian things, such as astrology, and Saturn in the 9th house shows the travel connection, as well as her promotion and publicity through the hotel owner. Converse transiting Neptune is conjunct converse progressed Ascendant, showing a time of personal transitions. Angular Neptune, linked to the Ascendant when in nice aspect, often manifests in dreams that materialize. Converse transiting Mars is trine her natal Midheaven, nearly exact. In both sets of chart, it is Mars and the Sun acting as timers.

These charts reveal even more when taking into consideration the sign and house positions, and by continuing to check for combined contacts. The above should suffice to illustrate the value of the technique. The converse progressed chart is in no way diminished in reliability because of the reverse system of calculation.

Red Flags, Retrogrades & Other Tips for Prediction

The traditional meanings of the planets should be kept in mind when doing a forecast. Conditions applying to the benefic planets and the malefic planets will be found to signify quite different kinds of events. The Sun, Jupiter, and Venus are usually very powerful for good, while Saturn, Pluto, Mars, and (usually) Uranus tell of challenging times. Mercury is neutral. The planet in closest aspect to Mercury easily influences it. Neptune can indicate either having dreams come true or total confusion and deception since much depends on its position and aspects in the natal chart as well as the type of aspect made by the progressions. Mars and Pluto show similar types of energies, and for this reason Mars' co-rulership of the Scorpio house can give more detail. Squares from Venus do not show harm unless there is a theme formed that indicates loss or sadness. Always look for the main theme in the chart.

A chart giving indications of hard times and problems in general would have several adverse progressed aspects in orb, including afflictions to the planet ruling the progressed Ascendant, plus a couple of transiting malefic planets making close stressful aspects to important places. Increasing the troublesome phase, the progressing Moon may be forming a series of difficult aspects.

Having several transiting or progressed planets form harsh aspects to one planet in the chart is an indication of trouble in the areas ruled or occupied by the planet. If it is a natal planet, check the house ruled by the planet in the natal chart to see where trouble is brewing. If it is a progressed planet receiving afflictions, check the progressed house that the planet rules.

The natal aspect between two planets should be given priority since this will often show how a later progressed aspect of the two will work out, no matter the type of aspect.

Watch for transiting or progressed planets to go retrograde. At certain times, they may end up at their point of station while in aspect to a natal or progressed planet or point. This means the aspect will last a much longer period of time and can therefore be set off by other transiting planets for the duration of the orb. Mars' transits and stations are especially important in this regard.

The planets that usually act as a trigger are the transiting Sun and Mars. By their nature of being the planets of vitality and energy, they bring these characteristics into the chart as they transit through the houses. If they make a trine to a long lasting affliction in the progressed chart, they may bring a temporary reprieve of the associated problems. When they make a square, opposition, or conjunction, however, they can set off the whole fireworks display.

It should be mentioned here that although the Sun and Mars play such an important part in the timing of events, the Moon is nearly always found to be transiting a sensitive planet or point at the time of important events. Many times it will be angular, or another angle will be contacted, such as the nodal axis, or the Vertex/Anti-vertex.

Using the progressed Moon, and the forming aspects it will make, helps to pinpoint the timing of events when other long-term aspects are in force. Difficult themes shown in the major progressions and transits may play out during the periods of the more difficult lunar aspects, while the best of the major progressions and transits are likely to be experienced during the months that the progressed Moon aspects are more favorable. The progressed Moon contacts are all very important. The Moon oversees the daily routine and domestic situation, the general conditions at the end of the day. As the progressed Moon changes signs or houses, it brings emphasis and focus to various departments of life.

Speaking of the progressed Moon, a red flag should be noted if it comes to a point of conflict with transiting Saturn or transiting Uranus, since these are usually indications of difficult times. These are times of sadness, loss, and depression with Saturn and times of upsets, problems, and when nothing goes as planned with Uranus. Everyone faces these delays or reversals at some point, and the contacts in the progressed chart show the timing. The speeds of the progressing Moon and that of the transiting planet determine how long they will remain in aspect. If the progressed Moon is moving along quickly and Saturn slows down, ready to make a station, then the length of time of the Saturn restrictions will not be long. The rate of speed of the progressed Moon and transiting Saturn are nearly the same, so if they come into a conflicting aspect at a time when the Moon is slow in motion, they could remain in aspect for some time. In this case, illness, business, or other losses can take a toll before the aspect is out of range.

In rare cases, there can be a situation where the speed of the progressing Moon continues to equal that of the transiting Saturn. This is called "Saturn chasing the Moon" and reprieves may come seldom from what can be a depressing influence. A case comes to mind of a woman who had this aspect for many years. While there was opportunity here for soul development, she chose to escape through drugs, thus ignoring the opportunity and compounding her problems. She spent those years in a disconsolate existence, and by the time the aspect was out of range, she had a serious addiction problem. These configurations can be made to work to the advantage of the individual once its limitations are accepted. (Refer to chapter 16 for more discussion.)

With Uranus, the speed of the progressing Moon is much faster than that of the transiting planet. Therefore, the aspect will not remain for too long, but severe reversals can take place in a short amount of time with Uranus. Remain flexible and avoid activities that could lead to scandal or injure the reputation.

Transiting Pluto is another planet that can foretell domestic and personal changes that can be quite complicated and intense when it makes a stressful aspect to the progressed Moon. It is an unsettled time. If other progressed aspects agree, forceful circumstances may come from outside influences of a powerful order, and one must deal with putting things back together with what is left to work with. This influence, again, is not very long lasting since Pluto moves much more slowly than the progressing Moon. The aspect is not terribly troublesome unless the Moon and Pluto were in a stressful aspect at birth, or in conjunction and afflicted, or other progressions and transits in the same time frame are problematic.

As troubling as they can be when forming adverse aspects to the progressed Moon, transiting Saturn, Uranus, or Pluto in favorable aspect to the progressed Moon can be especially helpful. Saturn in positive aspect to the Moon is a very fortunate foundation for any action that brings slow but permanent rewards. It is a favorable time to progress in domestic and vocational affairs. Uranus brings a spark to the life, where meeting new and interesting people create scope for unexpected opportunities and an up-tempo personal life. Pluto lends energy to expend in relation to the personal and domestic life. It's an excellent time to start new projects or ventures that will improve personal and domestic conditions. Masculine figures or powerful people are often helpful.

Aspects by any of the transiting planets to the progressed Moon are informative and can be read similarly as transits to the natal Moon, though with the exception of the outer planets, the influences are fleeting. Mars in aspect to the Moon is very similar to Pluto, described above. Its adverse aspects can be especially annoying, when caution is needed to avoid conflicts. Jupiter in fortunate aspect to the Moon is a time of optimism, expansion, and travel, and for domestic, business, and financial success. Relations with women are good

and this is an all around favorable influence for personal happiness. Adverse aspects of Jupiter to the Moon may mean domestic expenses. Aspects of Venus or the Sun are similar to Jupiter. With favorable aspects from Neptune to the Moon, the intuition improves, and one becomes persuasive and more magnetic. The adverse aspects of Neptune to Moon is a misleading influence, and strange experiences may come through some woman, often the mother or wife. Travel and general changes are favorable with nice aspects from Mercury, while the reverse is the result of poor aspects.

The hard aspects highlight much the same issues, but with less positive results than in the good aspects. Here, though, it must be kept in mind that the planet's nature in general will determine how bad the results can be. The negativity associated with Jupiter, for example, would be from excess or indulgence, something that can be controlled more easily than the restrictions coming from a planet such as Saturn.

Practice and study of event charts will give a clearer understanding as to how the aspects work out in various combinations. Chapter 14 gives descriptions of the aspects.

1. Evangeline Adams, *The Bowl of Heaven* (New York: Dodd, Mead, 1926; Santa Fe: Sun Books, 1995), A Grim Success, 31–37.

chapter two

Exploring the Finer Points
of the Progressed Chart

The nativity is the primary concern when considering the present or the future. Important events will occur only when a natal pattern is stimulated through repeating links among the progressed and natal planets, followed by transits, which touch these off and reinforce the pattern. The progressed chart shows how the natal potential is working out. When transits tie in, events are produced.

Since the progressions show which natal factors are coming under stimulation, they are fundamental and basic to any further chart types. Before doing Solar Returns or any other technique, the secondary progressed chart should be studied. It offers the plot of a story and lays the foundation for possible events that can be set off by the transits. All of the aspects formed in the progressed chart must be considered, and there will usually be a theme that stands out once all of the contacts have been tabulated. Since a restricted orb is used to determine the "working" aspects, a short list usually sums up the active influences at any given time. A summary of the aspects might describe credits and gains as in Ms. Adams chart in chapter 1, or they may describe joy and happiness, praise and honors, suffering and loss, or blame and ridicule.

If a planet is found to be heavily involved in progressed aspects, then something can be anticipated that will be related to the nature of the planet combined with its natal potential. Look to the natal chart and note what house(s) the planet rules, as well as the house position and aspects made. The more planets it contacted in the natal chart, the more important events may be in bringing out the natal potential, especially when it reconnects by progression to a planet it was linked to at birth. The house it rules will be an area where activity takes place.

Generally, the birth aspect will be most revealing in the way a progressed planetary pair will manifest no matter what new aspect is formed between them. A beneficial aspect between two planets in the birth chart will not be cause for alarm when they form a stressful aspect later on, unless it comes at a time when there is a complex of harsh aspects in the progressed chart.

Occasionally, there are opportunities to optimize natal potential. This comes about when a pair of planets form a new and improved aspect over the aspect formed in the natal chart. For example, Mercury and Mars squared in the birth chart is likely to form a sextile or trine at some time in the life. Both aspects show a dynamic use of communication skills, but the latter aspect will show a more positive and profitable use of the natal potential. There will still be challenges associated with the natal square, but the individual will handle them better. The mind is sharp but less inclined to impulsive errors in speech.

Some of the most opportune times come about when a pair of planets comes into beneficial aspect in the progressed chart that were not in aspect in the birth chart. While it is a temporary asset, it can bring tidings that are otherwise unavailable. This appears to be more spectacular if one of the planets is Venus or Jupiter, and especially more so if such an aspect forms while there are other positive indications in the chart. Similarly, slight difficulties may arise at a time when a pair of planets forms a stressful aspect in the progressions that were not in aspect at birth. This should not cause extreme problems, but will add light to a situation if it forms while there are other stresses in the chart at the same time.

Stressful natal aspects identify problems to solve or lessons to master. The planets, their signs and houses show what the lesson involves. When the progressions repeat a contact of these planets, it usually reflects a time when the issue will surface for attention. If we have not had enough experience in dealing with it or have not yet mastered the lesson, then we will still "tend" toward certain limitations or a weakness in the area. Up until we overcome this tendency through practice, there will be a certain amount of stress involved each time the pair of planets forms an aspect. The contact is a chance to work through the associated difficulties and bring the planetary energies into better harmony.

If the birth chart contains a square or opposition between malefic planets, the combination of the two in a later aspect offers an opportunity to bring the planetary energies into better integration. Even a conjunction between two malefic planets can be stressful, due to their incompatible natures. For a conjunction to be judged an affliction, take into consideration the aspects it receives and the prominence it holds in the chart. This is an extremely important factor for prediction purposes, and the concept is demonstrated in the chart delineations herein.

Each planet is symbolic of several things. For example, the Sun rules over honors, benefactors, strong male types, the father, the husband, as well as the vitality and life purpose of the individual. It can show a wealth of benefits if it is well aspected in the progressed chart. If it is very afflicted, and confirmed by similar aspects in the chart, the Sun may warn of trouble to the father or another benefactor, or the individual's health may be in danger. That is why a thorough study of the natal potential of each planet is necessary. Chapter 14 goes into the types of activities associated with each planet as it becomes active.

In progressions, the orb of aspect is very narrow, only one degree for the planets and other points. The Sun and Moon, or the Lights, are allowed an orb of one and a half degrees. Occasionally, it will be found that these latter two in particular appear to "work" even if beyond this one

and a half degrees of orb. It will also be found that in certain instances, a planet can pull in energies from another planet to make contact with a third. For example, let's say the progressed Ascendant is within orb of conjunction with Venus while also in orb of opposition to the progressed Moon. Even if Venus is not technically within orb of an opposition to the Moon, it may be pulled into the configuration by its conjunction to the Ascendant. This is most notable if the planet in question rules the chart or if one of the aspects links two planets that were in aspect at birth.

The primary aspects in the progressed chart to consider are any involving an angle. This can be a natal or progressed angle involved with a planet from either the natal or progressed chart. These help determine the most likely types of events for the period in question. Look to aspects of the progressed Ascendant to be most revealing. This new Ascendant is as important now as the natal Ascendant is all through life. This progressed Ascendant represents the physical apparatus, the outlook, attitude, experiences attracted, and so forth, so that aspects to this angle are top priority. Following the angles in priority are aspects involving the Sun, whether natal or progressed. Once these have been sorted, the remaining planetary aspects between the natal and progressed planets are considered. The chart ruler is given special consideration, as well as any particularly prominent planets from the natal chart. Without aspects involving an angle, the Sun, or the progressed Ascendant ruler, it will likely be a routine period.

While the progressed Moon aspects are very significant, they change fairly rapidly so that they must be considered relevant to the longer lasting progressed aspects in the chart. These lunar aspects do reflect the general tone and domestic conditions, according to the planet contacted and the type of aspect, so they are helpful in timing events.

Once the active progressed aspects have been tabulated, the transits must be taken into consideration. If a theme has been repeated among the progressed aspects and then the transits confirm and expand on the same theme, it is simple to ascertain that an event is coming due.

For a major event to take place, either fortunate or unfortunate, there will be multiple progressed aspects, many of which suggest a similar theme. At the same time, transiting planets will form aspects to the natal and progressed planets, and among themselves, which emphasize the theme. This will often be a specific set of planets that are linked by aspects several times. At least one of the transiting planets will be in close aspect to a natal or progressed planet when the event takes place. This aspect will frequently describe the event. Aspects from the faster transiting planets (usually the Sun and/or Mars) help time the event.

Unless stimulated by transits while within orb, the progressed aspects remain a background theme. They describe conditions and influences but are not necessarily event-producing without sufficient stimulation from transiting planets. Transits represent external circumstances. When external circumstances combine with progressed potential, events are produced. Some progressed aspects will remain within this one-degree orb for years, and changing progressions and transits will bring them more prominently into the chart (life).

Important transits to watch for are those of the outer planets making a hard aspect to the progressed Sun, Moon, progressed Ascendant, or its ruler. These can signify difficult times. The same general notes can be applied if it is the natal Sun, Moon, Ascendant or natal ruler that receives a hard aspect (conjunction, square, or opposition) from one of the outer transiting planets.

Blending Horary Concepts with the Progressed Chart

The transiting configurations that are used in conjunction with the progressions are calculated for as close as possible to the birth of the event, the question, or the issue involving the individual. The transiting Ascendant can be used to find out more about the person, the event, or what lies in the immediate future for the individual according to the next natal planet to rise to this Ascendant. As an example, in chapter 1, the chart of Evangeline Adams had the transits calculated for the morning of March 16, 1899, around the time she might have set out from home to relocate to a new state and all of the attending new arrangements. Around 8:00 AM seemed appropriate, and since Ms. Adams was born at 8:30 AM, that's the time that was used to calculate the transit chart for her big day.

The transiting Ascendant for this date and time was 21° Taurus, which meant that Ms. Adams' next natal planet to rise to this new Ascendant was Uranus. Uranus speaks volumes about the unusual set of events following her departure from Boston and upon her arrival in New York. In this case the event is over, and everyone knows what happened so this is all seen in retrospect. When working with a chart to determine a forecast for the future or for an event where all the details are not known, the method offers valuable information.

Oftentimes the astrologer has a knack for zeroing in on some significant factor at the time of the inclination to check the current planetary configurations in an individual's chart. The chart will be revealing about what is coming up next for the individual when this Horary Ascendant is used to find the individual's natal planet next to rise. Chapter 10 goes into specifics on the meanings of each of the planets being the first to rise and this technique will be illustrated in delineations throughout the coming chapters.

Delineation: Progressed Afflictions in the Birth Chart

It is easier to assimilate so much significance by seeing the progressions and transits at work.

The following chart, belonging to a child named Annie, will be used to show several events. This chart was chosen because it provides the opportunity to illustrate progressed aspects already within orb of influence at birth. These aspects prove to be of great significance in the life of an individual, and the events signified by such aspects begin to work out soon after birth. The illustrations further reveal how flurries of activity during a short span of time are always reflected in the progressed aspects.

This delineation is detailed to show which planetary factors are linked to the events taking place. For simplicity's sake, discussion of the converse progressions is limited. Emphasis is on the standard progressed chart, which is shown.

Annie's Story

Immediately apparent in Annie's horoscope is the stellium of planets on the Ascendant in the sign of Libra. This shows that cooperative efforts will be strongly emphasized throughout her life. Partnerships are of primary concern, and there's a desire for harmonious relationships. Venus in Libra leads the stellium. This gives a friendly demeanor and pleasing manner. People with strong Libra traits often make good mediators. A virtue is a sense of fairness and the ability to see any situation from the viewpoint of the other person.

Venus in the 1st house is a strong influence for good and should afford her much protection and love. The Moon in conjunction with Venus also ensures a measure of benefits and happiness.

Mars in Libra also shows a desire to act in partnership with others, although Mars in this sign indicates potential upsets in relationships. Other configurations give similar indications.

Her chart ruler Venus is square Uranus, suggesting upsets in love and possible divorce. There may be many love relationships or hasty marriages. There's a desire for partnerships but also the need to be free and independent, a combination that may be difficult to achieve. Creating balance in life is crucial for Libra.

The closest aspect in the chart is the square of the Moon to Uranus, an indication of domestic instability so that her early childhood may not provide her with the kind of emotional foundation and security she needs to easily trust and bond with others. Annie may be deprived of emotional nurturing from her mother, who may reject Annie, or be physically absent. Their relationship is complex.

The Moon and Saturn, ruling the 4th and 10th houses, are brought by close conjunction to the Ascendant. This indicates an unusually karmic relationship with her parents, and her relationship with them has a deep impact on her. This combination of the Moon and Saturn implies a serious and dampened quality within the home and between the parents. On the Ascendant, such circumstances will leave an indelible mark, and Annie tends to be emotionally chained to the past.

Uranus in square to Annie's stellium suggests disruptive forces and reversals. An unusual relationship with the parents is suggested, as well as an unusual home life in general. There are many moves and changes with family chaos and uprooting. Uranus square Moon, Saturn, and Venus show probable separations from her parents and from others she loves. On the cusp of the 10th house, Uranus suggests

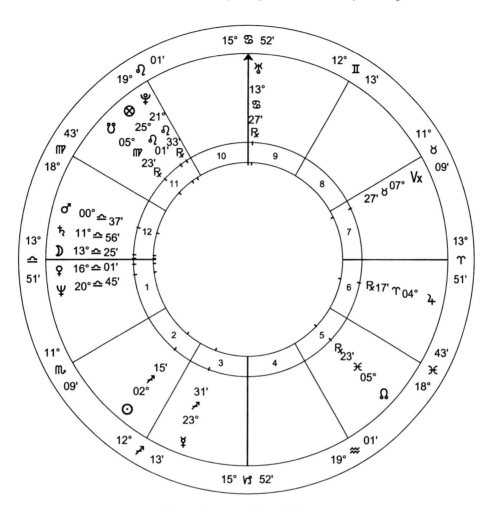

Figure 2a: Annie's Natal Chart
Nov. 25, 1951; 3:33 AM EST; 84W31, 39N05

that her life direction will be greatly affected by these personal events.

An aspect adding similar tones is her Sun in square to her North Node, indicating less than fulfilling experiences with her father.

These configurations will remain descriptive of Annie's home life and family situations throughout life whenever progressions and transits set off the natal potential.

A life lesson for Annie will be to learn how to break with the past, and to grow beyond the fears associated with unfamiliar situations and new experiences. This is shown by the prominent square between Saturn and Uranus. Saturn, being part of the stellium, casts the stronger influence. Uranus trine North Node also encourages Annie to see the advantage of change. Life comes at her in surprising ways to ensure she learns to become more progressive and to overcome a fear of change. Thus the early lessons signified by the stressful aspects of Uranus may be a necessary prerequisite for Annie's long-term growth and progress.

Uranus is parallel Pluto, similar to a conjunction. It will be seen to operate in a more profound way because of this connection to Pluto. When things settle down after Uranus has swept through, there is a quality of permanence in the new conditions. Pluto, like the Phoenix, brings the power to rise from ashes.

Saturn on the Ascendant shows that many trials and difficulties early in life will result in Annie's self-reliance. She is of a somewhat serious disposition, but will be tougher for having survived early adversity. She is sensitive (Moon on Ascendant) but emotionally reserved (Saturn conjunct Moon), and will need to overcome difficulties in establishing healthy emotional ties.

While these themes involving the stellium are most prominent because of the angularity, there are two other interlocking patterns in Annie's chart.

There are harmonious aspects among Pluto, Mercury, and Neptune/Venus. This pattern will not be activated through progressions for some time although it may turn out to be advantageous in the long run. Venus conjunct Neptune in Libra shows her to be inspired and artistic. Sextile Pluto, artistic potential is increased, and since Libra is an air sign, creative inspiration runs along intellectually motivated lines. A trine between Mercury and Pluto gives a natural affinity for research. This is fortunate for problem solving and concentration. This is emphasized with Mercury in close quintile to her Saturn and Moon. She may excel in communications fields, especially since Mercury trines her Part of Fortune from the 3rd house. She may do well in a teaching or writing capacity. With Mercury in Sagittarius, there may be publishing ventures.

Neptune ruling her Pisces North Node suggests mystical leanings. Annie might be interested in healing or counseling. Her North Node in the 5th house shows promise for doing independent work.

Uranus trine North Node also suggests a potential flair in new age fields. Uranus is strongly linked to her future growth. Eventually, talents associated with Uranus may be key to her professional success, suggested by its complexity of aspects and position on the Midheaven. The square of Moon and Uranus is creative, inventive, and Annie can utilize the aspect for conceptual understanding and clear insight of advanced concepts. The aspect also indicates original methods. Combined with the intellectual patterns, she may have talents along the lines of scientific research and an ability to present her insights artistically (Uranus ruling the 5th house). What appears early on to be her greatest liability may later prove to be among her finest assets. Saturn conjunct Venus also shows the capacity to bring form to artistic potential.

Much personal effort will be required to achieve her highest potential with the ruler of the 10th house (Moon) on the Ascendant. Since there's such a need to be independent, she'd do well to work for herself. Saturn on the Ascendant gives her the self-discipline and the organizing ability to do so.

Annie's third pattern involves the Sun, Mars, and Jupiter. The Sun in Sagittarius emphasizes a need to be free and independent. There's a trine between the Sun and Jupiter, which serves as protection against severe harm since the Sun rules the vitality and life-giving forces. Jupiter signifies guardianship and blessings. The aspect suggests the presence of many benefactors in Annie's life, and that she remains optimistic. A measure of luck and success is guaranteed. Since Sun trine Jupiter is a potentially lazy and self-indulgent aspect (as is Venus with Moon), the prominent Saturn in her chart will offset any tendency to avoid responsibility. She is resourceful and finds work fulfilling. She may enjoy working behind the scenes or in seclusion with Mars in the 12th house. Her Sun is also sextile Mars, fortunate for health, energy, willpower, and assistance from masculine types. The opposition of Mars to Jupiter, inclining toward impulse actions, is mitigated by the Sun in mutually assisting aspects. These beneficial rays to the Sun will be of great assistance to Annie in overcoming the many adversities she will face.

Overall, it should be noted that Annie has two benefic planets of strong influence. Venus rules her Ascendant, while Jupiter rules the sign of her Sun.

The following events, beginning early in Annie's life, will illustrate how the configurations of the natal chart are reflective of her life experiences. These events will have a resulting impact, and will further define her personality as set forth in the birth configurations. In addition, her experiences will ultimately lead to the mastering of life lessons as indicated in the horoscope features.

The very early experiences of a child are closely linked to the personal experiences of the mother. The movement of the progressing Moon, as well as progressions to the natal Moon, reflect these experiences. Similarly, during the earliest stages of childhood, the houses and indicators have a way of reflecting the activities of the mother while remaining descriptive of the child's experiences stemming from those.

The aspects present in Annie's birth chart already within the one-degree orb for progressions are: Uranus square Moon, Moon conjunct Ascendant, Uranus square Ascendant, and Venus square Midheaven. Since the Moon can be given one and a half degrees of orb, this brings its conjunction with Saturn into the list of aspects already matured at birth. The planetary natures and aspects describe a theme of disturbing family issues, which will erupt early in Annie's life.

Family Split

When Annie was eighteen months old, progressed Uranus had retrograded the small amount necessary to come into an exact square to her natal Moon. This testifies to unsettling domestic changes.

By now, the Ascendant of the converse progressed chart was at 12° Libra and had moved backward in the zodiac to come within the one degree orb of a conjunction with natal Saturn, while also still within orb to square Uranus. Saturn conjunct Ascendant suggests possible separations from, or loss of a parent or another close family member. *The converse Venus at 14° Libra has come within a square to converse Uranus*, an aspect descriptive of divorce. This aspect from the birth chart is now repeated in the progressions. The direct motion progressed Midheaven is square progressed Venus, suggesting difficulties in domestic affairs, separations, and possible scandal.

Transits that are linked are *Uranus squaring natal Venus* from the Midheaven, underscoring themes suggesting divorce or relationship breaks. Transiting retrograde Venus near the cusp of the 7th house opposes natal Venus, repeating such a theme, and shows a very personal effect on Annie from events taking place. *Transiting Venus squares natal Uranus. Transiting Uranus is in square to transiting Venus.* So, we see there are repetitions of Venus in square to Uranus, an aspect from the birth chart indicating upsets in relationships. Transiting Uranus is in a close square to pro-

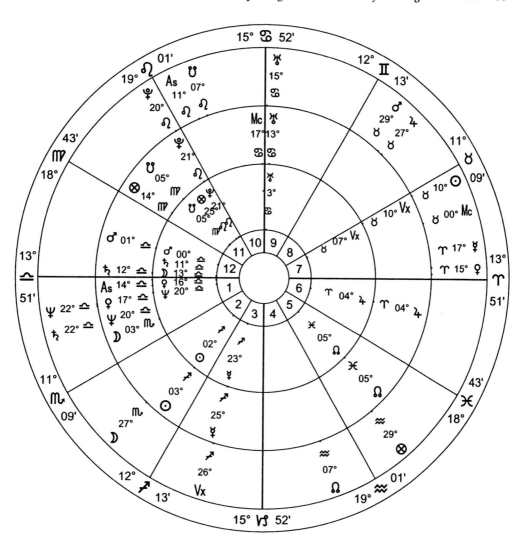

Figure 2b: Family Split

Inner Wheel: Annie's Natal Chart: Nov. 25, 1951; 3:33 AM EST; 84W31, 39N05
Middle Wheel: Progressed Chart: Apr. 30, 1953; 12:00 PM EST; 84W31, 39N05
Outer wheel: Transit Chart: Apr. 30, 1953; 12:00 PM EST; 84W31, 39N05

gressed Ascendant while transiting Venus opposes progressed Ascendant, suggesting sudden peculiar happenings and difficulties where attachments are concerned and again showing how circumstances involve Annie in a very personal way. Her ruler Venus and her progressed Ascendant receive many harsh aspects. These aspects describe the events taking place.

It was at this time that Annie's mother chose to get a divorce. She was in love with someone else whom she wanted to marry and start a new life with. While their parents were getting things sorted out, custody of Annie and her older brother was given to their grandmother, who lived in another state.

On the positive side, the astrologer will note the trine aspect now in orb between the progressed Sun and Jupiter. This indicates protection and the presence of a benefactor. Permanent and lasting attachments may be formed.

Several of the promises of the natal chart have now been fulfilled through the progressions. A domestic disruption and family upset has occurred. A marriage has split up and separation from her parents has taken place, yet Annie is still afforded with protection.

Sibling Split

About two months later, Annie's father took her older brother to live with him.

Since he could not afford to keep both children, Annie remained with her grandmother who had become very attached to Annie. Again this is reflected in the progressed trine of the Sun to Jupiter, showing that there is an assisting benefactor.

The chart themes of separation recurred in the children being split up. The progressed aspects had not changed much. The most emphasized among them still involved angular Venus and Uranus in square, suggesting unexpected developments that would affect Annie personally. At this point, transiting Sun and Mars joined transiting Uranus on the Midheaven in square to Annie's natal stellium. In particular they square her progressed Venus, suggesting sorrow or loss of a loved one, and suggesting disruptive domestic affairs. Sun and Mars indicate the influence and involvement of a male figure. They also square natal Neptune, which combined with transiting Saturn conjunct Neptune, describes confusion and a transition at hand. Neptune, when in prominent aspect, often means dissolving attachments or the dissolve of previous conditions. Transiting Venus squaring her natal nodes underscores themes of broken attachments and loss.

She did not see her brother again until two years later and then only for a brief visit.

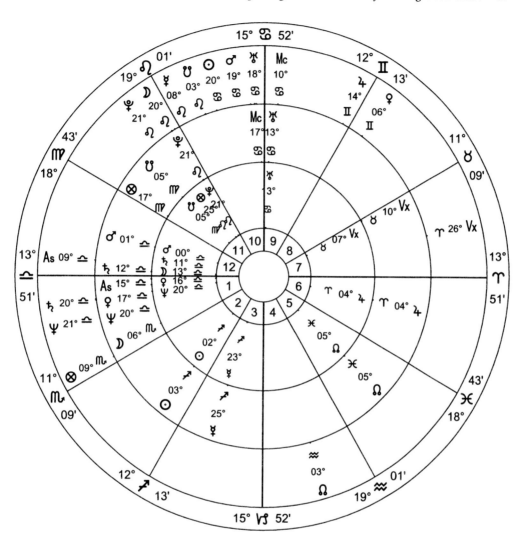

Figure 2c: Sibling Split
Inner Wheel: Annie, Nov. 25, 1951; 3:33 AM EST; 84W31, 39N05
Middle Wheel: Progressed Chart: July 13, 1953; 12:00 PM EST; 84W31, 39N05
Outer Wheel: Transit Chart: July 13, 1953; 12:00 PM EST; 84W31, 39N05

After her brother left, things were pretty quiet. Living in a remote area without television and few neighbors, Annie spent considerable time playing outdoors alone. Meadows and fields surrounded their little house, and the only sounds were the sounds of nature. She could walk a few hundred feet down the lane to pick fresh blackberries and fill her little tin bucket with the ones she didn't eat.

Annie recalls an experience from when she was only a few years old that had a lasting impression. She was kneeling on the ground in the tall grasses and had a metal ice cube tray next to her because she'd discovered a weed that had these little seedlings. It was fun to slide the weed through her cupped palm, scoop the seeds off, and deposit them in one of the ice tray cubicles. As she worked intently to fill the whole tray, a soft breeze wafted by. Annie sensed a presence and lifted her head. In that moment she felt enveloped in an awe-inspiring energy. She felt the energy move through her; she felt joy, she felt blessed, loved, and protected. She was filled with a sense that there was a special purpose for her in this world and that she would always have guidance. The experience lasted maybe only a minute, but it was uplifting and exhilarating. She looked up into the tall trees and began singing to the birds.

Her experience is descriptive of her natal Sun trine Jupiter, which was in close orb of influence at the time of her experience. It gives the sense of being blessed and watched over; a spiritual connection.

Pneumonia

When Annie was going on six, she was still living with her grandmother and had just started first grade. True to her chart, she had been spoiled, pampered, and overly protected by her grandmother, uncles, and cousins, but had very infrequent contacts with her parents. Having lived in a remote community with little interaction with children her age, she was shy (Saturn) and unprepared for attending school. It frightened her. The bus ride alone was frightening and for several weeks she had to be picked up and returned home shortly after the school day began.

This chart shows that progressed Saturn has moved into a closer conjunction with the natal Moon, thus also squaring the natal Uranus. This indicates a fear of change and of the new and untried. The progressed Midheaven is now squaring natal Neptune. This indicates a transitional phase that is often accompanied by confusion. Neptune can indicate fears, reflecting Annie's present state of mind about attending school. The element of fearfulness likely contributed to factors upon which an illness evolved, also a Neptunian issue, corresponding with 12th house elements of confinement.

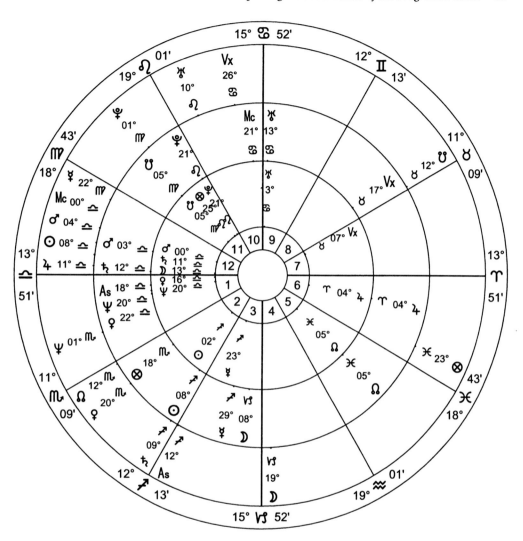

Figure 2d: Pneumonia

Inner Wheel: Annie, Nov. 25, 1951; 3:33 AM EST; 84W31, 39N05
Middle Wheel: Progressed Chart: Oct. 1, 1957; 12:00 PM EST; 84W31, 39N05
Outer Wheel: Transit Chart: Oct. 1, 1957; 12 PM EST; 84W31, 39N05

Neptune is also the key to Annie's 6th house of health. With her Neptune in Libra, imbalances in life create health issues. With Neptune near an angle at birth, some health issue might be expected at its first contact with an angle if other aspects give confirmation. Progressed Venus, her ruler, is near progressed Neptune while also in square to the MC (Midheaven). This brings Venus and Neptune angular, suggesting potential discomforts. Normally, Venus and Neptune together could show nearly blissful conditions. When together under stressful aspect, indications are magnified for disturbances. This combination indicates a period of poor vitality, lethargy, weakness, or physical vulnerability. Danger is likewise associated with her progressed Mars in close orb of opposition to her 6th house Jupiter.

The progressing Moon is moving into position to square each of the planets near the Ascendant in succession. It is already within orb to square the converse Ascendant and Venus at 9° Libra and soon squares natal and progressed Saturn.

There are a threatening combination of transiting aspects, from both Saturn and Pluto to the Sun. Pluto has moved within one degree to square the natal Sun. Transiting Saturn recently moved away from a conjunction to her natal Sun and has moved onto the progressed Sun. It is unfortunate to have transiting Saturn make a hard aspect to the natal Sun, followed closely by the same aspect to the progressed Sun. Vitality is usually at a low point with such a transit, and the individual is unable to rebound from the first pass of Saturn before the second aspect forms. These transiting aspects should be regarded seriously. Such a combination from these two malefic planets (Saturn and Pluto) to the Sun can bring serious illness and is hardly able to be overcome by good aspects when they form at the same time.

The aspects all agree that Annie is not well physically.

It was at this time that Annie became very seriously ill. Before she was over pneumonia, she contracted the measles. Her memories of this time period are few and vague (Neptune). She was confined and bedridden, attended by the doctor with medications and by her grandmother with Vick's vapo-rub and horrible cough syrup. She missed the rest of the school year entirely (also Neptune—a temporary retreat from the outside world).

The key aspects were the transits of Saturn and Pluto afflicting her Sun, combined with the square of Neptune and Venus to the MC and progressed Mars opposing Jupiter in the 6th house. The latter aspect was reinforced by transiting Mars conjunct her progressed Mars and opposite her Jupiter. Transiting Mars reflects the timing. The prolonged aspect of Pluto square her Sun reflects the long duration of the illness when combined with the stressful aspects formed by the progressed Moon over the coming ten months.

Kidnapping

When Annie was seven-and-a-half years old, she still lived with her grandmother, who by now had become a replacement mother. She had adjusted to school, and though they lived simply, Annie was happy.

In this set of charts, the progressed Ascendant has moved into a conjunction with Neptune, denoting a transitional period, often accompanied by a degree of confusion and sometimes involving deceptions. It's an aspect of dissolving conditions and new entanglements. Progressed Mars is still in orb of opposition to her Jupiter, a critical aspect denoting possible danger. In fact there had been an incident with a pony in a hailstorm during the orb of the aspect, when Annie came close to being trampled by the frightened animal.

Progressed Saturn is coming ever closer to conjunct natal Moon and square Uranus, tending to restrictions, reversals, and an unsettling period, with unexpected or upsetting events, including possible loss of a parent or another authority figure.

Other aspects chime in for potential upsets and unexpected developments. At this point Mercury has progressed to form a square with natal Mars, indicating conflicts, tempers, and potential problems connected with travel. The aspect is associated with impulsive but unwise actions and uncontrolled speech. It is an unfortunate time to make changes. Transiting Saturn is in conjunction with progressed Mercury and square natal Mars, so this progressed aspect is stimulated by the transit, an indication that it is key. Saturn on Mercury makes for difficulties in communications and sometimes means having to say goodbye. Saturn square Mars is an aspect of conflicts with those whose goals are counter to one's own. It is an aspect of setbacks. Saturn suggests that authority figures are tied in to any possible events along such lines.

The Aries Point is quite a stimulated factor in the present configurations and underscores the themes revealed by progressed Mercury square natal Mars. The zero degree of the cardinal signs, when occupied by a planet, indicates the involvement of people outside the usual circle of associations. When so occupied, any one of these cardinal degrees automatically signal activities associated with each of the remaining cardinal signs. One event has a domino effect, impacting the most personal areas of life associated with the 1st, 4th, 7th, and 10th houses. Being a critical degree, the initial activity is often due to unforeseen situations that arise. In these

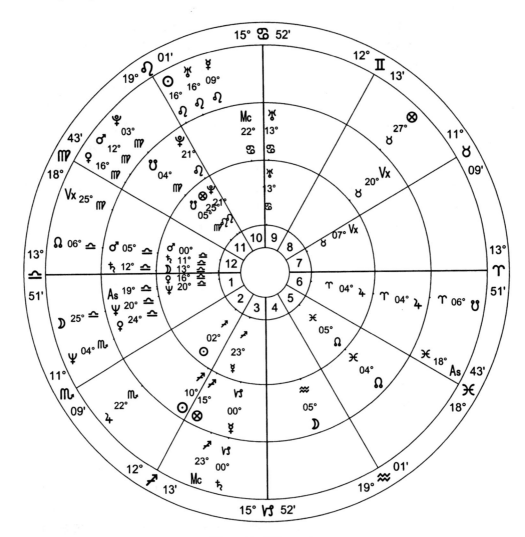

Figure 2e: Kidnapping
Inner Wheel: Annie, Nov. 25, 1951; 3:33 AM EST; 84W31, 39N05
Middle Wheel: Progressed Chart: Aug. 9, 1959; 9:00 PM EST; 84W31, 39N05
Outer Wheel: Transit Chart: Aug. 9, 1959; 9:00 PM EST; 84W31, 39N05

charts there are three important indicators in the zero degrees of the cardinal signs. Progressed Mercury and transiting Saturn are both at 0° Capricorn square the natal Mars at 0° Libra. The configuration suggests that aggressive action is needed from outside authorities (Saturn/Capricorn) to restore harmony (Libra). Additionally, this will be related to movement and/or agreements (Mercury/3rd house). (Refer to The Aries Point in chapter 16.)

An aspect of converse progressed Moon at 9° Cancer conjunct the converse Midheaven within one degree of orb is noteworthy. The progressed Moon conjunct the Midheaven is often a time when a personal issue becomes a public issue, and here it partakes of similar meaning as the Aries Point signatures. Converse progressed Moon is also square converse progressed Venus, an emotional time, and one of disagreements in family relations.

In checking the rest of the transits, Pluto squares natal Sun while Mars is square progressed Sun. Combined with other indicators these suggest power struggles, conflicts, and forceful elements. Transiting Jupiter is square Pluto, also indicating conflict, possibly of a legal nature. Transiting Neptune is square progressed Moon, leading to misunderstandings and possible deceptions. It is a difficult time emotionally.

The transiting North Node is making an unmistakable signature by its conjunction with progressed Mars. This Mars/Node combination indicates a dynamic thrust of energy, followed by some new and vital element in the life. Significant experiences revolve around a strong male figure. Transiting Pluto is also coming to a conjunction with Annie's progressed South Node. This is a transforming influence when circumstances are likely to be beyond one's control—when events occur suddenly, forcing one through changes. There's the need to adapt to new conditions and circumstances.

To summarize briefly the indications in the chart, there are conflicts of interest, travel, or legal problems, requiring outsiders to become involved. Disturbing family issues are at hand and may become public there are likely to be deceptive elements or confusion involved. Some forceful event will lead to a new life, requiring adjustments. The chart accurately reflects the circumstances and events.

The initial event that took place on the date of these charts was a visit from Annie's father, who had just gotten remarried that day and had his new wife with him. His plan had always been to have Annie with him as soon as he could care for her properly. Due to a couple of visits over the years, Annie was familiar with who her father was. Because she enjoyed the visits with her brother, and still missed him, she allowed her father to talk her into going home with him for a one-week visit. Once packed and in the car, however, by a slip of the tongue, the news was revealed to Annie and her grandmother that Annie would not be coming back.

Havoc broke loose, to say the least. Even with Annie and her grandmother screaming and crying, struggling to reach one another through the open car window, her new stepmother held Annie down as the car sped away into the night. Traumatized, this is the last Annie remembers for some time.

A neighbor, hearing the disturbance, called the police in town and described the car. The chief of police happened to be Annie's uncle. He had no trouble tracking down and arresting the couple, returning Annie to her grandmother. For the next several weeks, Annie was kept secluded at an uncle's home in another state so that her father could not find her. It was the beginning of a major custody battle.

Eventually everyone concerned was called into court, but the judge decided against Annie's wishes to remain with her elderly grandmother. She was given into the custody of her father. All this occurred within a little over three months, at which time she moved to another state and a whole new family. This was as transiting Saturn neared the 4th house cusp and began a series of hard aspects to her stellium.

The potential shown in the progressions have been fulfilled while also fulfilling those of the nativity.

Father's Death

This next event chart is set for a time when Annie was twelve. True to her chart, Annie had rebounded from the earlier upsetting circumstances and had adjusted to her new life. This is not to say that things had been easy. She missed her grandmother, who was heartsick after their separation. The best thing about this change was being with her brother. Still, he had been used to having his dad all to himself. Now he and Annie had a new stepmother who had two half-grown children to take care of. She had a young son from a previous marriage and soon a new baby boy entered the family. There was a lot to adjust to, and all of the stepfamily problems were apparent with a measure of dysfunction due to jealousies.

Even so, Annie and her father began to form a bond. This happened during what Annie calls her Cinderella years. As her chart shows, Annie had to learn responsibility at an early age so by the age of ten, she cooked meals for her father and her brothers while her stepmother worked second shift. She cleaned and helped with the younger children. On the bright side, she and her brother rode their bikes together after dishes were done, and their dad would often treat the kids from

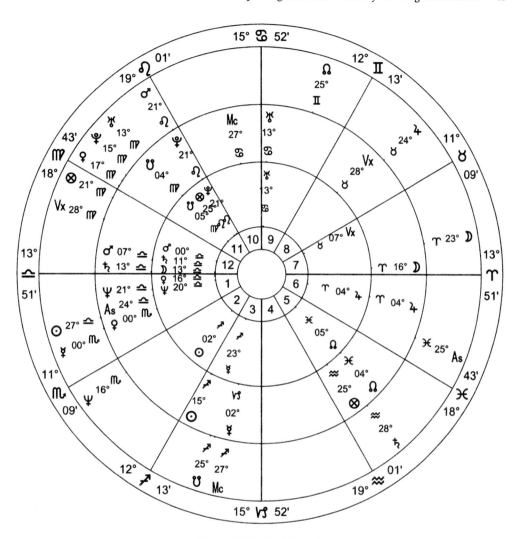

Figure 2f: Father's Death
Inner Wheel: Annie, Nov. 25, 1951; 3:33 AM EST; 84W31, 39N05
Middle Wheel: Progressed Chart: Oct. 20, 1964; 4:30 PM EST; 84W31, 39N05
Outer Wheel: Transit Chart: Oct. 20, 1964; 4:30 PM EST, 84W31; 39N05

the ice cream truck in the evening. They had some good times. This was during a period when Annie's progressed Sun was sextile her Saturn.

By now, though, progressed Saturn has moved in to make a closer conjunction to the natal Moon, still accentuating heavy responsibilities with restrictions affecting the home life and family members. Progressed Saturn is now in exact square to progressed Uranus. In the birth chart this aspect suggested sudden separations or loss of a parent or another authority figure. Saturn also rules the 4th house, accentuating the theme of loss of a parent. This is a key aspect at this time, being so close.

We see that progressed Moon in the 7th house has already formed hard aspects to her Saturn and Uranus, showing trouble brewing in the family, especially likely in connection with a parent. Now the progressed Moon is square the Midheaven, producing family stress, often involving the breadwinner of the family. Progressed Moon also now opposes Annie's natal Venus, an indication that sensitive circumstances are at hand and may cause sorrow.

Transiting Saturn is square natal Sun. Although retrograde at this point, it has spent the last few months in square to the natal Sun. This can mean restrictions for important masculine figures in the life. The father is ruled by the Sun.

In the converse chart, converse progressed Venus is conjunct converse Ascendant at 3° of Libra, and both are opposing natal Jupiter. Jupiter squares converse Midheaven at 4° Cancer. A general rule of thumb is that an afflicted benefic on an angle represents an interruption to harmony. The benefic planet represents ease and harmony, but when afflicted and angular, this represents conditions that are counter to harmony—thus we get dis-ease. Other aspects emphasize this theme and it appears that an authority figure or a benefactor is under attack, likely her dad. With two benefic planets opposing one another from the angles (Venus opposite Jupiter), the theme turns to one of grief and loss, similar to her progressed Moon opposing natal Venus.

Other transiting planets reinforce the themes indicating threats to her father. A transit of Pluto, Uranus, and Venus in Virgo are in square to the progressed Sun, with the square from Pluto exact. The same aspect is repeated in the converse progressed Sun in square to natal Pluto. As seen earlier, the square between Pluto and Sun may indicate severe illness, but now it is the father who appears to be in danger.

Transiting Jupiter in her 8th house is square natal Pluto, while transiting Mars is making an exact conjunction to natal Pluto, a timing factor. Annie's ruler Venus has just entered Scorpio in the progressions, the sign ruled by Pluto. With so many aspects involving Pluto, themes of transformation appear prominent. There is plenty of evidence of a possible loss brought about by death. Transiting Neptune is also conjunct the converse progressed Sun, implying weakness or frailty for her father.

It was at this time that Annie's father died after suffering from extremely invasive cancer, which he had been diagnosed with less than three months earlier. He was only thirty-seven. A Full Moon was forming between the transiting Sun and transiting Moon, sometimes bringing separations, occasionally broken attachments through death. The transiting Sun in Libra was exactly in square to her progressed Midheaven while the transiting Moon in Aries was opposite her progressed Ascendant at the time of his death.

The astrologer will notice that there is a sextile between progressed Sun and natal Venus. There are often one or two beneficial aspects in the chart when a death from illness occurs, to represent the harmony restored by the end of suffering. The aspect may also reflect the death benefits awarded Annie from her father's time in the military.

In her father's chart, not shown, the major indicators of death involved multiple afflictions to his natal and progressed Ascendant and their rulers, and his Sun.

Progressed Mars was in a close square to his natal Ascendant. Transiting Saturn was on this Ascendant while opposing his natal ruler. Transiting Neptune was square his progressed Ascendant ruler. Progressed Saturn squared progressed Sun. Transiting Uranus was afflicting progressed Sun and natal Moon, which were approaching an opposition.

Fire & Pregnancy

The next events in this series occurred when Annie was going on eighteen. She still lived with her stepmother, who depended on her help with the younger boys, although her older brother had gone to live with their biological mother a couple of years after their father's death.

Annie had become pretty independent following her father's death, and had worked to make her own money since she was thirteen. From thirteen to sixteen she babysat her little brothers while her stepmother worked, taking babysitting jobs on the side on weekends. By sixteen she attended high school on weekdays and beauty college on Saturdays (Venus in the natal chart). She also had two jobs: one on the weekdays, during her long lunch break from school, and another job she worked evenings and Sundays. This is Saturn in the natal chart, showing an ambitious nature, with self-discipline, working, and saving money.

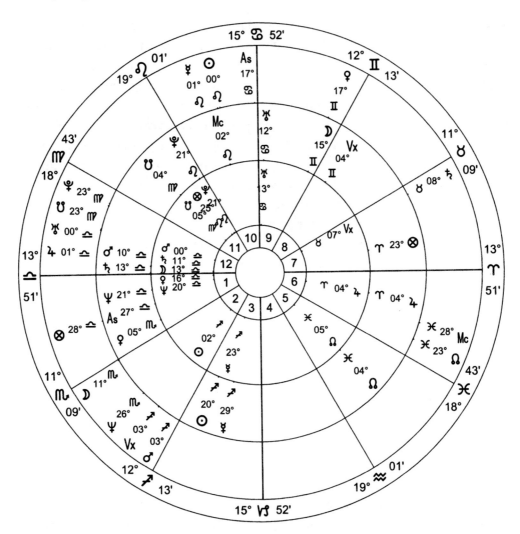

Figure 2g: Fire & Pregnancy

Inner Wheel: Annie, Nov. 25, 1951; 3:33 AM EST; 84W31, 39N05

Middle Wheel: Progressed Chart: July 23, 1969; 5:30 AM EST; 84W31, 39N05

Outer Wheel: Transit Chart: July 23, 1969; 5:30 AM EDT; 84W31, 39N05

After the many trials of early life, Annie had become somewhat reserved (Moon/Saturn). Self-protective, she had begun to build a wall of insulation, allowing few to get past it (Moon/Venus/Saturn). Extraordinarily sensitive, her guard is up for any who might hurt her. Aware of her own emotional vulnerability, she has extremely high ideals (Venus with Neptune in Libra) in close relationships. Since she has a need to know that there will be something in it for her over the long term, she has elevated expectations in relationships. Few can pass these tests.

One who did was her boyfriend, a young and successful musician, whom she began going steady with shortly after her father's death. Her natal chart suggests an early relationship, and Venus in Libra signifies an attraction to artistic types.

This set of charts reflects conditions at the time of three major life events. Since the events are all taking place so close together, delineation will be for the whole set of circumstances. A peculiar twist links the three events together. Notice the increased number of progressed aspects.

For a fire to take place, a number of aspects and afflictions involving Mars would be expected. This is the case in both the transits and the progressions.

The converse Ascendant is conjunct natal Mars, which is always a potential point of affliction.

Progressed Mars is conjunct converse Saturn, both at 10° Libra. While it gives drive to achieve through the application of personal energy, ambitions may be thwarted by circumstances. This can also be a dangerous aspect with physical suffering, sometimes from fires, burns, cuts, or fevers.

The converse Midheaven is square natal Mars. It's similar to the previous aspect. There may be a struggle between duties and personal interests, and trouble or disharmony through a male figure. It is also an accident-prone aspect. It indicates a time when conflicts will be brought into the open.

Converse Mars at 20° Virgo is square the forward motion progressed Sun, indicating a crisis period and a critical time for potential danger. The aspect between these two in Annie's natal chart is a sextile so this removes the degree of personal hazard that may come from the present square, but the square will still bring some repercussions. For a young person it can mean *hasty actions or getting into trouble*.

Progressed retrograde Mercury is square natal Mars, indicating conflicts in movement and communication. This aspect was present at the time of the kidnapping incident, and it is a repetition of the birth square, so there's accident potential. There's a tendency toward *premature or impulsive actions*.

There are already multiple indicators of dangers. With natal Mars also being transited by Uranus and Jupiter, there is a predominance of Mars' contacts in the chart, which could prove threatening. The natal chart shows Jupiter and Mars in an opposition, so this conjunction will express a more negative nature, especially with Uranus attending. Uranus and Jupiter, which were in a wide square aspect in the natal chart, are transiting in opposition to natal Jupiter. There's risk. The combinations suggest sudden unexpected danger and other sudden events. Mars as the dominant stimulated factor in the charts will be seen to work out in several manifestations.

The Aries Point is a factor in the present configurations, and the special significance of planets in the zero degree of a cardinal sign should not go unnoticed. People outside the usual circle become involved. The currently afflicted natal Mars is at 0° Libra, along with transiting Uranus. Several planets energize the point, thus emphasizing it. In Libra, the issue may be one of restoring harmony by calling in those who are experts in Mars' affairs. They may be Mars types themselves. Transiting Uranus in the same degree indicates that a sudden or unexpected situation will arise, necessitating these outsiders to be called in.

With this positioning of planets in the 12th house, something hidden, mysterious, or unknown is implicated. This reflects several specifics in the actual events that took place.

Progressed Mercury is brought into the picture with a square to the converse Ascendant, and it is in opposition to the converse MC. An event is due that involves movement and/or the written word.

The Nodes are active in this chart with the South Node transiting along with Pluto. Recall that Pluto was involved with the nodes at the time of the kidnapping. Pluto sometimes indicates a force of nature or situations out of one's control. With South Node, it suggests sacrifice. These are squaring the natal Mercury. There are inconveniences, stress, and anxiety.

Now another set of aspects exists involving the Sun and the Moon very harmoniously configured. The radical Sun is in trine to the progressed MC, and the converse Sun at 14° Scorpio is trine the radical MC and Uranus. The Sun involved in aspects with the angles is often a time of marriage for a woman, but here it may come suddenly or unexpectedly. The progressed Sun is sextile Neptune and trine Pluto. With such a prominent Sun, the very major events of life are forthcoming, and with beneficial aspects, some honors and fortunate times should follow. There are powerful people in assistance.

Transits include the Sun making beneficial aspects to the radical Sun, Jupiter, and Mars. These three are linked in the birth chart, so this is a consequential transit. Transiting Mars is conjunct natal Sun, trine Jupiter, and sextile Mars, a duplicating configuration. Transiting Jupiter is conjunct Mars, sextile the Sun, and opposing its own natal place, a third repetition of the natal links. This again suggests major life events. The general protection of Annie's health and well being shown in the natal Sun/Jupiter trine is heavily stimulated, and there is an implication of involvement with and benefits through masculine types.

The progressed Moon is in trine to all of her 1st house planets, and is in exact trine to Venus, a feature of the most feminine and womanly. Things of beauty and lace are combined with motherhood.

There are two themes here of very different natures. Mars aspects are definitely threatening an injurious event momentarily. On the other hand multiple aspects of the Sun suggest marriage. Mars rules her 7th house so its activity in the charts also reflects eventful happenings in the marriage sector.

In the early predawn hours, Annie's home caught on fire, and the family members were drugged into deeper sleep by smoke inhalation (12th house). Annie's youngest brother finally woke up and calling out from the next room got Annie to wake up. It was blacker than black. The two of them half fell, half slid down the stairs as they escaped through the thick hot smoke. Annie ran to a neighbor's to call for help as the rest of the family was escaping from the burning house.

The day before the fire, Annie found out she was pregnant, and she had tried all that evening to get up the courage to tell her stepmother. Although they had the best talk they'd had in a while, Annie was never able to spill the story. In relaying the story of the fire, Annie says she felt as if she'd somehow caused the fire because of her immense stress that night. The fire was actually caused by faulty wiring.

While temporary housing arrangements were being made for the family, Annie gave her stepmother the news that she would be getting married shortly. This worked out to be a very nice wedding just a week later through the efforts of her stepmother.

Many things can be seen in the exact aspect of Uranus on Mars. Because Uranus rules the 5th house of children, the hidden pregnancy (Uranus transiting the 12th house), and romantic involvement (5th house) leads to sudden marriage (Uranus conjunct Mars, which rules the 7th house). Uranus in the 12th house also shows the unexpected events taking place during the dark hours, and the contact to Mars suggested a fire (electrical). The several aspects formed by the progressed Moon from the 9th house of legal ceremonies to the 1st house stellium reflect the wedding when combined with the progressed Sun contacts suggesting the same.

Mercury was key in the quick move because of the link to Mars while strongly configured to the angles of the chart. Mercury in aspect to the angles was also key to a name change following marriage.

Marriage

Note that in the marriage chart a week later, aspects to Mars have settled down some. As the ruler of Annie's 7th house, the active Mars gave details to the configurations indicating marriage, one that came about hastily and under less than ideal conditions.

The Sun's aspects played two roles as well. It provided a protective element at the time of the fire, something that was promised in the nativity. The Sun also signified the important union of marriage.

Some illustrations of the magnificence of astrology are reflected in the marriage chart, which has Annie's natal Venus on the transiting Midheaven at the time of the marriage, representative of a wedding. Love has an elevated position for the time. Transiting Venus is trine her progressed Ascendant. Transiting Mercury was conjunct natal Pluto, again to indicate the name change. The Ascendant of the marriage chart was conjunct natal Mercury,

also reflecting the name change and suggesting that a trip would follow shortly (the honeymoon). Transiting Moon conjunct natal Jupiter reflects the legal ceremony and also suggests travel. All of the important links from the natal chart of Sun/Jupiter/Mars are still intact at the time of the wedding.

Supplement to Annie's Story

It is interesting to note that in the case of the fire, the younger brother, who is an Aries, was awarded for his bravery and heroic action.

In the case of the fire, all of the family members had chart afflictions involving Mars at the time. If a competent astrologer had seen the maps of all family members at the time, such an event could have been forewarned. Since family members usually have ties in the charts by planets near a specific degree, aspects to this degree tells of the experiences they might share as a group.

Annie's father's Saturn was placed on her Sun. Such an aspect can be unfortunate, and sometimes a relationship will not even develop between two people with this influence. The fact that they only spent four years together, and had just begun to get to know one another when he died, is reflected in the aspect.

The close square between the Moon and Uranus in Annie's nativity reflects the

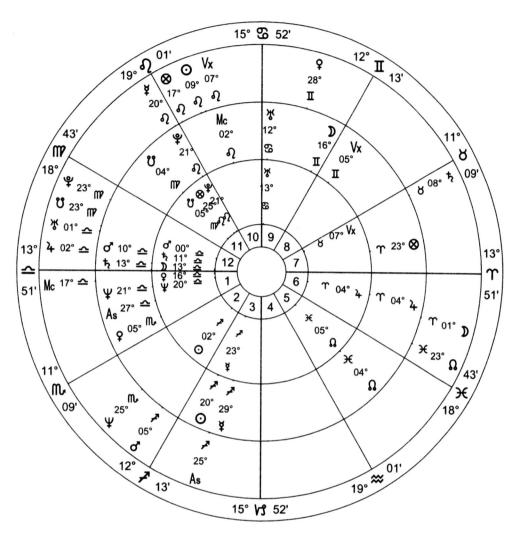

Figure 2h: Marriage
Inner Wheel: Annie, Nov. 25, 1951; 3:33 AM EST; 84W31, 39N05
Middle Wheel: Progressed Chart: Aug. 1, 1969; 6:00 PM EST; 84W31, 39N05
Outer Wheel: Transit Chart: Aug. 1, 1969; 6:00 PM EDT; 84W31, 39N05

early and permanent separation from her mother. Additionally, the only planet from her mother's chart that was friendly to Annie's planets was the mother's Moon. This represented Annie's mother's mother or the grandmother who raised Annie. While their relationship was formal and distant for many years, Annie and her mother eventually formed a mutually rewarding relationship. Their common bond was the woman who raised both.

Annie's baby was a boy, predictable by the sextile between her Sun and Mars and by the afflictions of the 5th house ruler to the feminine planets (Uranus to Moon and Venus). She soon had a second son.

Her marriage to the musician deteriorated after several years (Mars afflicted at time of marriage), and Annie remarried multiple times. A second and third failed marriage came during a period that her Sun and Mars were heavily afflicted. Her fourth marriage worked, and she found the security and settled conditions that eluded her for much of her life.

With her life and personal affairs better balanced, Annie was able to pursue her vocational interests. She did enter into metaphysical fields and became an astrologer, which is how we met. She especially enjoys research and writing, and in the last few years has had some success in publishing. In fact, you may one day read her books on astrology. She was happy to share her story here for other students.

chapter three

Love & Marriage

Romance is a subject of the 5th house, and marriage a subject of the 7th house. These houses and their rulers, along with aspects involving the Sun, Moon, Venus, and Mars, provide information about affairs of the heart. The natal chart shows the potential, and the progressions show when that potential will come to pass.

In the natal chart, the aspects of the ruler of the 7th house largely determine the chances for marriage. The sign on the cusp of the 7th house, its ruler, and planets in the house describe the nature of the partner. The condition of Venus, by sign and aspects, shows the extent of harmony with a partner.

For a man, the Moon and Venus symbolize the women in his life. Afflictions to these may deny, delay, or bring problems in relationships. If the Moon and Venus aspect one another, there is an attraction toward the female sex, and unless Saturn interferes, he will likely wed. If his Moon is in the 7th house, this may indicate multiple marriages unless the Moon forms an adverse aspect to the Sun or Saturn.

For a woman, it is the condition of the Sun and Mars that are the main indicators of marriage. She will likely marry if these two are in aspect to one another. When these or the cusp of the 7th house are very afflicted, marriage may be difficult to bring about. Saturn contacts might mean delay or marriage to an older partner. Uranus aspects can be disruptive and bring disconcerting effects to a relationship. For either sex, Uranus on any angular cusp or in any angular house is often a sign of being divorce-prone.

An aspect between the luminaries usually brings matrimony, as does Venus in aspect to Mars. Similarly, when the rulers of the 1st and 7th house are in aspect, marriage is likely. The better the aspect the better the chances for a happy union.

The 5th house rules love affairs. The condition of the ruler and planets in the 5th house shows how these affairs will go. A good aspect between the rulers of the 5th and 7th houses is an assist to the love life.

As for timing marriage, there must be aspects involving the 7th house ruler in the progressions for marriage to take place. Aspects involving planets placed in the 7th house should also be considered.

If a romance is signified instead of marriage, the 5th house ruler and planets therein are active in the progressions, but the 7th house indicators are not so prominent.

For a woman, the Sun is nearly always active in the progressed chart when events of such importance as marriage are coming due. As we saw in the preceding chapter, the Sun is often in aspect to one of the angles when marriage occurs, especially for a woman. Mars establishes the sexual union and is quite active, especially in a woman's chart, because it, along with the Sun, rules the men in her life. For a woman to have the Sun, Mars, and the ruler of the 7th house forming nice aspects at the same time is promising for a successful marriage. In the last chapter, Annie had some of these in place, but her 7th house ruler, Mars, was under affliction. So the marriage produced two children and lasted eleven years, but it eventually fell apart as signified by the aspects at the time of the marriage. It was rushed and premature.

Venus reflects a true love connection, and the Moon is active to show the changing domestic scene as a result of the union. These latter two are especially important in a man's chart since they rule the women in his life. There are usually multiple major progressed aspects involving these, as well as the ruler of the 7th house, when marriage occurs.

If a relationship is going to lead to marriage, other house rulers also become active to show how such a union will affect other areas. This is especially true of the 8th house, which often becomes active to show the pooling of joint resources and learning to work as a team.

When reading the chart for love or marriage potential, it's also important to watch the ruler of the progressed Ascendant. This planet shows by its aspects the types of experiences a person is likely to attract.

Let's take a look at Laura's chart to see what was happening when her boyfriend betrayed her.

Jilted

When Laura went to give her long-term steady boyfriend his birthday gift, his brother met her at the door. He had some shocking news to tell her. Brad, also known as the Dirty Dog, had ran off and gotten married earlier that day, without even telling Laura what he was up to! She couldn't believe it. How could someone be so capricious and thoughtless to another person, she wondered? She felt betrayed. She was confused and hurt; she'll never forget that evening. Born May 13, 1958, 9:10 PM; 113W59/46N52, her charts were revealing.

With her progressed Ascendant in early Capricorn, the ruler of Laura's progressed chart was Saturn. This ruling planet shows, according to its aspects, where a person is going in life and the kinds of events coming due. Saturn was opposed by her progressed Sun, an aspect of separation and estrangements. In fact she'd just lost her mother the previous year to brain cancer under the same aspect. The opposition of Sun and Saturn is often indicative of worry over a parent, and it usually brings some depressive circumstances and restricting conditions.

Her progressed Venus was closely semi-square her natal Moon. This aspect sometimes coincides with shattered romances or broken engagements. Venus is naturally associated with matters of the heart.

She also had a semi-square from progressed Sun to progressed Uranus, which suggests trouble through men; not the best aspect for the women in their relationships, whether married or single.

There is a trine from progressed Mars to her natal Ascendant, good for cooperative efforts, and a trine from progressed Uranus to natal Venus, which stimulates new love interests, new friends, group activities and joining clubs; not necessarily conducive to marriage unless other stabilizing aspects exist.

When the aspects of transiting planets are combined with the progressed aspects, which play up themes of separations, it's easy to see that there was pressure building up that was impacting Laura's Venus, planet of love. Transiting Uranus was in a close square to her natal Venus, an aspect of sudden or unexpected breakups. Transiting Neptune, planet of mystery, was in a wide square to natal Venus. It signified disillusionment through a romantic relationship, when the partner may be disloyal.

She also had an opposition from transiting Pluto to her progressed Venus in the natal 5th house. This aspect reflects the increasing difficulty she'd noticed recently in trying to understand Brad and their relationship. He had not been supportive when her mom died and had actually started to back off then, just when she needed emotional support the most. The relationship had begun to change, and she wasn't sure where they stood anymore.

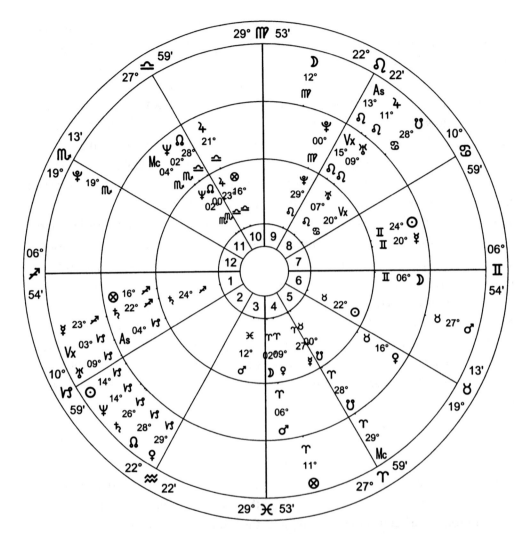

Figure 3a: Jilted

Inner Wheel: Laura's Natal Chart: May 13, 1958; 9:10 PM MST; 113W59, 46N52

Middle Wheel: Progressed Chart: Jan. 4, 1991; 7:30 PM MST; 113W59, 46N52

Outer Wheel: Transit Chart: Jan. 4, 1991; 7:30 PM MST; 113W59, 46N52

Transiting Saturn was square the cusp of her natal 5th house of romance. The transiting lunar nodes and transiting Venus also squared that cusp. The cusp is the most sensitive area of a house. Certainly, the rule of three or more similar aspects was met. Venus and the 5th house cusp, both signifying affairs of the heart, were meeting with multiple conflicting aspects.

Her progressed Moon was just coming into conjunction with her natal 7th house cusp. The Moon emphasizes areas of fluctuations and changes by its position, and this was another reflection of changes in her intimate relationships.

Transiting Moon was closely opposing her Mars, indicating a conflict or confrontation. Mars rules her natal 5th house of romance. Only in this case, Dirty Dog couldn't even do it himself. Instead, she learned the upsetting news by proxy through his brother as transiting Mercury crossed her Saturn/Sun opposition.

Her first natal planet to rise to the Horary Ascendant when she rang the bell was Pluto, an apt symbol for the painful process of having to purge Brad from her life in order to experience a rebirth.

Laura's natal chart shows Venus in Aries, the sign of its detriment. Venus is semi-square the Sun, and she has the South Node in the 5th house. Together, these showed the possibility of suffering a heartbreaking romantic loss at some point

during her life. The progressed aspects reflected when.

Something else that can be noted is that Brad's Sun was square her natal Venus, one indication that he might break her heart, especially since she had the matching semi-square between Sun and Venus in her natal chart, showing such potential. At the time he deceived Laura, Brad was under the influence of Neptune, shown here in the transits on his birthday, with Neptune conjunct the Sun. He was confused, under some illusions of his own. Uranus was in orb of conjunction to his Sun, when unusual ties may be formed or broken. Maybe that is why his sudden secretive marriage to his high school sweetheart only lasted two years. Guess Brad just couldn't deal with the reality of Laura's responsibilities at the time.

It took Laura a long time to get over the hurt she experienced. She couldn't believe Brad didn't even break off their relationship of many years before running off and getting married to someone else. Fortunately, she did have some distractions and responsibilities that helped take her mind off it during those first weeks afterward. These can be seen in the lunar aspects just after the incident, as the progressing Moon was sextile progressed Mars, sextile Uranus and sextile Venus. She was taking tae kwon do and other classes, and had her hands full with taking care of her family, including her father, who'd moved in with her after her mother died. He was of comfort, support and assistance through her heartbreaking ordeal, shown by her progressed Jupiter sextile to progressed Saturn. He helped keep her mind on practical matters. She also had the supportive trine of progressed Sun to her Jupiter, which helped her adopt a philosophical attitude about the experience.

Signatures of Romantic Compatibility

One of the best features for general compatibility, whether in a friendship or a marriage is for the Moon in one horoscope to be in the same sign as the Sun in the other. This shows harmony and understanding.

For marriage, some of the best aspects include: Moon of one conjunct the Moon of the other; Moon of one conjunct the Ascendant of the other; Venus of one conjunct the Ascendant of the other. Wide orbs work here, and often it is enough to have the two in the same sign.

When Venus of one partner is in the same sign as the Moon or Ascendant of the other, a strong bond of love is often felt. Venus in one chart in the same sign as the Sun in the other is also an indication of affection. This can mean a strong friendship or an ideal love between partners. The Venus person loves and appeals to the other.

A strong bond between the sexes involves Venus in one horoscope in the same sign as Mars in the other. This gives physical passion. The person who has Mars on the Venus of the other will play the role of the seducer. This is more promising for a hot affair than for marriage unless there are other supporting aspects. Squares or oppositions between Venus and Mars may give passion, but also conflicts.

Another strong sexual attraction occurs when the Moon of one individual falls in the same sign as Mars in the other. However, there may also be a lot of arguments or quarrels due to tension. The same holds true if the Moon of one person squares or opposes the Mars of the other.

As the Greater Fortune, when the Jupiter of one falls in the same sign as the Sun in the other horoscope, the Jupiter person will be generous and indulgent to the other. The Jupiter person plays a benevolent role and showers gifts on the other. There are quite similar themes if Jupiter of one falls in the same sign as Venus of the other, or if Jupiter falls on the Ascendant of the other. The Jupiter person tends to impress the other person with his or her importance as well. It is similar with Jupiter to Moon relationships. Jupiter treats the Moon person most generously while the Moon person honors and looks up to the Jupiter person. These are quite happy arrangements for both generally. However, if Jupiter forms adverse aspects in the natal chart it will play down the benefits.

The very opposite may be the case when the Saturn of one falls in the same sign as the Sun or Venus of the other. The Saturn person may be stingy. The Saturn person may also seem boring to the other or have a wet blanket affect. Sometimes there's an attraction between two who have these planets in opposite signs, though it is a bit of a heavy vibe. The Saturn person may need the Sun person to cheer him or her up, so that Saturn is willing to let the Sun take the spotlight, and the Sun person is willing to put up with the drag on his or her optimism that Saturn often causes.

If you want someone you can talk to, look for someone with their Mercury in the same sign as your Sun. Be prepared to do a lot of listening too. For fun and naturalness, look for someone who has their Venus in the same sign as your Mercury, or vice versa.

There is also a lot of talk and possible debate when Mars of one is in the same sign as Mercury in the other horoscope. Check the aspects to these planets in the natal horoscopes though, because with difficult aspects there, this feature could quickly turn ugly. If afflicted in the nativity, the Mars person might deal harshly and critically with the other.

When the Sun of one falls on the Neptune of the other, the Sun person can be misled, confused, or charmed by the other. Check the aspects to both planets in the nativities to see how this will go. Similarly, when there are Mars to Neptune connections, the relationship may be on the weird side or leaning toward the dangerous. If the aspects to either planet in the individual nativities are adverse, this combination in the comparison can lead to crime or scandal.

When Venus in one chart combines with Neptune in the other, it can mean an ideal love, but cruelty, contrariness, or difficulty may result if there are difficult aspects to either planet in the respective horoscope.

With the Sun of one in the same sign as Uranus in the other horoscope, the Sun person will find the other to be amusing and stimulating, or irritating, depending on the aspects to the respective planets in the nativities. These are out of the ordinary connections when the unusual or unexpected often happens, even though it is an exciting relationship. There is a similarity in relationships where the Moon of one is in the same sign as Uranus in the other. This, as well as Venus/Uranus combinations can lead to romance, and with Venus, it may mean a sudden attraction or even love at first sight.

Pluto is similar to Mars when joined with other planets. Pluto conjunct the Sun can indicate sexual attraction but a clash of wills. It is the same with Pluto and Mars joined. With Moon in hard aspect to Pluto, there can be attempts to remake the Moon individual by the Pluto person. Pluto in aspect to Venus signals strong romantic sexual attractions, and this acts in a similar fashion as Mars to Venus aspects.

When there is a planet of one person connecting to the Ascendant of the other person, this will cause similar reactions as if the planet was combined with the Sun.

When it comes to connections between the two Suns, it is generally found that compatibility or affinity exists between the fire signs Aries, Leo, and Sagittarius; between the earth signs Taurus, Virgo, and Capricorn; between the air signs Gemini, Libra, and Aquarius; and between the water signs Cancer, Scorpio, and Pisces. There is generally less affinity and more antagonism between the cardinal signs Aries, Cancer, Libra, and Capricorn; between the fixed signs Taurus, Leo, Scorpio, and Aquarius; and between the mutable signs Gemini, Virgo, Sagittarius, and Pisces. Usually the fire and air signs get along while earth and water signs get along. These are generalizations, however, and may be modified according to the strength and condition of the Sun in the respective horoscopes along with other combinations between the two charts. In some cases, having the Suns in opposite signs can be very complementary.

There are other combinations and aspects that shed light on compatibility, but these are some of the most informative that are easy to spot.

We can put these guidelines to work to find the compatibility of Lee and Trish, our next couple.

A Romantic Meeting

This next chart belongs to Lee, who recently met Trish and planned to give her an engagement ring on her birthday. The progressed chart and transits are set for the beginning of their first date. Let's look first at his natal chart to see his relationship potential.

Lee's Natal Chart

Lee's 7th house ruler is Mars, showing that relationships come about quickly. Lee is attracted to the more assertive types who somehow stand out above the rest (Mars). He is daring in the area of marriage. Even if upsets occur, he will not be afraid to get involved again. The house with Aries on the cusp shows where the urges and passions are strong. Other sacrifices or compromises will often be made for the sake of the opportunity to actively participate in the experiences associated with the

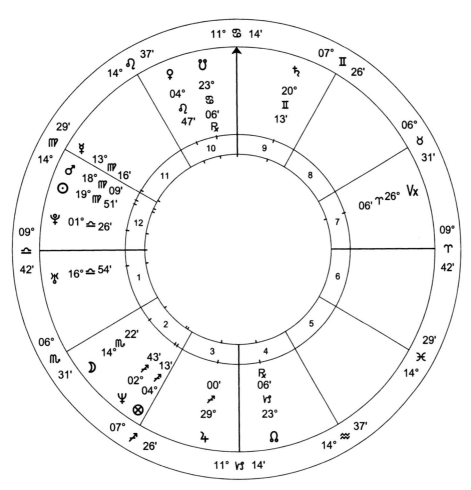

Figure 3b: Lee's Natal Chart
Sep. 12, 1972; 8:05 AM EST; 85W40, 40N33

Aries house. Lee's Libra Ascendant also shows that relationships are of a high priority for him.

Mars is conjunct the Sun and sextile the Moon. Already dynamic, Mars is more energetic due to the conjunction with the Sun. A relationship is a must for Lee to function at his highest potential. It would support and push him to pursue his life purpose and important goals. The sextile from Mars to the Moon shows that Lee enjoys the domestic scene afforded by such a partnership as marriage, and that he responds well to the nurturing qualities of a wife. With the Moon ruling the 10th house, his basic life direction is assisted by such a partnership, a repeat of the theme shown by the Sun.

With his Moon in Scorpio, Lee tends to take personal affairs very seriously, and this Moon sign can lead to possessiveness. There's a strong will, passion, emotional intensity, and plenty of potential to dominate the domestic scene, best if directed toward making constructive improvements.

A conjunction of the 7th house ruler (Mars) with Mercury in Virgo shows the potential to be critical of the partner and to engage in debates. The 12th house position of Mars suggests that disputes with partners are likely to remain a behind-the-scenes activity. The square from Mars to Saturn suggests that an excitable temper could cause serious arguments. With Sat-

urn ruling the 4th house, there might be a stand off within the home when these problems come up. This aspect suggests that some sorrows will be encountered through his intimate relationships. (Lee's first marriage ended in divorce, and there are two children from the marriage, thus confirming several of the natal promises.)

Venus rules the women in Lee's life whom he might wish to form a cooperative effort with. It is involved in a trine to Neptune and a sextile to Pluto. Such a combination indicates karmic or fated attractions, the possibility of finding the true soul mate, and idealistic expectations in matters of love. The only downfall is the tendency for Lee to over-idealize a partner. This can make it difficult for the partner, who may feel she cannot be accepted for herself, faults and all. Venus is sextile the Ascendant and trine the Descendant from warm and sunny Leo. In the 10th house, Venus shows that Lee is assisted in reaching success and pursuing life direction by associations with women—with marriage partners specifically. Lee would be attracted to more responsible types. His Venus is semi-square the Sun, Mars, and Saturn, so Lee is sensitive and may be easily hurt. As before, these indicate a measure of problems in his relationships.

Uranus rules Lee's 5th house, bringing the potential for sudden temporary love affairs. Uranus in semi-square to Neptune indicates that love affairs are subject to peculiar, elusive, and upsetting conditions from time to time. With Uranus trine Saturn, Lee is inclined to be romantically attracted to more serious types, and only serious relationships interest him romantically in the first place. Uranus is semi-sextile the Moon, showing spontaneity in his relationships. Uranus is semi-sextile Mars, which can help a marriage continue to be exciting and romantic. Romance and marriage are tied together very closely. Uranus ruling the 5th and Mars the 7th house may incline Lee to rush into marriage. When Lee becomes seriously involved romantically, it will be sudden and could easily lead to marriage. With Uranus in an angular house, he is also prone to divorce.

First Date with Trish

It is fascinating to look at the progressions and transits at the time of the first date. The most important factors are progressed aspects involving the Ascendant or Midheaven. These show the potential for important events.

Lee's progressed Mars, ruler of his marriage house, is sextile his progressed Midheaven, indicating that an important relationship could be formed at this time. The progressed Midheaven is conjunct natal Venus, again pointing to affairs of the heart. This Midheaven is trine progressed Neptune, a harmonious aspect indicating new entanglements and the possibility of a romantic dream come to life. The linking Midheaven reestablishes the trine between Venus and Neptune from the natal chart, energizing the potential for a spiritual connection. A repeating link involving progressed Venus in square to natal Neptune is found, bringing more emphasis to such themes.

Since Neptune is beginning to appear prominently, this square might cause one to suspect that Lee's natal tendency to idealize a partner or to have an otherwise unrealistic view of the relationship might become an issue. A square between Venus and Neptune is often found at times of *heartbreak or lost love*. This potential will need to be considered with the rest of the aspects, especially since Venus is Lee's ruler as well as ruling matters of love and partnerships.

His progressed Ascendant is approaching a sextile to natal Jupiter. Ceremonies are suggested and, with the Midheaven involved in so many aspects, a possible change of status. Venus has progressed to trine progressed Jupiter, an aspect showing important connections with women. The North Node transiting the natal Ascendant also suggests that Lee is entering a period of important personal crossroads. Mars is sextile his natal Venus by progression, a classic aspect of new love connections.

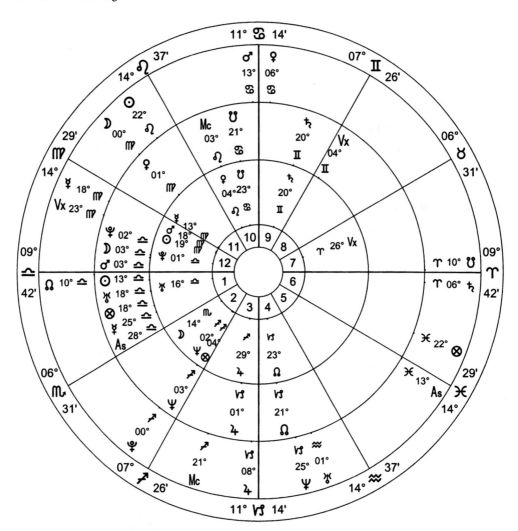

Figure 3c: First Date

Inner Wheel: Lee's Natal Chart: Sep. 12, 1972; 8:05 AM EST; 85W40, 40N33
Center Wheel: Progressed Chart: Aug. 14, 1996; 8:30 PM EST; 85W40, 40N33
Outer Wheel: Transit Chart: Aug. 14, 1996; 8:30 PM EST; 85W40, 40N33

Mars is sextile progressed Neptune, so Trish may charm him.

His progressed Moon is sextile his progressed Midheaven and natal Venus while it conjoins progressed Mars, showing event potential involving a new relationship. Transiting Pluto conjuncts natal Neptune. From there, Pluto forms a sextile to progressed Moon and progressed Mars while in trine to natal Venus, stimulating the most romantic patterns. While transiting Pluto is trine the radical Venus, it is square progressed Venus. Since these contacts repeat a natal theme, they become important in distinguishing that this relationship will fulfill the natal promise of a *fated* quality. Although these two are in good aspect in the natal chart, the current square may be problematic. There's a strong desire and urgency to find love but with Pluto square his progressed Venus, Lee may be *too hasty in choosing a partner.*

Converse progressed Mars is at 2° Virgo, conjunct progressed Venus, but square natal Neptune. The first aspect is significant of a passionate union, but the second aspect suggests misleading impulses and accentuates the themes of *unrealistic expectations,* increasing the chances for disillusionment. Transiting Pluto ties into this theme by square and conjunction and indicates that *manipulation, jealousy, or power struggles* for control within the relationship could

be a problem and might bring explosive situations.

Transiting Uranus will soon oppose Lee's natal Venus. This aspect can signify magnetism and spontaneity within the relationship at its best, but such an aspect can be suggestive of *breakups.*

Transiting Saturn in trine to natal Venus approaches the 7th house cusp. This may be seen at the time of serious commitments such as marriage. An individual may be ready to get involved "for better or worse."

Transiting Mars on the Midheaven is sextile natal Mercury and Mars. The link to Mercury repeats a contact in the natal chart, as does Mars in square to natal Uranus, linking the rulers of marriage and romance. The square suggests *impulsiveness.*

At the beginning of their first date, the transiting Moon conjoins progressed Venus, an indication that a romantic tie might be established immediately. A New Moon in Leo just occurred, suggesting new beginnings involving romantic relationships.

It is clear that the themes from Lee's natal chart concerning love and marriage are heavily activated. Lee will be quite taken by Trish and ready to go on to more serious and permanent arrangements even though there is plenty of potential for conflicts and likely some unrealistic expectations on his part. Overall, the aspects of Venus suggest that a relationship entered into at this time will be subject to a premature end. He would be advised to take things slow and easy.

Trish's Natal Chart

In Trish's chart, the ruler of her marriage house is Mercury, and Saturn is occupying the 7th house. These two are trine to each other in the natal chart, showing that she will be conservative, using logic and practical judgment in deciding on such things as marriage. These also point to the type she would be attracted to: someone who is talkative, serious, and a problem solver. With her 7th house ruler in the 11th house, a requirement in her partnerships is that her partner be a friend first and foremost. Mercury also forms a trine to Jupiter, ruler of her 1st house, indicating that harmony can come about through marriage as long as she is allowed to retain a sense of personal freedom.

With Saturn occupying the 7th house, marriage will be delayed for Trish. She might marry someone older or of a very different age group. At the very least she will be drawn to someone who is of a serious nature, and she can anticipate extra responsibilities as a result of a union such as marriage. He might be an executive with Mars trine Saturn. Since Trish had one serious relationship four years earlier that resulted in a child, but not in marriage, the delay factor shown by Saturn in her 7th house has been fulfilled at least once.

Mercury forms a square to the natal Moon, showing domestic disputes and arguments with partners. Mercury conjunct Mars stresses the point. This theme is repeated once again in the square from Mars to the Moon. With important rulers of the marriage house in Scorpio, Trish may have a tendency to try to remold partners into a more perfected form, or they may try to do the same to her. This brings about the potential for manipulation or control issues, suggested also by her Pluto in Libra. With her 4th house ruled by Mars and in trine to Saturn, she will want to take the lead in the home and the way it is run.

The ruler of the 5th house is Venus in Sagittarius. This sign position for Venus suggests someone who needs freedom in love and who is content with casual romances and friendships. This goes along with indications from the 7th house that she will not be inclined to jump into a serious commitment without taking time to judge all factors. In the natal chart Venus conjuncts the Sun in passionate Scorpio. Trish attracts partners who will spoil her but she would not take well to being tied down.

First Date with Lee

Trish's progressed chart shows that natal Mercury as ruler of the 7th house of marriage is now sextile the progressed Ascen-

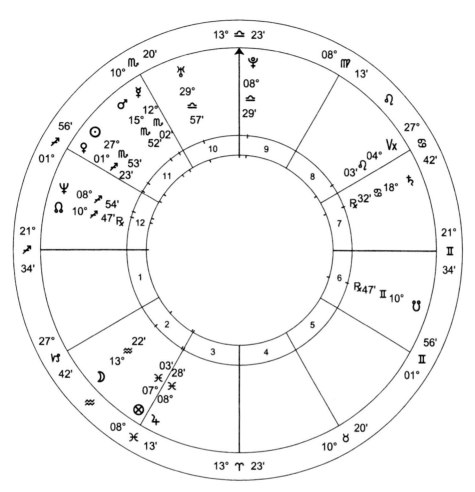

Figure 3d: Trish's Natal Chart
Nov. 20, 1974; 9:35 AM EST; 85W40, 40N33

dant. This verifies the possibility that an important relationship could be established.

The progressed Sun is approaching a conjunction to the natal Ascendant. This aspect is not yet within the allowed orb but is an aspect that is often prominent at the time of marriage for a woman.

Progressed Mars is conjunct natal Venus, indicating that the time is ripe for a romantic relationship to develop. Progressed Venus is sextile natal Uranus. As seen earlier, sudden magnetic attractions are typical under such an influence, although not necessarily permanent. Transiting Pluto is in conjunction to natal Venus and progressed Mars, showing the desire for a romantic attachment and that there may be some profound experiences that involve affairs of the heart and intimate connections.

Transiting Mars is trine natal Mercury and Mars, her natal 7th house indicators. This verifies the potential for a partnership to form when Trish meets Lee. Transiting Mars is opposing her progressed Ascendant; in other words, it conjuncts her progressed 7th house cusp, a decidedly stimulating aspect in relationships.

Other transits are Mercury, ruler of the natal 7th house, in sextile to natal Saturn in the 7th house, while sextile the natal Mercury/Mars conjunction.

Although Trish's romantic and marriage potential is stimulated, it is much less so than Lee's. It is mainly her 5th house ruler (Venus) that is active in the progressions. Her Moon, ruler of her progressed 7th house, is involved in no major aspects in the progressions and neither is Saturn, while Mercury is only involved in one aspect and her Sun not yet in orb of aspect to the Ascendant. There are not enough aspects to signify marriage at this time. She'd be inclined to hang onto her freedom and content with an exciting, fun, flirtatious, and sexy romance, especially since the recent Leo New Moon fell in her 8th house.

Chart Comparison & Summary

To quickly find connections between the two charts, Lee's chart is in the center wheel, Trish's in the second wheel and the transits for the time of their first date are in the outer wheel.

Obvious right from the beginning is that Trish's Pluto is conjunct Lee's Ascendant. This can be quite a profound influence. She will fulfill the natal potential in his chart as it calls for karmic ties, and she can bring about deep changes within him. Neither of them will be the same as a result of this relationship.

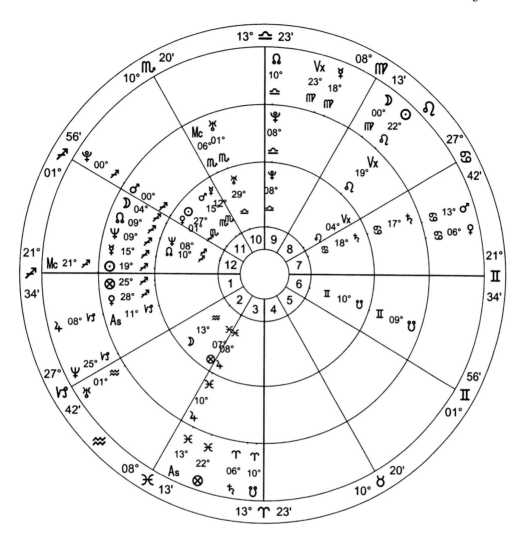

Figure 3e: First Date

Inner Wheel: Trish's Natal Chart: Nov. 20, 1974; 9:35 AM EST; 85W40, 40N33
Center Wheel: Progressed Chart: Aug. 14, 1996; 8:30 PM EST; 85W40, 40N33
Outer Wheel: Transit Chart: Aug. 14, 1996; 8:30 PM EST; 85W40, 40N33

These connections are often compelling, even obsessive for one or both partners. They may be unable to break apart, even if there is good reason. It can be a very profound and positive aspect, but if such things as manipulation, jealousy, and control become an issue, then a breakup can be quite a destructive one, and one or both partners are likely to be devastated.

Lee's Venus is conjunct her Vertex at 4° Leo, an aspect somewhat similar to having his Venus conjunct her Descendant. They both may feel it is a fated love.

Her Midheaven is conjunct his Ascendant, an angular connection that is karmic and often appears in the charts of married couples.

Her Saturn is conjunct his South Node, often a heavy, serious association where both persons tend to discipline and set boundaries for the other.

Here are the planetary aspects formed between the two charts that are most descriptive:

Lee's Moon is in the same sign as Trish's Sun; good for compatibility between friends or lovers.

Her Sun is conjunct his Neptune, so she is charmed by Lee.

Her Venus is conjunct his Neptune, so they might make ideal lovers.

Lee's Jupiter is in the same sign as her Venus so he would be indulgent with Trish.

His Moon is conjunct her Mars, so there is sexual attraction, but also tensions and quarrels.

Her Mars is square his Venus, fostering sexual attraction, but also a tendency to argue.

Her Pluto on his Ascendant suggests an intense relationship with potential control issues.

Her Moon is closely square his Moon, causing difficulties in understanding one another's feelings.

Her Moon opposes his Venus, so there's sexual attraction, but there may be problems relating, and the bond may be broken.

People who are attracted to one another frequently have similar configurations in the individual charts, showing an ability to identify with one another. Both Trish and Lee have Mars/Mercury conjunctions in their natal charts, which show how they relate in close partnerships. It has been demonstrated that each of them are prone to having disputes with partners, and that each of them leans toward being critical or controlling in a relationship. Not only do they each have this conjunction, but they also form a sextile to the pair in the other's chart. They might actually enjoy arguing. This theme is repeated with her Mars/Mercury conjunct his Moon. There is sexual attraction and

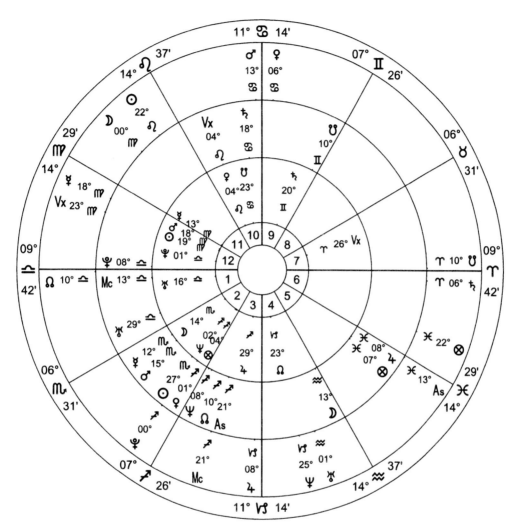

Figure 3f: Chart Comparison with Transits for First Date
Inner Wheel: Lee's Natal Chart: Sep. 12, 1972; 8:05 AM EST; 85W40, 40N33
Center Wheel: Trish's Natal Chart: Nov. 20, 1974; 9:35 AM EST; 85W40, 40N33
Outer Wheel: Transit Chart: Aug. 14, 1996; 8:30 PM EST; 85W40, 40N33

intellectual stimulation, but the drawback with the ties so far is that it could simply be a case of too much arguing and not enough understanding.

Although Lee and Trish conform to a few basic requirements of the other, more harmonious aspects between the two charts would be needed for a durable and healthy relationship. They may not be accepting of the other or willing to share in the control of the relationship. There are cautions of arguments and attempts to manipulate. With his progressed Venus square Neptune, Lee may not be viewing the relationship realistically. Overall, the individuals would be advised to go slow and easy before committing to anything serious. The attraction appears to be mostly physical and may not survive the harsher realities of life once that initial attraction has worn off. They may not be on the same page as to the direction of the relationship.

Nevertheless, at the time of the first date, the transiting Ascendant is in trine to transiting Mars and both form a close aspect to the Mars of each chart, reflecting the physical attraction that did result. Transiting Venus was alongside transiting Mars, so it too was applying to harmonious aspects to their Mars.

Update

The strong Plutonian factors seen in the charts came through in full force. Several breakups and makeups occurred between Lee and Trish. Both went through deep changes as a result of the relationship and attempts to make it work. They felt compelled to be together, yet had clashes of wills over the control and direction of the relationship. Their first big split postponed their engagement indefinitely. Lee was quite crushed by this first breakup, but he immediately began seeing someone else. He and Trish then got back together, but had another serious and final breakup. At that time Lee's progressed Moon came into orb with Trish's natal Pluto. The progression of Lee's Moon to Trish's Pluto signified the end of the romance.

A similar progression of one's Moon across Uranus in another person's chart is often indicative of separating trends. This will be more likely to represent a problematic separation if the relationship was primarily Uranian in nature to begin with and without strong stabilizing connections between the charts.

Trish went her way and Lee went his. With so many aspects in his progressions indicating marriage potential and stimulation, Lee did marry within a year, while the major aspects were still in play. Unfortunately, it was ill timed and the marriage didn't work out long term. The themes of unrealistic expectations in partnerships, and impulse, indicated by the aspects, best describes why the relationship didn't work out. He married a third time under better Venus aspects; this marriage has survived some rocky roads.

Synastry & the Sun

An excellent starting point in analyzing any relationship is with the Sun. The Sun rules the ego, and the way in which two egos mesh is a strong factor in determining how a relationship might go. Whether it is a love relationship you are inquiring about or one involving a child, parent, or boss, the house position of another person's Sun in your horoscope reveals your response to the association. In turn, you can find their response to you by considering the house position of your Sun in their chart.

If someone's Sun falls in your 1st house, there is an element of competition. These people get your attention and cause you to look at yourself in comparison to them. You may have the peculiar feeling that you must maintain your image and that you can never completely let your guard down around this person. There is a good chance that your actual meeting was in some competitive capacity, which is one of the healthiest relationships for this po-

sition. Many other kinds of relationships would feel this strain of competition in an uncomfortable manner. Friendly competition is likely between family members with this position.

Having the Sun of another person fall in your 2nd house is usually a fortunate position for a warm relationship. This person genuinely cares for you and supports your efforts. They do not judge you in any way, and as far as they are concerned you can do no wrong. To them, your talents and values are obvious and should be to everyone else as well. They want you to be paid for your real worth. The support you receive from them may be in the form of financial or monetary support, or they may simply have a way of putting your mind on your own resources with thoughts toward increasing or protecting what you have.

When someone's Sun falls in your 3rd house, there is mutual intellectual stimulation and much to discuss. There is an ease and comfort in each other's presence, as you tend to view life from similar perspectives. This person may feel like a natural comrade, such as a sibling might. You may have met due to living in the same vicinity, or through a mutual relationship with a third person. These relationships tend to be light and airy rather than deep. Your exchange with these people is nonchalant. Daily communication is the focal link and it usually isn't necessary to put a lot of attention on maintaining these relationships.

Having someone's Sun fall in your 4th house suggests a relationship borne from a domestic link. This position is common in family ties. There is a sense of security from knowing and associating with this person. There's a comfortable bond, as if they are family. Pleasures you share may center on the home or a shared domestic interest. At times you may find yourself asking for advice, as a child would ask a parent. A certain amount of respect is demanded from you, and you tend to take more from these people than you would from others. A pitfall is that you might end up resenting the way this person wants to run your life.

When someone's Sun falls in your 5th, there is an element of playfulness. This is a lighthearted relationship and usually much enjoyment results from the association. You may have connected through a mutual pleasurable pursuit, a hobby, or an activity related to entertainment. There is a youthful vibrancy in these relationships, as this is the house associated with romance. This is one of the best positions for friendships; a happy relationship that could last through thick and thin. This person awakens your creative adrenaline, and you tend to forget about the more serious aspects of life when in their presence. Sometimes they feel like

your child and you may find yourself indulging them.

If another person's Sun falls in your 6th house, you may feel the necessity of exchanging services or that one of you has a duty to perform for the other. Often, this appears to be an obligation you owe them for some long-ago favor or service they did for you. You may have the distinct feeling of expectation on their part. The underlying purpose for the two of you coming together in the first place is for this repayment of service. If you accept help from this person, you will be expected to repay them eventually, but the form of payment is something that only you will understand. In the meantime you will have their devotion and help.

When someone's Sun falls in your 7th house, you may hit it off well enough to become partners. This position has the opposite effect of the 1st, where you felt you must maintain face. Here, you have nothing to hide. You want to give of yourself, as it seems most natural to form an allegiance. You have great admiration for this person. Marriages often have this position, and it is an advantage for any serious partnership. This house also rules enemies, and the relationship must go one of two ways. If the other person is of the opposite sex, you'll tend more toward partnership, whereas same sex associations more often tend to become enemies.

If a person's Sun falls in your 8th house, you may go through deep changes as a result of the association. These relationships often develop because of a feeling on your part that a change is due. At best, this person will rekindle something that you had given up. There is an aura of mystery about this person that appeals to you, including sexual allure. An intimate relationship has the potential of becoming extremely sensual and erotic. Associations of the 8th house that do not work out have the potential for fireworks over shared property. This relationship can be revealing and uplifting, or it can be painful and disastrous.

If someone's Sun falls in your 9th house, you are of similar minds. Mutual interests may lie in areas of philosophy, travel, or religion. You may explore theories or beliefs, and your exchange is stimulating. You enjoy yourself immensely with this person, and the two of you center your discussions on the broader issues of life. Discussions are on an abstract level, and you may share common goals or visions. This relationship is not so good for everyday responsibilities. The magic may be lost if forced into any serious arrangement. This person is in a position to promote you to others, and you find it easy to let them become your teacher.

When someone's Sun falls in your 10th house, you regard the person as an authority figure. This person has the in-fluence to make or break you in regard to your vocational goals. They can make you look good if they so desire and generally are all for you, but you must be willing to give them the leading position. On the other hand, they may prefer to hold you in a subordinate position. In relationships with this position where the person is not an obvious authority, you still find that you do regard them as an authority in some area, and you will ask their opinion in their area of expertise, even if they are much younger.

When someone's Sun falls in your 11th house, you share common hopes and dreams. Common interests are often the basis for this friendship. You might have met through an organization, club, or group activity. These associations usually come about when there is a need for sympathetic encouragement, and the relationship is full of warmth. There is much to discuss and an openness between you. You allow this person to know about your motivations and goals, and you enjoy the opportunity to voice yourself. There are shared goals on a broad basis, rather than true intimacy. Your creative ideas flow in the presence of this person.

A person whose Sun falls in your 12th house appears to know more about you than anything discussed between you. They see beyond the superficial and are aware of your secret fears and weaknesses. You get the feeling they have been there. This person feels the same way about chances of reaching their personal ambitions as you do about yours, creating a sympathetic bond. A rapport exists that is sometimes comforting and at other times disquieting. Contacts between you may leave you feeling vaguely upset. You may be reminded of things you'd rather not think about. Still, they can be of assistance in times of trouble. To fully appreciate them, you may have to be going through a crisis, which is when they are most helpful.

In summary, the most cataclysmic relationships involve connections with the angular houses: the 1st, 4th, 7th, and 10th. These people will exert a decided influence over your affairs. The 2nd, 5th, 8th, and 11th house connections may be comprised of long-standing associations with people having some influence over your personal gains or losses. The service and communication houses are the 3rd, 6th, 9th, and 12th. These relationships tend to have the least influence, since they remain in the background of your awareness.

A good combination for love and marriage might be one Sun in the 5th house and another Sun in the 7th house. This suggests a romantic partnership and the best of both worlds. There are many possibilities though, and this analysis of the Sun will be most informative in matters of love when combined with the signatures of romantic compatibility given earlier in this chapter.

chapter four

Money & Success

Money and success signs in a chart are most often found in the 2nd house of resources and the 10th house of profession. However, each of the succeedant houses can be termed houses of resource, with each of them representing a different kind of resource.

The 2nd house tells of financial standing and represents money the individual is able to earn. This is usually through the 6th house of work and the 10th house of profession. The 2nd house includes not only money, but also all portable property and resources. These 2nd house resources come to the individual based on the personal abilities shown by the 1st house indicators. Many planets in the 1st house may show abundant talents and versatility.

The 5th house rules the money or resources that come to one as a return from speculation, risk taking, and gambling. The riches from this house are based on the confidence of the individual to take risks, and this confidence is a result of his or her subjective security shown by the 4th house.

The 8th house shows resources that the individual shares with one or more others—often marriage or business partner. With a good 8th house, other people support the individual's monetary needs. This house also indicates whether the individual is able to get loans from banking institutions and whether to expect gains through taxes, inheritance, wills, and insurance. The returns from this house are based on the relationships of the 7th house.

The 11th house shows resources available through employers as well as gains through associations and group affiliations. Valuable friendships in higher circles result from Jupiter here and in good aspect. Money from business is also shown here. The 11th house benefits come to the individual as a result of the recognition and achievement shown by the 10th house.

In addition to all of these, the 4th house is a house of resource as it relates to real estate holdings.

The signs that appear on the cusps of these supply houses describe the potential for wealth to come through that area. In general, the signs most often associated with an easy accumulation of wealth are Taurus, Cancer, Leo, Scorpio, Capricorn, and Aquarius. Sagittarius, the sign corresponding with Jupiter, could bring material wealth, but may bring spiritual wealth instead. Libra often shows benefits that result from a cooperative effort or partnership.

Beneficial aspects to planets in the supply houses show a connection to the particular benefits from that house. If planets in these houses are outer planets, or well configured with outer planets, the auspicious potential is increased.

Jupiter's position and aspects are most important in establishing the possibility of wealth since it is the Greater Fortune. Any of the planets in good aspect with Jupiter bring certain benefits and should be studied for potential. The outer planets combined with Jupiter are especially good for acquiring wealth.

There are some signature aspects as well as positions and signs that are more prominent in the charts of those whom we call "successful." For instance, aspects between Jupiter and Saturn can be very promising for attaining lifelong wealth. The same is true of Jupiter with Neptune, and this is called the "millionaire aspect." It represents a lavish lifestyle. In this case it does not seem to matter much what kind of aspect the two are making. J. P. Morgan had Jupiter in opposition to Neptune and a square from Saturn to both. The same is true in the chart of Hugh Hefner. Marilyn Monroe had an opposition between Jupiter and Neptune. Elvis Presley had the two planets in sextile, as does Bill Gates.

Pluto in beneficial aspect with Jupiter can be wonderful materially. It is favorable for amassing large sums of money. Such individuals may have the assistance of influential figures or gains may come from inheritance, insurance, or from entering raffles, lotteries, and so forth.

A good aspect between Jupiter and Mars assures that a person will make money faster than it can be spent. A good aspect between Jupiter and the Sun brings many benefactors into the life that can help them reach ambitions. It can bring material wealth or, at the very least, the individual is satisfied with the amount she or he has. These aspects, as well as Jupiter in good aspect to Uranus, are sometimes referred to as "lucky." With Uranus, involvement with advanced ideas or the latest methods brings excellent returns.

Jupiter well configured with Venus is a promise of an elite social life, and suggests existing resources that allow for a rich lifestyle. Jupiter in nice aspect to Mercury gives sound judgment and a knack for saying the right thing at the right time. Jupiter in good aspect with the Moon is one of the most auspicious aspects for financial success. Such a person is lucky, favored, and protected. Benefits often come through women.

Jupiter in its own sign of Sagittarius is very promising, but would depend on other factors for fulfillment. A prominent position of Jupiter or of a planet well configured with Jupiter increases the possibility of attaining wealth.

The aspects of the Sun are important in determining success potential, for it gives stamina and endurance to succeed in life when forming good aspects, while many barriers may prevent this if the Sun is heavily afflicted. There are many benefactors among those in a position to be of assistance when the aspects of the Sun are favorable.

If the natal chart shows promise of returns through any of the resource houses or aspects, then the progressions and transits will show when such good fortune can come about. The progressions involving Jupiter are most revealing. Venus, Lesser Fortune, is often found stimulated at such times, and the aspects of the Sun are also important.

On the other hand, if the natal chart denies luck, say through the speculation or gambling of the 5th house, then a lucky transit will only stir the individual to believe that a windfall will come about, but it often corresponds with heavy losses instead.

Since there are so many factors involved, an assessment of the nativity might determine that an individual could be very successful in one area, while not so successful in another. This is usually the case. While it would be fairly uncommon, if all of the areas of resource are favorable by sign and aspect, this is all the better for the individual.

Each nativity must be thoroughly studied to find the potential for wealth. A few charts are delineated in the following pages, one of a good friend, who started with very little and became exceptionally successful, and the other charts belong to a pair of lottery winners.

A Self-Made Millionaire

Howard's Capricorn Sun is a good starting point to describe the potential for a poor Kentucky coal miner's son to climb to the very top of the corporate business ladder and on to ultimate success.

Saturn, ruler of Capricorn, is often indicative of obstacles and restrictions met by the individual early in life. For Howard, the wide square between the Sun and Saturn indicates self-consciousness and his lack of confidence during his youth. Difficulties in school are shown in the afflictions to Mercury from Saturn and Uranus. Combined with those, the square of the Sun to his Neptune reflects his poor health in childhood. The Sun/Saturn square and the Sun/Neptune square suggests that the authority figures in his youth suffered hardships or ill health and were not in a position to be of particular help in his life direction.

The restrictions and limitations signified by Saturn's square to the Sun usually ensure that the individual becomes highly self-reliant and is driven to achieve worldly success—whatever it takes to ensure that the future holds no similar threats to those of the past. Steady and unrelenting in the ambitions to attain increased status, the individual often attains an elevated position later in life. Saturn is also said to take care of its own and provides rewards for those earlier trials. It is the planet of big business and organization, and many of those born under the Capricorn sign wield authority over others.

Howard's Capricorn Mercury emphasizes these traits. He's of a practical mind and much concerned with material accomplishments. He has organizational, managerial, and executive potential.

Howard's chart, with many of the planets angular, shows that he makes a strong impression on others. Such people do not long remain in the background, but ride the mainstream of life and are involved in many changes. The cardinal signs are prominent as well, and indicate that Howard is a "doer." He gets things going, and, with his 7th house Sun, is able to get others to follow his lead. Sun sextile the Moon shows his ability to get along with others.

When we check for his wealth and success potential, Howard has Leo on the cusp of the 2nd house, an auspicious sign for money he can earn for himself. It is ruled by the Sun, which forms some challenging aspects, helped only by a wide sextile to Jupiter. Pluto is in his 2nd house, sextile Neptune, but square the Moon and opposing Mars. It would take effort. He'd have to work hard and make sacrifices.

His 5th house has Libra on the cusp. Ruling Venus is sextile his Midheaven from the 7th house. Partners play a supportive role in his advancement, especially his wife. The Moon is in his 5th house. It forms many aspects. It is trine his Ascendant, widely trine Uranus, and widely sextile Venus and Sun. Although it is a wide trine between his Moon and Jupiter, Howard's Jupiter progresses rapidly and will trine his natal Moon around age fifty-six,

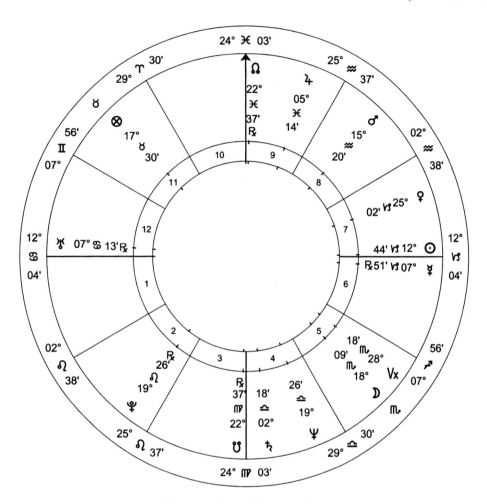

Figure 4a: Howard's Natal Chart
Jan. 3, 1951; 4:20 PM CST; 83W10, 37N02

so this gives a promising outlook for long-term growth and future earnings, especially as these depend on his willingness to take risks. In Scorpio, the Moon increases his determination and gives shrewd financial judgment. The Moon square Pluto and Mars in money houses represent conflicts over money at certain times in his life (divorce).

Jupiter is quite impressive in Howard's chart. Jupiter in Pisces is fortunate. This can bring unlimited potential to Jupiter's material side. Jupiter is co-ruler of Pisces, the sign on his Midheaven.

A close aspect of Jupiter in trine to Uranus is one of the lucky aspects. And, Uranus rules his 8th house, another of the supply houses! Uranus suggests that some lucky breaks come his way. These may have a direct bearing on an increased status and good reputation. The aspect promises long journeys, material good fortune, and luck with speculation. Howard is blessed with an intuition that allows him to take advantage of sudden or unexpected opportunities. When he does take risks, they have a way of working out in his favor. Mars in his 8th house in trine to Neptune also lends intuition when it comes to investments.

Howard definitely possesses wealth potential. The North Node on the Midheaven is also auspicious for material gains and success, especially with Venus in sextile. Jupiter and Uranus are most impressive.

Uranus, ruling the 9th house, points toward travel as an important factor in Howard's life. This is emphasized by Jupiter's placement in the 9th house. With Mercury sextile Jupiter, he is very fond of travel. He may travel in connection with his job and professional duties.

Uranus suggests that Howard is independent and advanced in his outlook. Mars in Aquarius agrees. Unafraid to go where life leads him, he tends to be daring with Sun opposing Uranus. Resourceful and inventive, he has a quality of charisma about him that draws others to him. In touch with a powerful inner purpose, he possesses an incredible will to achieve.

Uranus in opposition to Mercury in the natal chart with the mediating aspects from Jupiter increases Howard's wit, humor, and amusing manner. It increases his originality and inventiveness, and also shows that he loves going in new directions and into the future. He is ahead of his time and knows how to make his original ideas work for him. Jupiter sextile his Mercury gives good judgment.

Howard's magnetism and popularity is evident. Jupiter trine Uranus promises renown and it bestows exceptional creative abilities. Uranus in Cancer in a wide trine to the Moon suggests musical talent and a well-developed sense of sound and rhythm. Venus trine his Saturn in Libra also gives a sense of balance in music and composition. Mars trine his Neptune in Libra adds to his creative potential and increases his charm. In his teen years, Howard was a lead singer and guitar player with a successful young group. It was during this time that he began to build confidence and self-esteem.

Howard was unable to afford college but always looked for ways to be successful. When he found he had a knack for machine shop, he changed directions from music and threw himself into these classes. Though his musical talent and aptitude for electronics combined with charismatic qualities and public appeal suggest he might have been successful as a musician if he'd taken such a direction, Howard determined that a music career did not guarantee the stability he was aiming for. This decision exemplifies his Capricorn traits.

Immediately upon graduation from high school, Howard moved to a more lucrative area for his ambitions and got a reliable job. With support from his wife, and lots of hard work, he got through trade school to be a mechanical engineer. Much of this potential comes from his Aquarius Mars placement. He took flying lessons and acquired his own plane. He bought his first home in an elite area and a few years later he opened his own business.

Opened Business

Howard's company makes engine and transmission parts for some of this country's largest diesel manufacturers. When he launched his new company, Jupiter was actively involved in aspects. Progressed Jupiter was trine his natal Ascendant and sextile his natal Sun. Jupiter suggests advancement and an increase in status.

The progressed Jupiter in sextile to the natal Sun shows a successful and prosperous period. Opportunities presenting themselves and activities undertaken now can increase his earnings and future growth. It is a good time to expand. Progressed Mercury is sextile his natal Midheaven. This supports him in making wise business decisions. It is helpful for new enterprise when extensive dealings with others are required. Mercury is also near conjunction with his natal Venus. These aspects favor dealings with merchants and in employee relations.

Progressed Mars is applying to trine his natal Ascendant. This will be of great help to him going forward, giving a boost to his energy and his self-confidence. It stimulates his ambitions and is good for gaining cooperation in business partnerships.

Progressed Mars is also now conjunct his progressed Jupiter, showing that even though there are many expenditures involved in the opening of a new company,

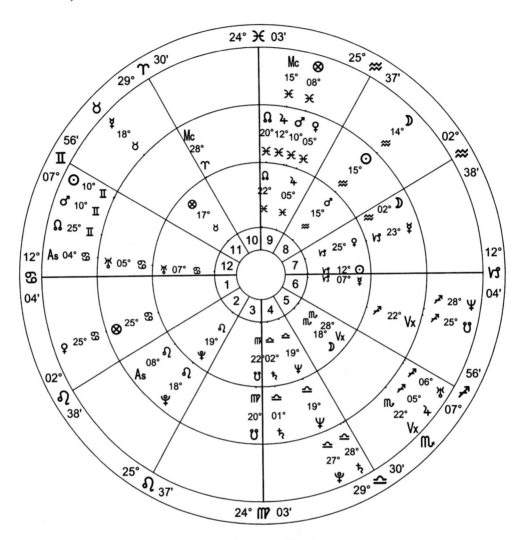

Figure 4b: Opened Business

Inner Wheel: Howard's Natal Chart: Jan. 3, 1951; 4:20 PM CST; 83W10, 37N02
Middle Wheel: Progressed Chart: June 1, 1983; 8:00 AM CST; 83W10, 37N02
Outer Wheel: Transit Chart: June 1, 1983; 8:00 AM EDT; 83W10, 37N02

Howard is still able to bring in adequate resources and thus is not restricted in his normal lifestyle. Progressed Mars is in sextile to the natal Sun, and progressed Sun is conjunct natal Mars, giving the necessary energy and drive to follow through on the physical requirements of undertaking new ventures. These aspects reflect an important new enterprise.

Uranus, which showed so much promise for him to attain material wealth and status, is trine his natal Jupiter by progression. This is among the most outstanding aspects from the natal chart now within orb and coming ever closer to produce dividends. Taking this risk will pay off.

Progressed Venus is now conjunct natal Jupiter and trine progressed Uranus! This is a sure promise of blessings coming his way. Venus increases all of that lucky natal potential. Success is fairly guaranteed.

Another important aspect often in evidence at times of increased status and the achievement of ambitions is seen in Howard's chart—the trine between progressed Moon and his Saturn. This aspect reflects the good timing for long-term success in the opening of the new business.

Howard's progressed aspects lean toward advancement and increase. New ventures are favored.

When we bring in major transits, we see that Neptune is trine his progressed Midheaven. Neptune suggests a change to more service-oriented work. Pluto and Saturn are opposite his progressed Midheaven. These represent dramatic changes in his life. He is entering a new phase of activity following much preparation. This will have important consequences in the future as he begins to make a gradual climb.

When Howard's company started, several transiting planets repeated themes from his natal and progressed charts that promised opportunities and growth. Transiting Jupiter and Uranus are conjunct, repeating a connection from the nativity and in his progressions (the trine). They are trine his progressed Ascendant. There are new contacts, new opportunities, and enthusiasm. Transiting Sun and Mars are traveling together, repeating two of his progressed aspects that promote new ventures. They are sextile his progressed Ascendant. They also trine Howard's progressed Sun on his natal Mars, where even the transiting Moon gets in the picture. The stars are bright for new enterprises. There are no boundaries to the amount of wealth to be gained.

Entrepreneur of the Year

By early 1995, success stories began to appear in newspapers and business journals about Howard's business technique and the prosperity of his company. Later in the

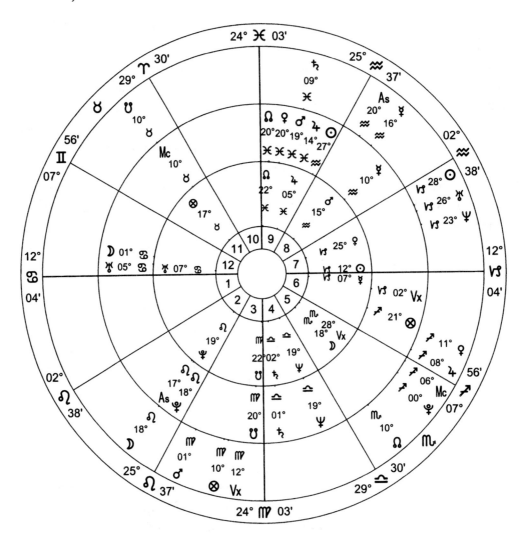

Figure 4c: Entrepreneur of the Year

Inner Wheel: Howard's Natal Chart: Jan. 3, 1951; 4:20 PM CST; 83W10, 37N02

Middle Wheel: Progressed Chart: Jan. 18, 1995; 9:00 AM CST; 83W10, 37N02

Outer Wheel: Transit Chart: Jan. 18, 1995; 9:00 AM EST; 83W10, 37N02

year, he was nominated for Entrepreneur of the Year. By this time his company had an annual growth rate of 40 percent a year, and its revenue for 1994 was $8.5 million dollars.

In checking his progressions, we see that progressed Jupiter was sextile his natal Sun for the last several years, an aspect from his birth chart (wide sextile) that helped him improve his material circumstances.

Now, his progressed Midheaven is advancing to trine his natal Sun. This suggests he is entering a period of honors with an elevation of status and influence. Howard's progressed Ascendant is coming into orb of conjunction with his Pluto. This represents a milestone, giving Howard exceptional powers of endurance to make accomplishments and effect wanted changes in his life. He still has progressed Uranus trine his natal Jupiter, closer in orb at this point, increasing his sphere of influence through his associations. Overhead, progressed Venus is conjunct progressed North Node, appropriately reflecting honors coming his way. Progressed Venus is also conjunct progressed Mars, the entrepreneurial planet.

Transiting Saturn is moving upward toward the Midheaven, often bringing professional rewards for past hard work and efforts. It has just made contact with natal Jupiter and Uranus and is approach-

ing the conjunction to progressed Jupiter, which it reaches at the time of his nomination.

Transiting Neptune and Uranus are sextile his natal Midheaven while conjoined with his natal Venus, also suggesting unexpected honors and promotion.

When Howard received the award, the progressed Moon was near conjunction to his natal Uranus, while also in trine to Jupiter. These are repeat aspects from the natal chart, and the trine of Moon to Jupiter is most auspicious for monetary success. Over the course of the coming year, the progressing Moon forms a trine to progressed Jupiter, Mars, Venus/Node and natal Midheaven while also in nice aspect to his natal Moon. It was during this time period that Howard invested in his second home in Key West.

The headline of one success story calls Howard unorthodox. Among his unusual business methods is the policy to give the customer the ultimate in good service, no matter what it takes. Every single employee has the authority to spend whatever it takes to solve a customer's problem. When an airline lost a shipment of parts to a customer, threatening to shut down its production line, he delivered new parts himself, using his own plane and incurring considerable cost. By this time Howard had upgraded his plane. As promised in the natal chart, travel has enhanced his potential for business success.

Much of his treatment of his employees comes from his recollection of how it feels to be from "the other side of the tracks." He is sensitive to the way his employees are treated, and he has each of them sign a mutual respect contract.

Howard, who laughs a lot and always mentions taking time to smell the roses, says he feels lucky, almost guilty at times, that he has the best job in the world. He is still a bit awed by his success.

Update

Howard continued for the next decade to build his company and his increasing wealth. He invested in more properties and now owns multiple homes. He came under some extremely favorable planetary conditions early in the new millennium, and his prospects for money and success multiplied. This was during a phase when progressed Jupiter completed the trine to his natal Moon, a most desirable aspect for financial success. In 2006 he was able to sell his company for top dollar. During this period, his progressed Sun was trine his Uranus, while transiting Uranus and Jupiter assisted. In trine to one another, they recreated his natal trine. Jupiter, approaching his natal Moon, was trine progressed Sun. During his preretirement

years, he started a band and once his business sold, Howard retired to Key West and got back into music professionally. He never lost his charisma and his band is thriving, with several CDs already. Howard is enjoying the best of the good life that money can buy. He is still down-to-earth though, with an authentic southern hospitality, and the most contagious laugh.

Lottery Winners

Next, let's take a look at the charts of a couple of big lottery winners and the aspects in their charts at the time of their winning. These are British National or U.S. lottery winners whose information was collected from the National Lottery website in Britain and other official sources by an interested astrology student. Of the twenty winners whose information was collected, only a few included the birth time in the data reported. Here are two of them.

Lottery Winner # 1

Our first winner, who won twenty-seven million dollars, has the "millionaire aspect" Jupiter trine Neptune. His Jupiter is conjunct his Moon, and in turn is in trine to Neptune, an affluent configuration. The millionaire aspect suggests a rich and lavish lifestyle and the Moon's involvement emphasizes promises of luck, favor, and

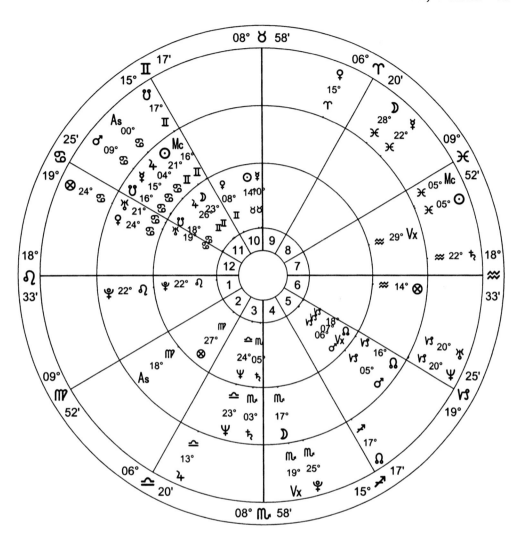

Figure 4d: Lottery Winner # 1

Inner Wheel: Winner #1 Natal Chart: May 5, 1954; 12:19 PM EDT; 71W09, 42N21
Middle Wheel: Progressed Chart: Feb. 23, 1993; 12:00 PM EDT; 71W09, 42N21
Outer Wheel: Transit Chart: Feb. 23, 1993; 12:00 PM EST; 71W09, 42N21

success. This configuration suggests a harmonious domestic situation. Neptune can mean blissful conditions and easy conditions when forming beneficial aspects. Our subject was likely doing pretty well for himself before he won the lottery since he'd have had a great deal of help and assistance early on, suggested by the excellent aspects to his luminaries.

With Leo rising, his chart ruler, the Sun, is elevated in the chart and in good aspect, showing he will make a rise in life. The Sun in Taurus is promising for material acquisition, and assisted by the trine of Mars, he gets a boost of vitality, willpower, and competitiveness to ensure he makes something of himself. Those with this aspect usually win in life, especially when they enter into competitions or contests.

Jupiter rules the 5th house of gambling and speculation, with Sagittarius on that cusp, so its trine to Neptune suggests potential wealth through speculation. Mars is in our subject's 5th house in Capricorn. It is sextile Saturn, also auspicious for money coming through gambling. His North Node in the 5th house also shows potential growth through 5th house activities. Mars in the 5th house trine his Sun emphasizes these themes.

Though out of orb at birth, his Jupiter is also in a wide, out-of-sign trine to Saturn, and it is an applying aspect. This aspect gives the potential for *life-long wealth*.

Checking the ephemeris, progressed Jupiter comes into orb to trine his natal Saturn roughly thirty-seven days after his birth, equating to thirty-seven years of age, and it will continue its orb of trine to Saturn until about age forty-six.

Howard was thirty-nine when he won the lottery. His trine from progressed Jupiter to Saturn was in orb, and at this point his progressed Mars was sextile his natal Saturn as well. Mars was a promising indicator in his natal 5th house, so these aspects greatly *increased his luck*.

His progressed Ascendant ruler is Mercury and is now sextile his natal Sun. This aspect recreates a link of these two in the birth chart (the conjunction), and is an indication of business success. Connections with solicitors and agents are profitable.

His progressed Moon in Scorpio plays up themes relating to financial affairs, and it has now come to sextile his progressed Ascendant and a sextile to his natal North Node. The latter two are in trine. This suggests *a favorable turn of events*.

There are a number of excellent transiting aspects. Transiting Saturn trines his natal millionaire aspect (Jupiter trine Neptune), increasing his chances to acquire lifelong wealth. Transiting Pluto trines his progressed Venus, which suggests amassing property and resources. There are multiple indicators of luck. Most noteworthy for timing, however, is the transiting Sun.

On the day of his win it is in sextile to his progressed Mars, in trine to his progressed Jupiter, and in trine to his natal Saturn, the three planets that were most promising in his natal chart for a win through risk taking.

Lottery Winner # 2

For our second winner, who won thirteen million dollars at age thirty-four, we see that he has natal Jupiter with Neptune and North Node in his 4th house. This suggests a life of luxury in his later years. His Moon widely trines his Jupiter, also auspicious. Pluto is sextile his Jupiter and Neptune, increasing this picture of contentment and serenity. Pluto rules his 5th house of speculation with Scorpio on the cusp, so Pluto's promising aspect shows luck at acquiring material wealth through risk and speculation. His intuition is a gift that increases his luck. He also has Mars in his 5th house in Sagittarius and Mars is trine his 1st house Uranus, one of the lucky aspects. Mercury in his 5th house is sextile his Jupiter, and this may assist him in his timing for playing in raffles or lotteries.

He has auspicious signs on each of the supply house cusps, and he is a Capricorn. Up until his luck came through he'd have had to work very hard and without a lot of help from others since his luminaries, especially the Sun, gets little in the way of assisting aspects from other planets. He

might have been self-denying and hard on himself, with a heavy sense of responsibility. A sense of scarcity may have added to his drive to acquire material possessions and security with his Saturn opposing his Moon. His South Node in the Midheaven also suggests trials and burdens early in life.

The natal features that stand out as far as showing promise of a big win are the arrangements involving Jupiter, Neptune, Pluto, Mars, and Mercury. Jupiter and Pluto appear to be the central figures, since Pluto rules the 5th house while Jupiter co-rules the 5th house and disposes of the planets therein. So, let's see what the progressions were reflecting when he reached age thirty-four and won the thirteen million.

His progressed Ascendant is in Virgo and now in conjunction with natal Pluto. This aspect reflects major personal transformations. Both progressed Ascendant and Pluto are sextile his progressed Jupiter. Jupiter in sextile to his progressed Ascendant means a lucky streak with good hunches, especially auspicious for games of chance. Jupiter in nice aspect to Pluto stimulates luck, and suggests the potential to amass large sums of money, especially through such means that require luck, like the lottery. These themes are of emphasized importance since Pluto rules his natal 5th house.

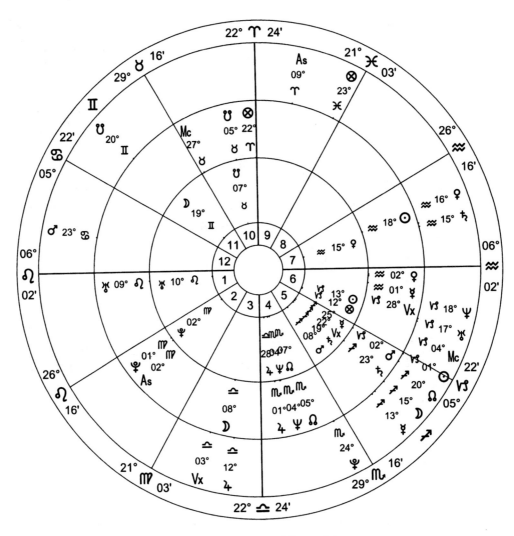

Figure 4e: Lottery Winner # 2

Inner Wheel: Winner #2 Natal Chart: Jan. 3, 1958; 6:16 PM EST; 71W20, 41N48
Middle Wheel: Progressed Chart: Dec. 22, 1992; 12:00 PM EST; 71W20, 41N48
Outer Wheel: Transit Chart: Dec. 22, 1992; 12:00 PM EST; 71W20, 41N48

Both Pluto and his progressed Ascendant are trine his progressed Mars. These show positive changes ahead and new areas of endeavor. It is especially good for an improvement in financial situations made possible by money coming in from dividends, the lottery, or other joint financial involvements. In turn, progressed Mars is sextile his progressed Jupiter. Although slightly beyond the accepted orb, the aspect again suggests sudden strokes of luck. His ruling planet, Mercury, is conjoined now with progressed Venus, the Lesser Fortune. Progressed Mercury is square his progressed Jupiter, recreating a link of two planets that were connected by sextile in the natal chart that suggested his good timing.

His progressed Sun is trine his natal Moon, a harmonious blend. His progressed Sun is sextile his natal Saturn in his 5th house of gambling. His progressed Uranus is trine his natal Mars in the 5th house, while progressed Moon forms a sextile to both. There are multiple progressed aspects suggesting the same thing—*his winning potential is at a peak.*

Transits include a trine from the Sun moving through his natal 5th house to his Pluto and progressed Ascendant while the Sun is in sextile to his progressed Jupiter and conjunct his progressed Mars. There are other transiting aspects but these are most reflective of the timing of his big win.

There are similarities between our two winners. Both have Leo rising and both have planetary activity in their 5th houses and much evidence for a potential win through speculation.

In each case, the transiting North Node was transiting their 5th houses in the sign of Sagittarius when they won, a transit that coincided with major progressed aspects that built upon the natal potential to experience a win.

Both winners have a natal aspect between the Moon and Jupiter that was harmoniously stimulated on the day of their win. This came from a transiting planetary link between Jupiter and Venus, the Greater and Lesser Fortunes. They were in opposition on the day of Winner #1's lucky break, and they were in trine on the day of Winner #2's big day. In each case, this pair of transiting planets formed a complementary aspect to the natal Moon, with transiting Jupiter in a wide trine. This recreated a planetary link from the natal chart that promised financial success— Jupiter in good aspect to the Moon.

All three of our millionaires had their Moon and Jupiter in fortunate aspect in the natal chart.

If you know someone who has won big, take a look at his or her chart to see where the win was promised and what progressed aspects and transits triggered their win. If you are fortunate enough to have winning luck, find the times the potential is stimulated in the progressions and transits. If you aren't lucky in speculation, find your best bet for creating money and success by studying your supply houses, the planets ruling those houses and their aspects, as well as planets in the resource houses and their aspects. Check your Jupiter and Sun aspects. Then you'll know where to invest your energy for the greatest returns.

chapter five

Children

The indicators of children are chiefly the condition of the 5th house in the chart, and in a woman's chart, the Moon. The planet ruling the 5th house and any planets placed within the 5th house are significators. The number of children can be found as well as characteristics about them. In a marriage, both charts must be studied, because while the chart of one of the partners may show children, the other might deny them for that marriage. A trickier determination is to find the sex of offspring by carefully considering the signs ruling the significators. Certain planetary aspects also give clues. A woman having the Sun in aspect to Mars is likely to produce male children, for example.

Multiple births, such as twins, can be found by significators in dual signs: Gemini, Sagittarius, and Pisces. A whole study can be done on this one area of the chart.

For a woman, the number of aspects made by the Moon is important in determining whether she will have children. The more aspects made by the Moon before leaving the sign it is in, the more children are possible. If the Moon is void of course (making no major aspects before leaving the sign it's in), then children are more likely to be denied. The overall condition of the 5th house significators, blended with that of the Moon, shows what to expect in regard to children. If the individual is denied children, this will show in these configurations. For an example, the chart of Evangeline Adams (see Chapter 1) shows that she would not have children of her own. Her first astrology teacher, Dr. Heber Smith, told her this based on her chart.[1] She has the Moon ruling the 5th house while separating from an opposition to the Sun and void of course.

The sign on the cusp of the 5th house is important. Some signs are fruitful for children, while some are not. Water signs are the most fruitful if on the 5th house. Leo, Capricorn, and Aries are least fruitful. Gemini and Sagittarius sometimes produce twins, although they are not otherwise fruitful. While aspects from Venus or Jupiter to the ruler of the 5th house increases chances for children, aspects of Mars, Saturn, or the Sun decrease these chances. In a female chart, the Sun in Capricorn, Aries, or Leo and making a stressful aspect to Saturn may indicate childlessness. A prominent Saturn in a man's chart that forms stressful aspects to the Moon and Venus may show sterility.

While the traditional malefic planets in the 5th house do not deny children, if afflicted, they may indicate problems concerning them. Saturn suggests having children later in life, or that there is some delay to parenting. Added worry and responsibility may be involved in raising them. Mars in the 5th house and afflicted may show stress connected to children. Mars, Uranus, or Pluto in the 5th house may indicate children with a rebellious streak or headstrong attitudes. Uranus in or ruling the 5th house may indicate that children are unplanned for, come as a surprise, or are of a disruptive influence. If Uranus is ruling the 5th house, its prominence in the chart and aspects it receives will indicate to what extreme the disruptions might extend. It may decrease the number of children but shows that the children have a unique quality.

An afflicted 5th house Neptune sometimes reflects a situation where a child is absent from the parent during the formative years, such as when a child is adopted. Pluto, in or ruling the 5th house and afflicted, or involved in progressed afflictions to 5th house indicators at the time of pregnancy, might show a miscarriage or abortion. Of course the progressions would be useful in each case of pregnancy to discover any possible complications or other significance.

It is imperative to keep in mind that the majority of people have children and raise them successfully with varying difficulties. The chart must be considered as a whole and, unless there are significant themes to the contrary, a common child rearing experience should be anticipated. The 5th house significators can be useful in determining the particular nuances of the experiences.

Each of the planets indicates the tendencies, possible aptitude and talents of children when positioned in the 5th house. For instance, Neptune in or ruling the 5th house may show a child gifted for show business or the theater. Venus here, combined with Neptune or alone, may show a child of exceptional beauty or artistic talents. The Sun suggests that the child is a leader, and that she or he enjoys being in the limelight. Mercury may show a talkative or an intellectual child. Uranus signifies children with quick comprehension of new technologies, and sometimes shows genius along a particular line. Mars might indicate a child who is a natural athlete. Mars or Pluto may show children with a knack for using sharp instruments, such as those used by surgeons, or another field where precision work is required. Saturn might indicate a child who appreciates responsibility at a young age, or who shows maturity beyond his or her years. This child may have a natural sense of business. Jupiter suggests a fortunate child: well-educated, philosophical, traveled, and reaping honors. The Moon may mean a sensitive, changeable child.

By fully delineating the charts of the parent(s) and child, more particular information may be found regarding an appropriate and rewarding career or special talents of the child.

Childbirth is assisted by favorable aspects involving the Sun, Mars, and Jupiter, and will often take place when such aspects are formed among the transiting planets, especially if they repeat an aspect found in the natal chart of the mother. Venus becomes quite prominent at important times connected with the birth of children, such as conception and labor.

Venus and the Moon often form appropriate aspects during happy occasions, including the birth of children. Besides these, important links between the charts of parent and child will be in evidence at the time of birth.

An interesting phenomenon is that aspects and peculiarities of horoscopes appear to work out down the course of generations. Prominent planets in a parent's chart will often show up as prominent in the charts of their children. This is due in part to the fact that strong natal configurations are repeated at times of important events, including the event of giving birth.

Obviously, the similarities from a parent's chart to the child's chart are also partly a reflection of similar conditioning, education, and environmental elements. Many studies have shown that someone who comes from a home where abuse was a part of their own upbringing is more prone to inflict abuse. Similarly, someone who comes from a broken home or from divorced parents is more likely to become divorced and pass the broken home syndrome down to their own children.

Motherhood

Let's take a look at Danielle's prospects for motherhood. In her natal chart, Libra appears on the cusp of her 5th house. This gives the benefic Venus as a significator

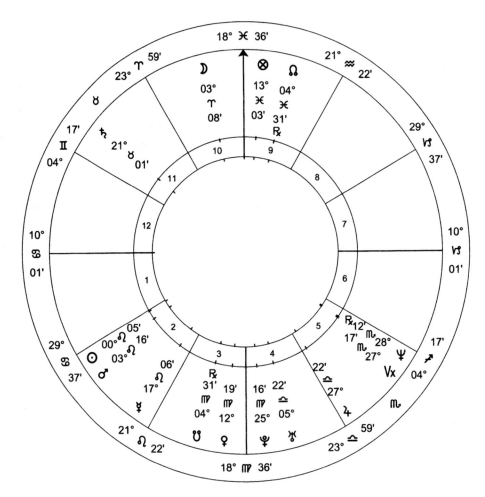

Figure 5a: Danielle's Natal Chart
July 23, 1970; 4:58 AM EDT; 85W40, 40N33

of children. Jupiter, another benefic, is in her 5th house and becomes another significator of children. These planets tend to support her chances for motherhood, and Venus is in sextile to her natal Ascendant. Neptune is also in her 5th house of children. Neptune's trine to her Moon and its placement in a water sign are further indications that she will likely have children.

The Moon, a key indicator of children for a woman, and her chart ruler, is in the Midheaven, suggesting that motherhood will be an active part of Danielle's life. In early Aries, the Moon is closely trine her Leo, Sun, and Mars. The Moon will form several more aspects before leaving the sign it is in, so Danielle's prospects for motherhood appear quite good.

The Moon/Uranus opposition in her chart reflects that she came from a broken home. Separated from her mother soon after birth, Danielle was raised by an aunt. It also represents sudden upsets to the domestic scene as they unfold throughout life at times of stimulation among the progressed and transiting aspects. It also indicates that children may not be exactly planned for, thereby creating a need for flexibility in regard to them.

With the Sun in Leo, Danielle would be quite a protector over her children, and fiercely so if they should come under threat. The link from the Sun to the Moon shows the warm closeness she will enjoy with her offspring.

From all indications, chances appear slightly more favorable for Danielle to have boys. This is suggested by the Sun/Mars conjunction and from the aspects of the Moon to these masculine planets. However, Venus and Neptune also show potential for girls.

First Child—It's a Boy!

When her first child was born, a boy, Danielle's chart shows major activity involving all three of her 5th house significators. Her progressed Ascendant is forming an angular aspect to her natal Jupiter, in square. At the same time, her progressed Ascendant is closely trine her Neptune. Her progressed Venus is conjoined now with her progressed Uranus. Events connected to children are due. While the trine of progressed Ascendant to the planet Neptune often brings pleasant happenings, the other aspects involving her 5th house significators suggest untimely expansion and sudden developments.

With progressed Venus conjoined with progressed Uranus, this new arrival and bundle of joy brings excitement and comes amid changes. As suggested in her natal chart by her Moon/Uranus opposition, this pregnancy was unplanned, requiring adjustments and altering plans. A new

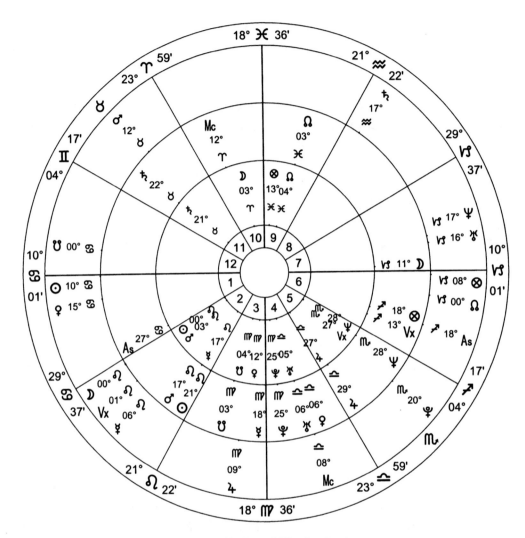

Figure 5b: First Child: It's a Boy!

Inner Wheel: Danielle's Natal Chart: July 23, 1970; 4:58 AM EDT; 85W40, 40N33
Middle Wheel: Progressed Chart: July 1, 1992; 6:33 PM EDT; 85W40, 40N33
Outer Wheel: Transit Chart: July 1, 1992; 6:33 PM EST; 85W40, 40N33

romance had sprung up suddenly when progressed Venus conjoined her natal Uranus the year before, leading to this pregnancy and a sudden marriage.

When she had her baby, there was a great deal of appropriate Moon and Venus activity in the progressions and transits that often appear during periods of happy occasions.

The progressed Moon is trine to her natal Venus, a time of warm emotions, happy affections, and increased socializing. Transiting Jupiter near her natal Venus is trine her progressed Moon, emphasizing a happy occasion and this joyful event.

Transiting Sun and Mars are also forming close favorable aspects to her natal Venus. On this day, transiting Mars is even in trine to her progressed Moon. This is a repeating planetary link from her natal chart (the trine) and is an important clue to timing.

The transiting Sun, Mars, and Jupiter are forming sextiles and trines among themselves, helping to pinpoint the timing for an easy childbirth. The transiting Sun and Mars in sextile to one another repeat a connection found in Danielle's natal chart (the conjunction) and thus also help to establish the timing of the important event. They play up themes from her birth chart that suggests the birth of a boy.

The transiting Moon is conjoined with Danielle's natal Sun. This recreates a link of the two Lights as in her natal chart (the trine). This is a third indication to closely pinpoint the timing of her son's birth. This mutual aspect also suggests that she and her son will have a close and mutually loving relationship.

The conjunction of the transiting Moon to her natal Mars also repeats a pattern from her birth chart, and for her child, his Leo Moon suggests that his mother will be dynamic and energetic. She presents a good image to the public, and will be a positive force in his life. Further, other women later in life will have these same attributes and will be of benefit and support to him. This theme is emphasized by his Sun/Venus conjunction in the sign of Cancer. He will be both family oriented and fun loving, and well appreciated for it.

The astrologer will note that Danielle's progressed Sun is square her Saturn while this pair is afflicted by transiting Saturn and Pluto. These aspects are partly reflecting the death of the aunt who raised her, from cancer, shortly before the birth of her son.

There are several indicators pointing toward travel in Danielle's chart. Progressed Mars is conjunct natal Mercury. Progressed Mercury is angular, on the cusp of her natal 4th house. Transiting Pluto, Uranus, and Neptune stimulate her progressed Mercury. These aspects reflect the relocation made by the family a few months after her son's birth, just as transiting Jupiter moved across her progressed Mercury on her natal 4th house cusp.

Second Child—It's a Girl!

When Danielle gave birth to her second child, just over a year later, several similar connections can be seen in the progressed chart involving her significators. This time, however, she had a beautiful little girl.

She still has the progressed Ascendant in strong aspects to her Jupiter and her Neptune. Progressed Venus is still near a conjunction to her progressed Uranus. While the aspect was still in orb, she'd gotten pregnant for a second time. Again, this child was unplanned, as suggested in Danielle's natal chart.

Now, instead of the prominence of the Sun and Mars in the transits, we notice numerous aspects involving the Moon and Venus, depicting the birth of a girl.

Venus in its transit is conjunct Danielle's natal Sun and Mars from where it forms several aspects. Transiting Venus is trine Danielle's natal Moon and sextile her progressed Venus, while the transiting Moon is trine to her progressed Venus and in sextile to her natal Moon. There is usually quite a bit of Venus activity during such happy occasions as there were for her son's birth, and now the numerous Venus aspects reflect the birth of a girl. There is even a repeating link between Venus and the Moon in the transits: the opposition.

Transiting Moon is trine natal Uranus, creating an important link from the natal chart, and acting as a timer for the event. Transiting Venus is applying to a sextile with her natal Uranus, repeating an aspect in her progressions: the conjunction of her progressed Venus and Uranus. The transiting Ascendant when she gave birth is sextile to her progressed Venus. This shows a close relationship with her daughter.

This child's extraordinary beauty is shown by the conjunction of transiting Venus to the transiting Ascendant at the time of her birth, which becomes her natal 1st house. In the sign of Leo, she fairly radiates charm, and she will come to enjoy the attention of others. She is artistic, creative, and imaginative with her Moon in aspect to Venus and Mars. North Node trine her Ascendant will be an assist throughout her life. It gives spunk. With her Moon trine Mars, her mother will be of great support and benefit.

There are still signs of travels with progressed Mars on natal Mercury and progressed Mercury angular in the chart. Progressing Moon is square her Jupiter and opposing Danielle's progressed Ascendant and is ready to make a series of aspects so there are many changes on the horizon. These aspects accurately reflect that the family moved again when the new baby

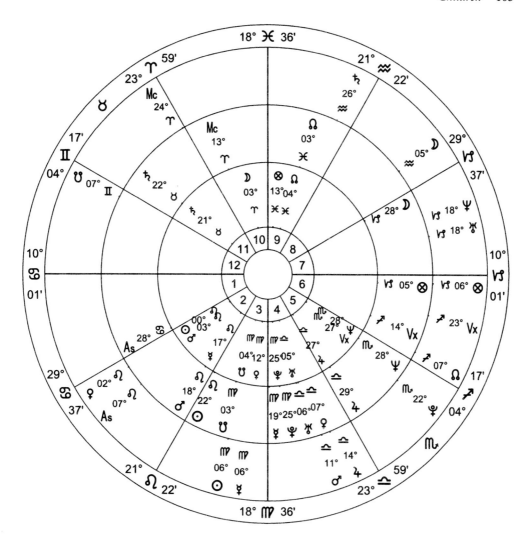

Figure 5c: Second Child: It's a Girl!

Inner Wheel: Danielle's Natal Chart: July 23, 1970; 4:58 AM EDT; 85W40, 40N33

Middle Wheel: Progressed Chart: Aug. 29, 1993; 3:45 AM EDT; 85W40, 40N33

Outer Wheel: Transit Chart: Aug. 29, 1993; 3:45 AM EST; 85W40, 40N33

was a few weeks old, as transiting Jupiter moves across her progressed 4th house cusp.

There is evidence of conflict in Danielle's marriage besides her applying lunar aspects. There are afflictions involving Saturn, with Saturn ruling the 7th house of Danielle's chart. Her progressed Sun and Saturn are in square. Transiting Saturn puts stress on both. Transiting Pluto squares her progressed Sun; one of the planets ruling the men in her life, as it also opposes her Saturn. The afflicting aspects indicate domestic upsets, brewing problems, and possible separations. The aspects reflected marital problems, which resulted in divorce a little over a year later. The parents share equally in the custody of the children. In reflection, this is often the result of a marriage based on the sudden attraction of the Venus/Uranus aspects.

Vasectomy Versus Children

Mike's chart reflects his decision to have a vasectomy soon after reaching adulthood.

The natal chart shows that his 5th house ruler, Uranus, is prominent on the Midheaven and in Cancer, the family sign. It makes only afflicting aspects in his chart. The opposition to Venus, ruler of his 1st house, shows that Mike may be counter to the idea of children. This aspect, combined with his Scorpio characteristics, is among the most illustrative of his decision to get the vasectomy. His Sun in Scorpio is square Pluto, so he is fearless and willing to take chances.

The Moon, attributed closely with the wife in a man's chart, is conjunct his Ascendant in the late degrees of Virgo. It applies to make no major aspects before leaving the sign it is in. This reduces the chances for his wife to have children. The Moon is also square the 5th house ruler, Uranus, showing that his wife may either be opposed to having children or unable to have them. These configurations involving the Moon will be seen to operate in two marriages. The fact that the 5th house ruler (Uranus) opposes Venus is another reflection that Mike's wife may be unwilling or unable to have children since Venus rules his wife.

Early in his adult years, Mike felt that the world was not a very good place to bring up children, that they would have a reduced standard of living and not many chances for a good life.

Some of his personal childhood experiences probably influenced these feelings. Uranus on the Midheaven points to the possibility that an authority figure, such as a parent, may have been a source of upset for him. His Sun square Pluto also suggests defiance against authorities.

Although he leaned toward such beliefs and was mostly against having children,

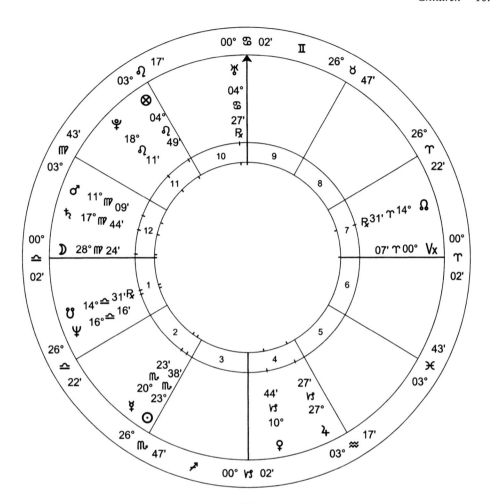

Figure 5d: Mike's Natal Chart
Nov. 16, 1949; 2:58 AM EST; 84W31, 39N05

Mike's first wife was absolutely opposed to them. This is largely what influenced him to have the vasectomy when he did.

The Vasectomy

When Mike had the vasectomy, the progressed Moon had returned to pass its natal position and was on the Ascendant in square once again to Uranus, his natal 5th house ruler.

A solar eclipse on the cusp of the 8th house had just occurred, the 8th house corresponding to surgery. His 8th house ruler, Mars, was sextile his progressed Midheaven, so this aspect to an angle means eventful happenings in connection with 8th house matters. Mars also rules Mike's 7th house of marriage, and this is one aspect showing his recent marriage. However, without enough favorable aspects, the marriage did not last.

Transiting Pluto, naturally associated with surgery, was in conjunction with the natal South Node, another indicator for such transformations. This is a regenerating influence and, occurring in Mike's 1st house, suggests some self-sacrificing and personal attempts to initiate changes. This aspect often means the end of a power struggle, so his steps to get the vasectomy were putting issues to rest in his marriage.

The 8th house ruler, Mars, is transiting in opposition to progressed Mars. Such a Mars transit will stir the aggressive urges, and Mars transits his 6th house, bringing a focus to health-related actions. Mars is square his progressed Sun, but trine his natal Scorpio Sun. These aspects are associated with initiating action and taking decisive steps, so we see the themes suggesting a surgery of the individual's choice.

Venus has progressed into his natal 5th house. Venus is squared by transiting Uranus and is opposed by transiting Saturn. This configuration is descriptive of restrictions imposed in the area of children and the removal of such chances. The repeating link of Uranus to Venus is a clue to the timing.

Progressed Mercury is opposing natal and progressed Uranus, stirring up a restless discontent and a desire to break free from regulations. This aspect is key. It often gives some eccentricity and abruptness of actions. These planets are in the signs of parenting: Capricorn and Cancer. The signs give clues as to the consequences of actions and decisions. The fact that Uranus rules Mike's 5th house points to his decision to have the vasectomy.

In such a case, it becomes a moot point whether biological fatherhood would have occurred without the vasectomy having been done. Certainly, he did not have configurations to indicate sterility. However, the chart indicators for children are

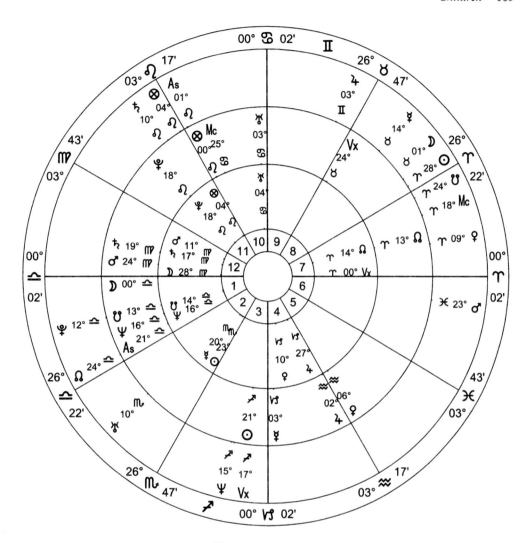

Figure 5e: Vasectomy

Inner Wheel: Mike's Natal Chart: Nov. 16, 1949; 2:58 AM EST; 84W31, 39N05
Middle Wheel: Mike's Natal Chart: Apr. 18, 1977; 12:00 PM EST; 84W31, 39N05
Outer Wheel: Mike's Natal Chart: Apr. 18, 1977; 12:00 PM EST; 84W31, 39N05

so very restricting, he might have chosen a partner who was unable to conceive or there may have been other problems surrounding children.

Twenty years later, Mike and his second wife want children. Becoming successful with his own business, he realizes that he would be able to provide for them, and give them the confidence they need to succeed at anything. The one thing he regrets is his impulsive decision to have the vasectomy. Such impulsiveness is the way of Uranus, especially involved in the affliction to Mercury at the time.

Since it was too late for a successful reversal of the vasectomy and since their age was a negative to adoption agencies, they used artificial insemination combined with fertility treatments in the hope of producing a child. Eventually their efforts were successful and twins arrived on the scene, a girl and a boy.

With Uranus ruling Mike's 5th house, these methods to bring about parenthood totally fit his natal chart. By the time the twins were born, Mike's progressed 5th house had 17° Pisces on the cusp, a fruitful sign, ruled by Neptune, denoting the potential for twins. Transiting Mars and Saturn afflicted his Neptune, however, and transits at the time of the twins' birth showed Mars and Saturn in opposition, the Sun opposing Uranus and Neptune, and Mercury opposing Moon and Jupiter. With Gemini rising at their birth, Mercury rules the twins and the Sun rules their 3rd house. The difficult aspects of Mercury and the Sun reflected learning disabilities and their need to attend special classes. The twins are their father's pride and joy.

Miscarriage & Caesarian Birth

Teri has Aquarius on the cusp of her 5th house. Ruling Uranus in the 1st house gets a trine from the Moon, which gives reason to believe she will become a mother and that she would be close to her children and do her best to create good ties with them. She also has the benefic Jupiter in the fruitful water sign Pisces in her 5th house that gets a trine from the Lesser Fortune, Venus, increasing her chances for motherhood.

Her Moon does not form many aspects as it is leaving an opposition to her Sun, reducing the number of children possible. Her 5th house Jupiter is also in a close square to her lunar nodes, so this may mean limited opportunities to conceive or give birth. Her 5th house ruler, Uranus, receives a square from Mercury, which could mean that a child has learning difficulties or it might mean unexpected accidents in connection with children or with giving birth to them.

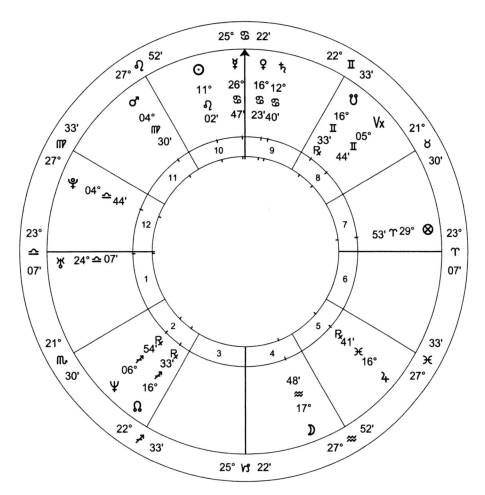

Figure 5f: Teri's Natal Chart
Aug. 3, 1974; 11:51 AM PDT; 117W23, 33N12

Miscarriage

When Teri had her miscarriage, we see that transiting Mercury is indeed in opposition to her natal Uranus, repeating a link from the natal chart between the two that indicated potential difficulties.

The miscarriage chart shows that the progressed Midheaven is sextile Uranus, her 5th house ruler, so this is a time that activity relating to children is stimulated. Her progressed Ascendant links by trine to her natal 5th house Jupiter, showing increases in connection with children. Progressed Venus is sextile her natal Ascendant as it approaches her progressed Midheaven, soon forming a sextile to natal Uranus. Venus is often highlighted when happy events like the birth of children take place, and this latter aspect specifically connects to Uranus, the natal ruler of her 5th house. There are multiple harmonious indicators for her to give birth to a child, but there are hazards showing in the rest of the current configurations. The time isn't right.

The progressed Moon has come to conjunct natal Jupiter in the 5th house, but at the same time it is square the natal nodes, which often coincides with health concerns. Blockages impact the emotions, often leading to feelings of inadequacy. It is an emotional low point. The progressed Ascendant is square her natal Moon, further indicating a low point for her vitality, when her health may suffer.

Neptune rules Teri's progressed 5th house with 26° Pisces on that cusp and transiting Mars is closely opposing her Neptune, complicating the pregnancy and creating danger. Transiting Uranus, moving through her natal 5th house, is square her Neptune, setting up accident potential. At the same time, transiting Uranus opposes her natal Mars, which is square natal Neptune. Conditions are very unstable for matters of health and childbearing. In looking at the transits, we see that Mars and Jupiter are in square, which is counter to the type of easy aspect between these two that we'd see for an easy childbirth. Mars and Jupiter as well as Uranus fall into alignments that put her Neptune in a Grand Cross. It is not a good time for her or the child. Indeed, according to the doctor, her hormones were completely out of balance, creating anxieties.

Transiting Venus was approaching the dreaded Pleiades, aptly describing that there was something to weep about.

Teri was emotionally impacted by the loss of this baby, a boy, because her husband wanted very much to have a child, and they had been trying to get pregnant for a few months. This was a new marriage for her and she was contented with her beautiful five-year-old daughter from a previous marriage, but she didn't want

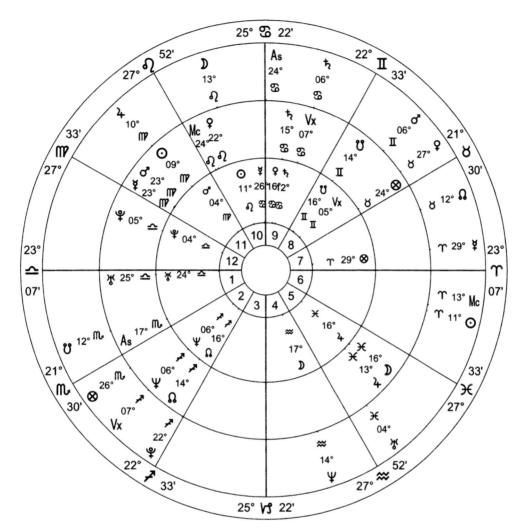

Figure 5g: Miscarriage

Inner Wheel: Teri's Natal chart: Aug. 3, 1974; 11:51 AM PDT; 117W23, 33N12
Middle Wheel: Progressed Chart: Mar. 31, 2004; 12:00 PM PDT; 117W23, 33N12
Outer Wheel: Transit Chart: Mar. 31, 2004; 12:00 PM PST; 117W23, 33N12

to wait a long time if she were to have another child. There are aspects in the chart suggesting some conflicting feelings about having another child. A recent Full Moon between her progressed Sun and Moon across the 5th and 11th houses tied in to her Neptune in the 2nd house, suggesting a compromise was made, with concerns about finances as well as the energy it takes to have and raise a child. With progressed Saturn on her Venus, ruler of her natal chart, there is a deep sense of responsibility and feeling the need to care for others. It is a weighty feeling.

Part of her hesitation and the reason for having second thoughts is because she had extreme difficulties during her pregnancy with her first full-term child and there had been a miscarriage prior to that. Transiting Pluto was on her Neptune at the time of the earlier miscarriage and progressed Moon was square Pluto, while transiting South Node moved over her 5th house Jupiter. The doctors told her then that it was probably not a good idea to get pregnant again. With her daughter, born about a year later, she had toxemia, gaining thirty-five pounds in one week—this happened when transiting Venus crossed her Jupiter in the water sign Pisces. No wonder she had conflicting feelings about having another child.

They felt somewhat relieved when, not long after this latest miscarriage, Teri and her husband took a weekend trip to Sedona, where they consulted with a psychic who told them that this baby had not been ready to come—that it wasn't the right time, but that they would get pregnant again within the year and have a healthy child. The psychic told them the same things the charts showed.

Many of the favorable major aspects among the progressed planets in Teri's charts that indicated expansion revolving around children remained intact in the progressions, and a year later when her progressed Midheaven formed its exact sextile to progressed Uranus, another boy was born—this time a healthy, rambunctious little cutie. The extra time had given Teri more time to process the whole decision about whether she wanted a child and she was okay with the idea, anticipating the birth.

Caesarian Birth

For this birth, the transiting Mars, Sun, Venus, Mercury in Teri's 6th house fell into nice aspect with Neptune, ruler of her progressed 5th house, while transiting Jupiter approached her natal Ascendant. Still, there was a semi-square from her progressed Ascendant to Pluto. Since Pluto rules her progressed Ascendant, this is a significant health risk aspect for her. Transiting Sun opposing her Pluto increased the danger. Her progressed Ascendant was

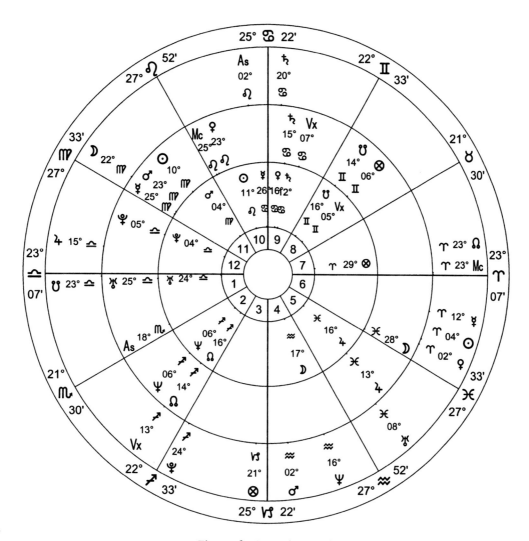

Figure 5h: Caesarian Birth

Inner Wheel: Teri's Natal Chart: Aug. 3, 1974; 11:51 AM PDT; 117W23, 33N12
Middle Wheel: Progressed Chart: Mar. 24, 2005; 1:06 PM PDT; 117W23, 33N12
Outer Wheel: Transit Chart: Mar. 24, 2005; 1:06 PM PST; 117W23, 33N12

also still in orb to square her natal Moon, presenting health risks. Transiting South Node was moving toward natal Ascendant, tending toward health vulnerabilities.

The child was breech and the doctors decided to take the baby by caesarian to avoid complications. The pregnancy had not been easy. With progressed Ascendant trine to her progressed and then to her natal Jupiter for the last few years, Teri had gained a lot of weight, which made this pregnancy extra strenuous.

At this point, the little one is three years old. His Mercury in Aries with Sun shows that he is rambunctious and headstrong. With Moon square Pluto he's been known to throw tantrums, and he wants his way.

His parents are feeding him a special diet to calm him down naturally and are having good results. They suspect he has ADD but are hoping to avoid prescription medications. The Sun and Mercury oppose his Jupiter, so he is impulsive and somewhat prone to accidents. He comes home from preschool almost daily with fresh scrapes from normal play. He is excitable and has a short attention span that requires mental training and discipline. Saturn on the Ascendant in sextile to his Moon is settling though, giving good control of the emotions, and helping him cultivate self-discipline.

1. Evangeline Adams, *The Bowl of Heaven* (New York: Dodd, Mead & Co, 1926, Santa Fe: Sun Books, 1995), 25.

chapter six

Physical Health

The primary indicators of health come from the 6th house and the 1st house, the condition of the rulers of these houses, and the condition of the luminaries. The 8th house also provides health information.

The 6th house ruler and planets within the 6th house have much to do with the overall health of an individual through the aspects they make at birth. If stressful aspects are present in the nativity involving any of these planets, the progressions will show when such health problems are likely to occur.

The luminaries furnish information about the subject's general health. When the Sun forms good aspects, the body is healthy and strong. Afflictions to the Sun show health defects and constitutional weaknesses. The Sun rules the vitality and life-giving forces, while the Moon rules the functional processes. An afflicted Moon may mean disorders arising after birth. Lunar afflictions can be quite critical during early childhood. If there are assisting aspects to an afflicted luminary by Jupiter or Venus, this can help overcome an affliction, although much depends on the comparative strength of the aspects.

The 1st house is an important indicator of health and vitality as well. While the 6th house rules the general health factors that are part of the physical makeup, the 1st house rules the physical body. Afflictions to the ruler of the Ascendant can be threatening, and when these afflictions are stimulated through the progressions and transits, health problems can flare up.

Good health is indicated if the Moon is free from affliction, gets good aspects from the benefic planets, and the Ascendant is not occupied or afflicted by a malefic.

If the ruler of the 1st house or either luminary is in the 6th, 8th, or 12th house and afflicted, this can mean prolonged ill health. The same is true if a rising malefic afflicts either luminary. The most serious health threat comes from an angular malefic afflicting both luminaries.

The Sun is often quite afflicted when an illness strikes. In severe cases the Moon and ruler of the Ascendant might be under adverse aspects along with the Sun. Very serious illness, followed by death, sometimes occurs when malefic planets afflict all three of these at the same time.

The most often afflicting planets involved when illness strikes are the malefic planets. Mars in affliction may bring feverish complaints, wounds, cuts, burns, or problems from over exertion. Saturn is commonly part of the themes at the onset of an illness, and represents the restrictions forced upon the individual by the illness. If Saturn is the afflicting planet, there may be colds, chills, sluggish vitality, falls, sprains, or dislocations. With Uranus as the afflicting planet, there may be asthma, bronchitis, allergic reactions, or nervous tension. Neptune is associated with wasting illnesses, coma, hypersensitivity, or hypochondria. Pluto may mean eliminative

disorders or deep-seated toxic conditions. The latter two planets as the afflicting planet may mean an illness that is hard to define or diagnose. With an afflicted Pluto ruling the 6th house, there could be dramatic effects on the health.

Pluto appears to be of significance in cases of fibromyalgia, either in or ruling the 6th house or afflicting the Sun, although there would be agreement found elsewhere in the chart: perhaps a luminary in the 12th house or another indicator of prolonged ill health. Mars or Pluto with the South Node may have particularly debilitating effects if in or ruling the health houses.

Sign Associations

Each zodiac sign has an external, an internal, and a structural rulership, corresponding to a specific body part(s), specific area(s) of the body, and the planet ruling the sign that governs the associated bodily functions. If the Sun is afflicted, the sign it occupies suggests particular health vulnerabilities and dangers. In addition to determining possible health risks indicated by an afflicted Sun, based on the following descriptions, the signs on the cusps of the 6th and 8th houses reveal vulnerabilities and tendencies.

Aries rules the head as a whole. Externally it rules the head, face, nose, and eyes. Internally it rules the brain and nerve centers, and structurally it rules the cranium and facial bones. Mars governs the blood, red blood cells, and arteries in the brain and head, as well as adrenaline production. If the Sun is afflicted in Aries, an individual may be prone to inflammation, fever, headaches, acne, rashes, abnormal blood pressure, or a tendency to put excessive strain on the body.

Taurus rules the mouth, throat, neck, chin, lower jaw, inner ear, thyroid, and base of the brain, while Venus governs the mechanism of swallowing and digestion related to saliva and taste. With an afflicted Sun in Taurus, there may be problems with the throat or tonsils, or one of the associated areas, and such an individual may make a slow recovery from any illness owing to Taurus being a fixed sign.

Gemini rules *all of the body's pairs*, including the brain and lungs, and Mercury governs their functions, including the upper respiratory system and the part of the brain controlling thought processes and the substance of the brain. If the Sun is afflicted in Gemini, an individual may be prone to respiratory problems, lung cancer, or nervous complaints. One might deal with two health issues at the same time.

Externally, Cancer rules the breasts and pectoral region, internally it rules the stomach, digestive organs, and womb; and structurally it rules the ribs and sternum, while the Moon governs the digestive processes and all the fluids in the system, including tears and secretions. The Moon also rules the senses, providing food for the mind to function. Aspects of the Moon show how sharp and accurate the senses are. With an afflicted Sun in Cancer, there might be cravings for alcohol, ulcers, or trouble with digestion.

Leo rules the heart while the Sun governs the circulation through the heart and the arteries around the heart. The Sun is associated with the back and chest area, and it governs the vital flow of energy and life-sustaining qualities, as well as the ability to recuperate. If the Sun is afflicted in Leo, an individual may be prone to heart and cardiovascular disease.

Virgo rules the intestines, gall bladder, pancreas, spleen, and abdomen, while Mercury governs the assimilation of foods and the functions of the bowels. A child with an afflicted Virgo Sun may have colic during infancy. Later problems might be appendicitis, or irregularities of the bowels and intestinal functions.

Libra rules the hips, kidneys, and bladder, while this sign and ruling Venus influence the distillation processes, keeping the balance in the system by separating the poisons that are carried off in the urine. An afflicted Sun in Libra may bring problems in the lower back, hypoglycemia, or diabetes.

Scorpio rules the reproductive organs, the anus, sphincter muscle, and lower bowels, and Pluto governs the reproductive and excretory systems, elimination, endocrine activity, and the regenerative organs and glands. With an afflicted Sun in Scorpio, there may be problems with the prostate, ovaries, sexually transmitted disease, hernia, or other problems of the generative body parts.

Sagittarius rules the liver, sciatic nerve, and thighs, while Jupiter governs the related functions: processes of detoxification, conversion of waste products, fat assimilation, and general growth. An individual with an afflicted Sun in Sagittarius may tend toward a weight issue, liver disease, toxemia, or problems with the hips.

Capricorn rules the knees, bones, skeletal structure, skin, and teeth, while Saturn governs the absorption and assimilation of calcium and other minerals. Colds, bad teeth, bone deformation, or rheumatism are among the problems that might be the result of an afflicted Sun in Capricorn.

Aquarius rules the lower legs, calves, ankles, and nervous system, while Uranus governs the assimilation of oxygen and the function of the diaphragm. It has a connection to the fluid-carrying vessels of the body, the lymph glands, and the circulation of blood. Obscure nervous disorders, asthma, allergies, cramps, twitches, spasms, or paralysis might result with an afflicted Sun in Aquarius. Afflictions in this sign often arise suddenly. Accident-prone tendencies are particularly tied to Aquarius and its ruler, Uranus.

Pisces rules the feet, and the glandular and lymphatic systems, while Neptune governs the related functions: the immune system, the lymph system, and excretory fluids. There may be low resistance to disease, fainting, frailty, tobacco or narcotics craving, or general physical weakness with an afflicted Sun in Pisces. For this sign, with Neptune ruling, ailments tend to be mysterious, stemming more from psychic or mental effects than from purely physical effects.

Blending an afflicted planet with the sign it occupies can be informative. For example, if Jupiter is in Libra and afflicted, there may be a predisposition to diabetes. Or, if Jupiter is in Cancer, there may be a predisposition to obesity, while anorexia might result if the Moon were in Cancer and afflicted by Saturn. Saturn afflicted in Aries may mean a tendency to Alzheimer's disease.

Medical astrology is a complex subject that requires extensive specialized training in order to get the best results. The purpose of this chapter is to cover some basics—enough to enable the student astrologer to estimate the potentialities in connection with health and disease and to recognize problems when they appear.

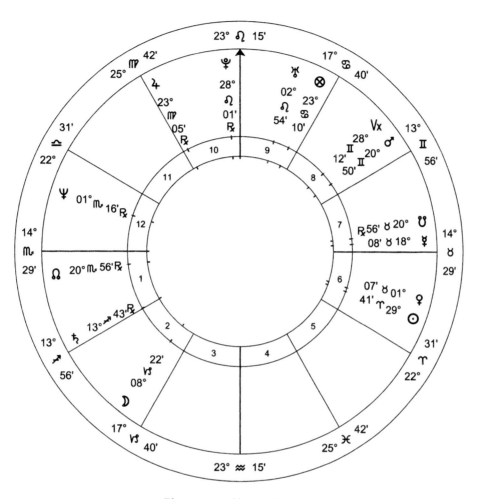

Figure 6a: Rob's Natal Chart
Apr. 19, 1957; 8:15 PM EST; 81W01, 38N55

Or, when they might disappear. For example, our first subject, Rob, started out with poor health, but he eventually built his health up against great odds. Delineating his chart allows us to easily see the planets in action as they influence health conditions.

From Sickly Child to Robust Adult

Rob's natal chart shows that his Sun is in the 6th house. The Sun forms several aspects. It is trine Pluto, conjunct Venus, opposite Neptune, and square Uranus. The trine of Sun to Pluto can give extraordinary strength and a robust body, but this aspect is separating. Pluto is retrograde and moving backward while the Sun is moving forward, so the full benefits of this aspect are not yet available. By progression, his Sun first meets with Venus by conjunction at the same time it opposes Neptune. These aspects are soon followed by a square of his progressing Sun to Uranus. The Sun afflictions to Neptune and Uranus indicate hypersensitivity and possible allergies or asthma when combined with his Sun in Aries, suggesting conditions affecting his face and head areas. There is also a minor afflicting aspect from Saturn to the Sun, suggesting that health issues will restrict him. Rob's natal

chart, with his Sun afflicted in the 6th house, suggests prolonged ill health. Since Uranus and Neptune also afflict his Venus, the conjunction of the benefic Venus to his Sun may be of little help in overcoming the afflictions.

The ruler of his Scorpio Ascendant, Pluto, forms helpful aspects to his Sun, Venus, and Neptune. However, if using Mars as the traditional ruler of Scorpio, it is placed in the 8th house. It is square Jupiter, opposite Saturn by a wide orb, and forms a semi-square to Uranus. The house placement of Mars and its aspects again suggest *prolonged poor health*. Both Rob's Sun and Mars, ruler of the physical body, are in affliction with Saturn and Uranus. Mars afflicted in Gemini, the sign corresponding with the lungs, especially with Uranus as an offending planet, emphasizes potential problems with breathing, asthmatic conditions, or bronchitis. An affliction from Jupiter to Mars in Gemini is also associated with asthmatic conditions, and since Mars also rules Rob's natal 6th house, it becomes doubly important as an indicator of his health.

Asthmatic Bronchitis

Rob was indeed very sickly as a kid. At nine months of age, he developed severe asthmatic bronchitis and spent much of his childhood coughing, wheezing, and

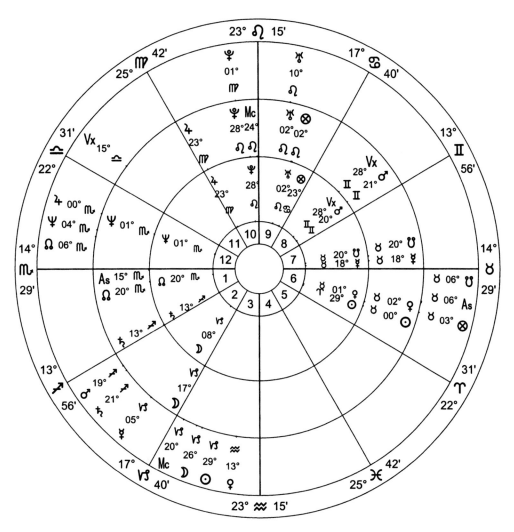

Figure 6b: Asthmatic Bronchitis

Inner Wheel: Rob's Natal Chart: Apr. 19, 1957; 8:15 PM EST; 81W01, 38N55

Middle Wheel: Progressed Chart: Jan. 19, 1958; 12:00 PM EST; WV; 81W01, 38N55

Outer Wheel: Transit Chart: Jan. 19, 1958; 12:00 PM EST; Oak Hill, WV; 81W01, 38N55

blowing his nose. He struggled to breathe and couldn't play with the other kids. All through school he did very little in physical education classes. He was in and out of hospitals, and doctors told him he'd have to have an indoor job and a controlled atmosphere with little physical activity. They advised him to watch what he ate because certain foods during certain times of the year might trigger an attack.

In checking the charts for the aspects in play at age nine months, Rob's Sun was in orb of conjunction to Venus and in orb of opposition to Neptune, showing a frail condition, while progressed Venus was square Uranus and so was of no help. Transiting Jupiter opposed his Sun and Venus. Transiting Saturn opposed his natal Mars. There is an assortment of afflictions to two important health indicators (Sun and Mars), indicating a vulnerable time for Rob's health. When transiting Mars joined Saturn to oppose natal Mars, it triggered the potential for the asthmatic bronchitis. The transiting Sun squaring its natal place was also relevant to timing.

Rob's Sun and Mars remained quite afflicted during his early years, with the progressing Sun applying to square Uranus while Mars progressed to square Jupiter. Transiting Uranus moves along to square his natal Mars. By age ten, transiting Pluto conjoins his Jupiter and squares his Mars. Due to retrograde motion, progressed Ju-

piter moved backward, coming closer to closing in on the square to his Mars. At the same time, transiting Neptune was on his progressed Ascendant, an aspect that reflected his frail condition. Soon after that, transiting Saturn moved through his 6th house and over his Sun, extending his problems.

Rob Builds His Strength

As Rob's story goes on, however, it gets better. Around the age of twenty-one, Rob began reading about modern homesteading: building one's own home and raising one's own food. The idea interested him so much that he quit a good-paying job at the post office and moved into the heart of Appalachia, securing a job at a sawmill. He learned how to use a chainsaw and built his own home, eventually setting it up with solar and hydropower, although he lived for several years without electricity. It took about ten years to complete the home, and Rob explains he had a terrible time at first. He became deathly ill several times with pneumonia and pleurisy, but his attitude was to just keep going. He learned from his mistakes.

Around 1981, when he was twenty-four, his body began to strengthen, although he stayed sore all the time for a couple more years. He had always been thin, but over a span of about four years

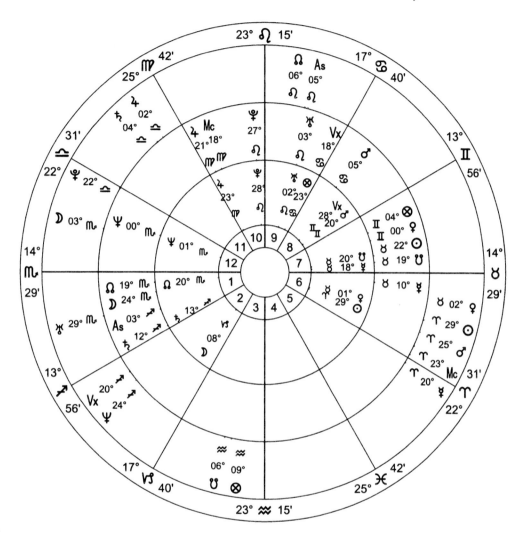

Figure 6c: Rob Builds His Strength

Inner Wheel: Rob's Natal Chart: Apr. 19, 1957; 8:15 PM EST; 81W01, 38N55

Middle Wheel: Progressed Chart: Apr. 19, 1981; 12:00 PM EST; 81W01, 38N55

Outer Wheel: Transit Chart: Apr. 19, 1981; 12:00 PM EST; 81W01, 38N55

he went from being spindly and frail to being defined and muscular. He outgrew his clothes. Rob says it is hard to describe just how radically his health and fitness improved.

The charts reveal how and why such an improvement took place when it did. By the age of twenty-one, Rob's progressed Ascendant had changed from Scorpio to Sagittarius, making Jupiter his new ruler. Soon after his progressed Ascendant moved into the venturesome sign of Sagittarius, he became interested in the prospects of homesteading and transitioned into an adventurous new life. His progressed Sun in Taurus was just coming into orb to trine his progressed Jupiter, a doubly beneficial aspect that supported him in his efforts and gave him the stamina to undertake such a big project. Jupiter also rules general growth.

There was an opposition from transiting Neptune to his Mars during those first few years, which coincided with his problems with pneumonia.

By age twenty-four, when he really began to build his strength, his progressed Sun came into trine with his natal Jupiter while his progressed Ascendant formed a trine to his Uranus. Transiting Neptune moved beyond the afflictions to his Mars and Jupiter. Transiting Saturn and Jupiter joined to sextile his new Ascendant. With his progressed 6th house now ruled by Venus, with 12° Taurus on the cusp, progressed Venus forms a sextile to Uranus from early Gemini. So, we can see quite a dramatic change in Rob's health indicators, with afflictions moving out of the picture and multiple beneficial aspects coming into view.

As to his life-long condition, Rob says that his lungs just don't work like they should unless he makes them work by staying active. He says he has to be consciously aware of his breathing, making his lungs go in and out, like steering a car. Otherwise, his breathing is shallow and irregular. Such symptoms and difficulties stem primarily from his afflicted Mars in Gemini. But, he had a complete physical a few years ago, and he is in excellent shape. Though the benefits were delayed, the natal trine from Pluto to his Sun is clearly evident in his ability to build his strength and his body. At this point his progressed Ascendant is in the late degrees of Sagittarius, the portion of Sagittarius that is co-ruled by the Sun, so he is reaping the benefits of that natal aspect now. Rob says he loves hard work and feeling the blood move within him.

Using Decans

To get additional information about health, it is quite useful to check the degree of the progressed Ascendant and identify the planet that co-rules this portion of the sign. This planet becomes an important co-ruler for an individual. The condition of this planet is revealing about health and general well being.

Also called decanates, the decans are subdivisions of each sign. The signs are divided into three subsections, ten degrees each. These are called decans; referred to as the first, second, and third decan. The first decan extends from 0° to 9° 59" of a sign. The second decan goes from 10° to 19° 59" of a sign. The third decan consists of the remaining ten degrees, from 20° to 29° 59" of a sign. The planetary ruler of the sign is the ruler of the first decan. The second decan is still ruled by the planet ruling the sign but it is also co-ruled by the planet ruling the next successive sign of the same element. The third decan of the sign is still ruled by the primary ruler of the sign, but it is co-ruled by the planet ruling the next successive (the last remaining) sign of the same element. Here are the decan rulers:

Aries: Mars rules the first decan of Aries.

Mars rules and the Sun co-rules the second decan of Aries.

Mars rules and Jupiter co-rules the third decan of Aries.

Taurus: Venus rules the first decan of Taurus.

Venus rules and Mercury co-rules the second decan of Taurus.

Venus rules and Saturn co-rules the third decan of Taurus.

Gemini: Mercury rules the first decan of Gemini.

Mercury rules and Venus co-rules the second decan of Gemini.

Mercury rules and Uranus co-rules the third decan of Gemini.

Cancer: The Moon rules the first decan of Cancer.

The Moon rules and Pluto co-rules the second decan of Cancer.

The Moon rules and Neptune co-rules the third decan of Cancer.

Leo: The Sun rules the first decan of Leo.

The Sun rules and Jupiter co-rules the second decan of Leo.

The Sun rules and Mars co-rules the third decan of Leo.

Virgo: Mercury rules the first decan of Virgo.

Mercury rules and Saturn co-rules the second decan of Virgo.

Mercury rules and Venus co-rules the third decan of Virgo.

Libra: Venus rules the first decan of Libra.

Venus rules and Uranus co-rules the second decan of Libra.

Venus rules and Mercury co-rules the third decan of Libra.

Scorpio: Pluto rules the first decan of Scorpio. (Mars may be used as a secondary ruler.)

Pluto rules and Neptune co-rules the second decan of Scorpio.

Pluto rules and the Moon co-rules the third decan of Scorpio.

Sagittarius: Jupiter rules the first decan of Sagittarius.

Jupiter rules and Mars co-rules the second decan of Sagittarius.

Jupiter rules and the Sun co-rules the third decan of Sagittarius.

Capricorn: Saturn rules the first decan of Capricorn.

Saturn rules and Venus co-rules the second decan of Capricorn.

Saturn rules and Mercury co-rules the third decan of Capricorn.

Aquarius: Uranus rules the first decan of Aquarius. (Saturn may be used as a secondary ruler.)

Uranus rules and Mercury co-rules the second decan of Aquarius.

Uranus rules and Venus co-rules the third decan of Aquarius.

Pisces: Neptune rules the first decan of Pisces. (Jupiter may be used as a secondary ruler)

Neptune rules and the Moon co-rules the second decan of Pisces.

Neptune rules and Pluto co-rules the third decan of Pisces.

Consider the main ruler of the progressed Ascendant sign primarily, especially the aspects of this planet by progression, but then look to the co-ruler and its aspects for more defining information. These planets tell by their aspects much about personal developments, just as in Rob's case, and they, along with the aspects of the luminaries, are among the most dependable indicators when it comes to health matters.

Leukemia

The following chart is used to illustrate the natal factors that were present in a shortened life due to unusual, extreme ill health. At the time of this birth and illness, the medical field was not nearly as advanced as it is today, however, the natal configurations are alarming.

This little girl, named Rita, appeared to the doctor to have only a lingering cold at the time. On the evening before her first birthday, a party was held in her honor. She was not feeling well and soon became so listless that the doctor was called in. She died early the next morning, on her first birthday, from what turned out to be leukemia. Relatives say her blood turned to water.

Rita's Natal Chart

Her natal chart shows severe afflictions. First of all, the Sun and Moon in the same sign suggests a frail condition in the early years. Many times these conditions are associated with the sign occupied by the luminaries, and the vulnerabilities increase if the Sun and Moon form bad aspects. Aquarius is associated internally with the circulation of the blood through the system. The Sun and Moon in Aquarius act upon the lymphatic system and the nutrition of the tissues. Afflictions to planets in Aquarius may tend to disturbances in circulation and impure blood. Agreement comes from the remaining severe aspects.

Mars is on the Ascendant. Mars is always an afflicted point, and this is a threatening position for it to hold in the nativity. Mars is the planet ruling the blood.

Two malefic planets oppose the Sun and Mars, Saturn and Pluto, and they are angular. Each of these planets alone show serious threats to the health when afflicting the Sun, but the two of them together are difficult to overcome by more positive aspects. Since Mars corresponds to the 1st

house and rules the physical body, and the Sun rules the vitality, with both on the Ascendant, the configuration of the oppositions poses a total of six afflictions. It is additionally threatening that her ruler, Saturn, is in conflict with the life-giving properties of the Sun. This aspect gains strength rapidly in the progressions. Mars may bring about a crisis very quickly as it progresses swiftly to the Ascendant. Rita's constitution and vitality are very weakened by the configurations. Pluto in conjunction with her ruler, Saturn, also implicates the threat of death. Pluto also widely opposes her Moon so that both luminaries are afflicted by an angular malefic.

Mercury is in the Ascendant with the Sun and Mars, and is similarly afflicted. It rules the 8th house of death. In Aquarius, death may come suddenly and unexpectedly, likely due to some unusual conditions. Mercury co-rules the third decan of Capricorn, becoming her co-ruler with the last degree of Capricorn rising. There seems to be no help.

Venus rules Rita's 4th house of the end of matters, including the end of life, and it is in a close opposition to Uranus and applying rapidly in strength. This aspect again suggests that her death may happen suddenly. Such an aspect between Venus and Uranus equates to temporary attachments and sudden separations, and

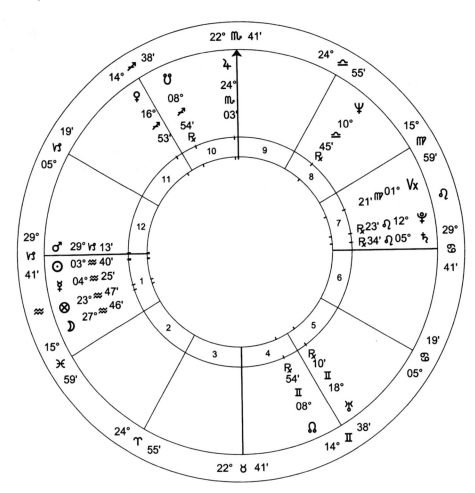

Figure 6d: Rita's Natal Chart
Jan. 24, 1947; 7:05 AM EST; 73W56, 40N38

reflects the untimely separation from her family with Venus ruling the 4th house.

The Moon rules the 6th house of health and is square Jupiter, with both of them angular. The Moon rules all the bodily fluids, and Jupiter is associated with detoxification processes. The Moon in Aquarius suggests that health conditions might be unusual, and would act suddenly upon the physical body (Moon in 1st house). The Moon square to Jupiter also shows the sad situation as it connects to her family.

Rita's Premature Death

At the time of Rita's death, the progressed Sun had moved into a close orb to oppose Saturn, one of the major afflictions in the birth chart. The Sun and Saturn in opposition show restrictions on the health, especially severe with the two planets angular and so vital to her health.

Although Rita's nativity shows Mars within a degree of the Ascendant, at the time of her death it had progressed across the cusp to a position just inside the 1st house, associated with the physical body. As a malefic, Mars poses a great threat. In its progressed position, Mars was in the first degree of Aquarius, associated with the circulation of the blood, while Mars rules the red blood cells. These afflictions in Aquarius suggest blood impurities.

Her progressed Ascendant has changed signs, now in Aquarius, giving Uranus as her new ruler. Progressed Venus is now in very close opposition to Uranus and Venus rules the 4th house of endings. Transiting Jupiter links into the aspect by a conjunction with Venus while opposing Uranus. This stimulates themes from the birth chart suggesting a sudden and unusual death.

Her natal Moon is widely opposed by transiting Saturn, while her progressed Moon is opposed by transiting Mars so that her progressed Ascendant and its ruler are afflicted at the same time both luminaries are afflicted. The combination of afflicting aspects reflects the very serious consequences.

The transiting Sun stimulates progressed configurations, and with its transit across the afflicted planets on the Ascendant, it did just that. Nearing her birthday, it is stirring up the natal afflictions while punctuating and closing the gap on that most serious exact progressed opposition between the Sun and her Saturn. That natal opposition created a double affliction, with progressed Sun moving forward to oppose her natal Saturn while natal retrograde Saturn was progressing backward to oppose her progressed Sun. The transiting Sun is the main timer of the event. Thankfully, she didn't suffer long.

To estimate the health potential of an individual, run through the checklist at

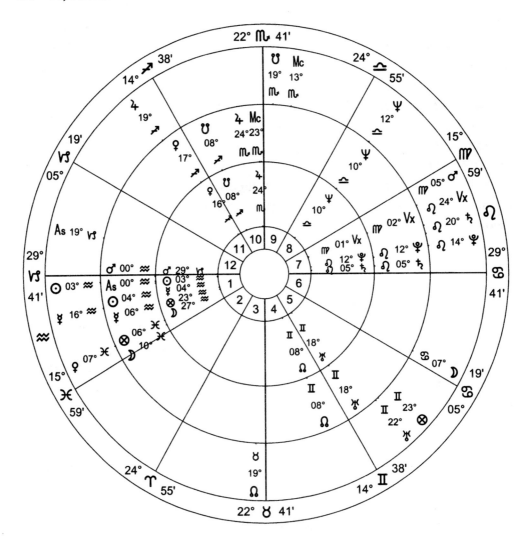

Figure 6e: Rita's Premature Death

Inner Wheel: Rita's Natal Chart: Jan. 24, 1947; 7:05 AM EST; 73W56, 40N38

Middle Wheel: Progressed Chart: Jan. 24, 1948; 6:30 AM EST; 73W56, 40N38

Outer Wheel: Transit Chart: Jan. 24, 1948; 6:30 AM EST; 73W56, 40N38

the beginning of the chapter. Then, for current conditions, check the active aspects among the health indicators. The sign associations may be used to get more detail.

chapter seven

Mental Health

Mental health is judged based on a combination of factors. The condition of Mercury, the 3rd house, the Moon, and the Ascendant are the most reliable indicators of mental health.

Mercury & the 3rd House

The planet Mercury, by sign, house position, and aspects, shows how a person's mind works. It shows an individual's type of mentality and his or her approach to intellectual activities. The characteristics of Mercury's sign influence the thinking, giving clues to the matters that occupy the mind and the kind of information a person regards as significant when making decisions. The house occupied by Mercury indicates the affairs that occupy the mind and the kinds of activities and subject matter that provide fuel from which ideas are drawn. If afflicted, the house occupied by Mercury gives clues to nervous or mental complaints. Stress, strain, tension, and worry stem from afflictions to Mercury.

The planet in closest aspect to Mercury has a very strong influence because Mercury is a neutral planet and picks up the vibrations of that nearest planet. It describes how the mentality is influenced.

For instance, with Saturn in closest aspect to Mercury, the mind may be slow and serious, but steady and with good concentration. With the better aspects, a person is capable of profound thought and is mentally organized. With less favorable aspects from Saturn, there may be excessive worry. Anxiety is common, and a suspicious or fearful outlook could prevent these people from making the most of opportunities. Even the poorer aspects of Saturn to Mercury have benefits, ensuring depth of thought. However, depression or pessimism is often a disadvantage. Similar themes apply if Mercury is in Capricorn, according to Mercury's overall condition in the sign.

With Mercury in closest aspect to Uranus, a person may be inventive, original, and witty if the aspect is easy, whereas if Mercury is in an afflicted aspect to Uranus, a person may be abrupt in speech or given to erratic and unconventional thinking. Similar themes apply if Mercury is in Aquarius, according to Mercury's aspects.

If Jupiter forms the closest aspect to Mercury, the better aspects suggest optimism and good judgment. Such a person may have an extraordinary knack for saying the right thing at the right time. With Mercury in affliction to Jupiter, a person may not think things through sufficiently, thus he or she may be prone to errors. Details may trip one up. Mercury in Sagittarius is similar, based on aspects.

If Neptune is in closest aspect to Mercury a person may be creative and imaginative, an inspiring dream weaver, or off in a dream world, prone to confusion, forgetful and unreliable. Some may be mental

escapists with the poorer aspects. Similar themes apply with Mercury in Pisces, depending on Mercury's condition.

With Mars in closest aspect to Mercury, an individual may be swift in decision-making processes and good at making a convincing argument, or an antagonist who is harsh in speech. Similar to Mercury in Aries, such an individual tends to think in competitive terms.

Aspects from Pluto to Mercury are similar to those of Mars. The better aspects produce a determined and resourceful mind, excellent scientific and research abilities, problem-solving skills, and make for a good strategist. If these two are in an afflicting aspect, it can make for a secretive and cunning mentality that could be particularly destructive. Mercury in Scorpio gives similar themes, according to Mercury's condition in the sign.

Mercury is only able to form two major aspects to Venus: the conjunction and sextile. These promote diplomacy and thoughtfulness in general, and may give a melodious or soft-spoken voice, nice handwriting, and exceptional artistic talents. Mental activities are frequently carried on in partnerships. The ability to communicate is often an avenue from which money can be made. Often there are mathematical skills. If in conjunction, aspects to this pair are most important. If afflicted, the mind may be inconsistent or fickle. Similar themes apply to Mercury in Taurus or Libra, according to Mercury's condition.

Aspects between the Moon and Mercury reveal a competent intellect with excellent communication skills and a good memory, or confused thinking and forgetfulness, according to the nature of the aspect. With afflictions, these people tend to believe that whatever is done or said is directed toward them personally. Much of the mental processing takes place on an unconscious level. Mercury in Cancer gives similar tendencies, according to the condition of Mercury.

The only major aspect that Mercury can form to the Sun is the conjunction. This gives mental energy and creativity. The mind is quick, sharp, and constantly engaged. Such individuals like to be considered authorities. If the conjunction is afflicted, it may affect objectivity. Mercury in Leo is similar.

In its own sign, Mercury in Gemini indicates great curiosity. These individuals want to know everything. They are knowledgeable on a number of subjects, versatile, fact seeking, and unbiased if Mercury forms good aspects, or they may be busybodies, chatterboxes, or with a tendency to get sidetracked if the aspects are poor. Those with Mercury in Virgo are not as talkative. There's a concern with precision, accuracy, and details. Such people are interested in ideas for their practical appli-

cation. These people often acquire specialized skills. Poor aspects to Mercury in this sign may cause an over concern with trivial matters or losing sight of the main issue.

Although the planet in closest aspect to Mercury is most influential, each aspect to Mercury is revealing and tells about the mind and memory, whether sharp and clear, or dull and slow. These aspects, including minor aspects, tell about speech, fluency, communication skills, handling paperwork, handwriting, about the ability to be logical and objective, and about the handling of business.

The better the condition and aspects to Mercury, the greater the chances for an individual to attain a high position due to the coordinating of so many factors that is done in the mind. With Mercury receiving many difficult aspects, there are likely learning problems, a speech impediment, faulty memory, bad penmanship or communication skills. Such a person may be prone to argument, sharp in tone, sarcastic, thoughtless, or given to fabricating and deceit.

Mercury by house position gives characteristics similar to the sign and planet naturally associated with that house. Mercury in the 1st house is similar to Mercury in Aries, or like Mercury in closest aspect to Mars. Mercury in the 2nd house is similar to Mercury in Taurus or in aspect to Venus, and so on.

The condition of the 3rd house shows the faculties of conscious thought based on perceptions. It shows how information is assimilated and processed. Planets in or ruling the 3rd house are influential.

Severe afflictions to the 3rd house cusp or to planets in this house may denote mental instability, or in extreme cases insanity. Saturn is likely to be prominently linked to the 3rd house by rule, occupancy, or afflicting the 3rd house ruler when mental deficiencies are in evidence. Deficiencies may also result from a water sign on the 3rd house cusp or intercepted in the 3rd house while malefic planets are within. Neptune in this house, or ruling it and afflicted, may tend toward deficiencies.

The Luminaries & Ascendant

The Moon rules the sense impressions, providing food for the mind. The Moon, together with Mercury, rules the substance of the brain. A much-afflicted Moon nearly always accompanies mental instability. For females, this luminary is closely connected to the general health.

Similar to Mercury, the Moon is a variable planet and takes on the nature of the planets with which it is closely configured. Each planet in aspect to the Moon is descriptive of mental health, according to the nature of the planet and by the type of aspect it forms.

For example, if the Moon forms an unfavorable aspect to Saturn, the senses are somewhat dulled, whereas the better aspects incline to sobriety and seriousness. Saturn in a hard aspect to the Moon in the natal chart is an indicator for potential nervous complaints; aspects are often in evidence in the progressions when problems arise.

A poor aspect between the Moon and Neptune indicates confusion, while a strong and dignified Neptune forming a fortunate aspect to the Moon may signify good psychic powers or intuition. Mental disorders often arise from a natal affliction between Neptune and the Moon. Neptune is quite involved in psychic disorders, psychotic episodes, or paranoia, frequently afflicting the Moon, the Ascendant, or the ruler of the 1st house.

When the overall aspects to the Moon are favorable, the senses are sharp and accurate, physical functions are efficient, and the public image is good, due to a peace loving and mild-mannered nature. With unfavorable aspects to the Moon, these themes are reversed. The senses are undependable, the temperament causes unpopularity, and there may be a lack of common sense, carelessness, laziness, or cravings for alcohol.

The aspect between the Moon and Mercury is most important for determining mental health. This aspect reflects an efficiency of the mind, the communication skills, and memory. Any aspect between them is good for mental expression. If the Moon and Mercury are conjunct, the aspects they receive as a pair are crucial.

Many close aspects to the Moon and Mercury give much versatility, although if these consist of mostly stressful aspects, it can interfere with concentration. Nervous disorders stem from afflictions to the Moon and Mercury, although a favorable aspect from a benefic planet can help overcome afflictions, depending on the comparable strength of the aspects. (A square or opposition to the benefic Venus from Mars or Saturn in the natal chart may indicate mental deficiencies in and of itself.)

The best indicator of good mental health and proper functioning of the mind and mental powers is a favorable aspect involving the Moon, Mercury, and the Ascendant, especially a supportive aspect from Mercury to both.

The least favorable scenario is no link between the Moon and Mercury at birth, which tends to weakness when neither Moon nor Mercury aspect the Ascendant and yet receive severe afflictions from malefic planets. Such conditions reflect mental deficiencies. In rare cases, insanity may result.

Because the brain is in the head, it is ruled internally by the sign Aries, the sign associated with Mars and the Ascendant.

Aspects to the Ascendant affect the brain and the expression, and color the outlook. Extremely severe afflictions to the Ascendant may indicate brain damage. Extremely severe afflictions involving Mars, especially to the Sun or Mercury, may reflect actual madness.

If the Moon rules the 1st house and is severely afflicted, the effects on mental health could be dire.

Instability may be noted if the Moon is afflicted in the 1st house, the severity depending on how seriously the Moon is challenged without benefit from Venus or Jupiter. The Moon in any angular house often tends to general restlessness and moodiness.

The Sun, as the life force that offers its vitalizing rays, feeds the nerves of the brain. Beneficial aspects it forms to Mercury, the Moon, to planets in or ruling the 3rd house, or to Mars or the Ascendant are helpful in terms of the mental health. Cases of hysteria may be marked by afflictions to the Sun, especially by the Moon. This aspect creates inner tension.

Nervous Breakdowns & Mental/Emotional Meltdowns

The cases that follow illustrate the natal potential for mental instability and the conditions when the potential manifested.

Particularly interesting is the fact that two of these women had what each described as a "nervous breakdown" near the same time, in reflex to a major transiting planetary alignment that triggered their breakdowns when conditions in the progressions were prime.

Dixie

Raised by a mentally ill mother and an alcoholic father, Dixie's life had been full of challenges, but it wasn't until her fifty-first year that Dixie suffered a nervous breakdown that sent her into group therapy and required her to take eight weeks off from her job as an advertising salesperson for the city newspaper. The job and her boss were extremely demanding. She was handling an extra territory and under increased pressure to meet her quota and make bonus.

This particular day had been productive, and she was in a good mood when she returned to her office after making her daily calls on prospective advertisers. Who knows what had been happening for her boss that day but he immediately called her out for a recent error in her paperwork, and he had written her up for it. Had he known all that she'd been dealing with lately and the reaction she would have, he might have taken a different approach. Besides the job and other stress, Dixie was withdrawing from an an-

tidepressant medication, Effexor, and her boss's timing couldn't have been worse.

The Moon reflects early childhood experiences, especially those directly related to the mother and other women. In Dixie's chart, the Moon forms an opposition to Mercury. The aspect suggests harsh handling by women, and it reflects her mother's mental health deficiencies. It symbolizes the difficulties in their communication and the confusion caused by her mother's flawed teachings. For example, Dixie was taught that the reason it was dangerous to touch the space heater was because there were mean dogs behind it that would jump out and attack. She was taught that it was wasteful to flush the toilet after a single use. Moon opposing Mercury also reveals the mental health of Dixie's siblings (Mercury). Her twin sisters have undergone therapy for schizophrenia, and her brother suffers from panic attacks.

The square of her Moon to Mars and the wide opposition between the luminaries is descriptive of conflicts within the home as a result of her father's drinking. Further reflecting her father's illness and the resulting strained circumstances is the square from Mars to her Sun in the 4th house. The square of Jupiter to Moon and Mercury also reflects family problems and stressful experiences through relatives. There were two long episodes of sexual abuse at a young age, one after the other

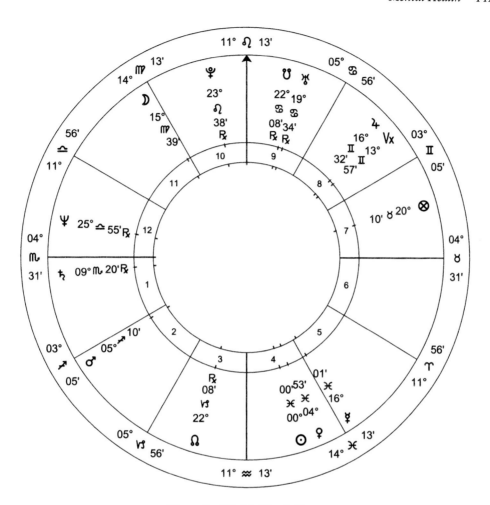

Figure 7a: Dixie's Natal Chart
Feb. 18, 1954, 10:43 PM CST; 85W40, 40N33

(see Chapter 8). In both situations, the abuse came from relatives who were temporarily caring for the children while their parents were unable to. She later suffered from panic attacks (Sun opposing Moon) as a result of psychological counseling to deal with the abuse issues. Mars is square Venus, another indicator of potential mental meltdowns, as well as being a component in the abuse issues that lie behind them.

Dixie's Breakdown

No, it hadn't been easy. Dixie has dealt with food issues (Jupiter square Moon), an extensive assortment of health problems, and periods of depression, the latter so serious as to lead to her long journey to find the right combination of drug therapies and antidepressant medications to enable her to cope. As a Pisces with an afflicted Sun, her health issues are affected by the sign Pisces, outlined in Chapter 6.

Dixie has natal Saturn on the Ascendant and in Scorpio. As a hard worker and a perfectionist, responsibilities are taken seriously and at an emotional level. In trine to Mercury, Saturn is a fortunate and steadying influence, although she tends to take a serious view of life. Saturn trine Venus gives a good business sense.

A deficiency in the transmission of data between the mind and the senses is noted with the hard aspects of Moon to Mercury so that unconscious emotional patterns from the past can interfere with an ability to communicate objectively. Agreement comes from Dixie's Mercury in Pisces, where the mind may become trapped in memories. Memories may be visualized so vividly that they distort present reality. Perceptions floating up from the unconscious mind influence mental deductions. Criticism is taken personally and with Mercury in the 5th house, especially if her intellect or ability to analyze is questioned.

The Jupiter aspects to her Moon and Mercury suggest that details might trip her up. Her newspaper ad sales job that required so much attention to detail might easily lead to frustration and stress. Her Sun square Mars indicates a predisposition to mental irritability, often suppressed.

Dixie and her parents enjoyed better relationships in the later years of their lives. She played the role of guardian during their final years when they were confined to nursing homes due to mental and health problems. Finally, with her parents dying a year apart, she had not had the chance to fully mourn their deaths due to her job pressures and heavy schedule. She especially missed her mom and the anniversary of their deaths was approaching. Finally, the combination of stress from so many directions became too much.

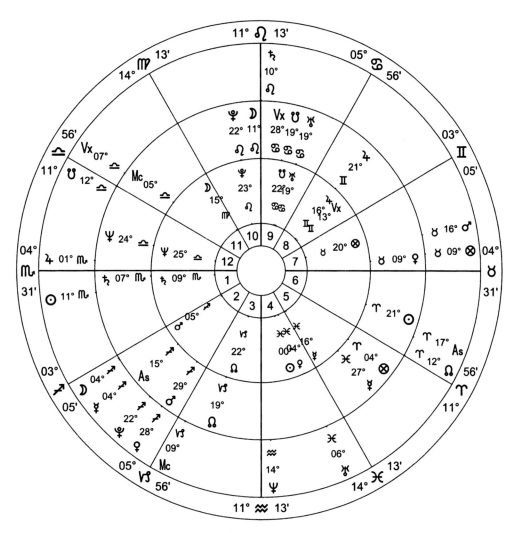

Figure 7b: Dixie's Breakdown

Inner Wheel: Dixie's Natal Chart: Feb. 18, 1954, 10:43 PM CST; 85W40, 40N33
Middle Wheel: Progressed Chart: Nov. 3, 2005, 4:30 PM CST; 85W40, 40N33
Outer Wheel: Transit Chart: Nov. 3, 2005, 4:30 PM EST; 85W40, 40N33

In looking at her chart for the day of her emotional crash, we see that her progressed Ascendant at 15° Sagittarius is square her natal Moon/Mercury opposition. This is the major aspect from her birth chart showing potential mental health deficiencies, and the current angularity is an indication that the potential is ripe to manifest. The progressed Ascendant in square to Mercury gives a high degree of nervous tension internally. The tendency is to excessive worry, often over small matters. The square of progressed Ascendant to the Moon brings emotional depression and concerns over family members, often connected to the loss of an older female. It is a generally unpopular time, when the greatest care is needed in business dealings.

With her progressed Ascendant in Sagittarius, her ruler is Jupiter. Her natal Jupiter is square her Moon and Mercury. Again, this brings to prominence aspects from the birth chart that suggested potential emotional and mental imbalances. Creating further disturbances and the potential for things to go wrong is the opposition of her ruling planet (Jupiter) to her progressed Ascendant.

Transiting Saturn conjuncts her progressed Moon, often coinciding with depressing periods or troublesome times in life. Such an aspect represents trials or hardships. Her recent stress and depression is also noted by the separating square of the progressed Moon to her natal Saturn. Transiting Saturn is also on her Midheaven, associated with potential troubles with superiors or in connection with vocation, especially since transiting Saturn squares her natal Saturn on her Ascendant, indicating a time of tests and trials having a significant personal impact.

As ruler of her natal 3rd house, natal and progressed Saturn receives multiple challenging aspects. The combination of progressed Venus opposite her Saturn and transiting Saturn on her progressed Moon suggests deep melancholy.

The opposition from transiting Neptune to her progressed Moon reflects the problem with medications, increasing chances to be incorrectly diagnosed or prescribed for. This is a key aspect. Since her progressed Sun is nearing an opposition to natal and progressed Neptune, such potential problems will require careful monitoring in the years ahead. Having been on her latest antidepressant for only six months, her doctor took her off abruptly just thirty days earlier, in order to switch her to another drug; this added confusion to the pressure on her mind. Some of the most common side effects of Effexor include anxiety and nervousness, however, Dixie asked to be taken off because her panic attacks had returned, and she'd begun to have bowel movements in her sleep, which really frightened her. Transiting Neptune opposing progressed Moon may produce not only sensitivity to drugs and chemicals, and strange moods, but the soul is often world-weary and ready for an escape.

At the very moment she lost it and blew up at her boss before storming out of the building, the transiting Moon had hooked up with transiting Mercury, repeating a planetary link from her natal chart that was most significant of problems stemming from mental stress. The original aspect of Moon to Mercury in the natal chart that suggested problems with objectivity due to unconscious emotional interference is emphasized now throughout the chart.

Also at the time, the transiting Moon/Mercury pair was conjunct natal Mars, increasing potential for a flare-up. They reactivated the natal square of Mars to Sun and Venus. The transiting Sun is conjunct her natal Saturn and square her progressed Moon. There are hints of challenges with someone of the opposite sex, likely an authority figure.

Following her loss of control when she gave her boss a piece of her mind and walked out, she entered group therapy at a stress center, making a daily round trip of more than a hundred miles for the next eight weeks. She says she cried for a month. Finally, she had the time to prop-erly mourn the loss of her parents and feels better as a result. During her time off, Dixie was also baptized; something she always wanted but never had the opportunity to do because she was affiliated with no specific religion or church. This is reflected in Jupiter's prominence and aspects, making possible the resolve of an old issue.

Dixie returned to work, but eventually quit her job at the newspaper, took a pay cut, and got a job as a restaurant hostess. It suits her soft Pisces demeanor, and she feels her quality of life has improved.

Katy

Katy dealt with many issues as a result of early abuse and living with an alcoholic parent. By the time of her breakdown in her forty-fifth year, when work frustrations combined with confusing personal and family problems, Katy was taking three prescription medications for depression and anxiety. She began the drug therapy after being diagnosed with mental illness several years earlier.

Having worked for the same bank as an investment operation service representative for a few years, Katy found it to be a rewarding job in many respects. However, she'd been involved in numerous clashes with supervisors and three of her immediate supervisors were let go in succession. She now felt she was regarded as a trouble

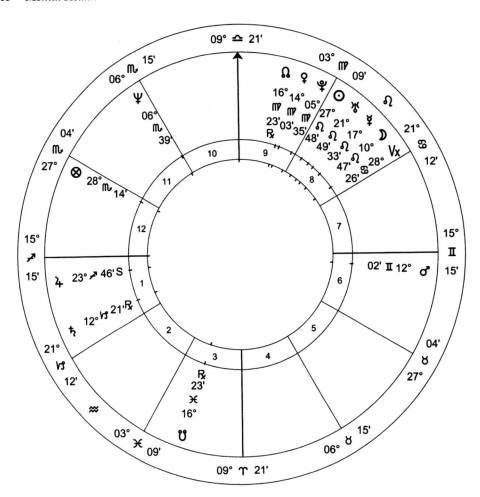

Figure 7c: Katy's Natal Chart
Aug. 20, 1960; 3:50 PM CDT; 93W06, 44N57

source because she had brought attention to questionable practices within her department that she thought should be exposed. The fact that she had an impact on the fates of her earlier supervisors gave her a certain sense of satisfaction, but now her new supervisors evidently felt her to be a threat, and Katy was moved to new departments on numerous occasions.

All spring, summer, and into the fall, she felt mounting tensions in her workplace and no longer knew who she could trust. Then, without warning, her computer was removed from her workspace, and she found she was being moved to yet another department. She blew up at her supervisor and walked out. The next morning she called in sick, and the day after that Katy checked into a mental hospital.

The first feature one notes in Katy's natal chart is the group of planets in the 8th house, aptly describing her responsibilities managing other people's money. Interests lie in corporate finances, and with Mercury here, she has the ability to uncover secrets. She presents a strong public image with her Moon sextile Mars.

Raised by a mother addicted to alcohol, Katy feels she has to take care of her mom instead of the other way around, and she resents it. Issues with her mother have been ongoing her entire life. Neptune square Moon shows her mother's addictions and indicates an irresponsible mother who may

have had a demoralizing effect on her. Her mother sexually abused Katy during a period of heavy drinking, an issue Katy spends a great deal of energy trying to work through. She had her own problems with alcohol addiction for many years, and she suffered for a decade from bulimia. Her bout with bulimia followed a prolonged conjunction from her progressed Ascendant to her natal and progressed Jupiter that brought substantial weight gain.

Katy has two brothers also dealing with problems, indicated by her 3rd house ruler, Neptune, square the Moon.

The conjunction of Moon and Mercury in Katy's chart is a similar planetary link as in Dixie's chart, except a conjunction rather than an opposition. The Moon and Mercury are in Leo, suggesting a need to be admired and appreciated, a flair for dramatic expression, and high intelligence and executive ability. This conjunction indicates a direct link between the unconscious mind and the conscious reasoning mind. It gives an intellectual awareness of one's emotional nature and responses to other people. At the same time, there is great sensitivity to what others think and interpersonal communications have an immediate effect upon the emotional responses. Unfortunately, Neptune in square to the Moon creates confusion. Neptune can interfere with practical judgment as it increases imagination, which may not always be reliable.

Such an aspect may cause an individual to be touchy and nervous, with a tendency for their feelings to override objective reason. These influences are especially relevant to Katy's thought processes due to Neptune's rule of her 3rd house. Neptune clouds the picture, and the unconscious mind may play tricks on the conscious mind. At the time she was diagnosed as mentally ill, this square was activated, with her progressed Moon square natal Neptune from the 8th house.

With her Moon/Mercury conjunction in the 8th house, Katy is busy seeking information that will bring transformational healing, often becoming involved in so many therapies at the same time that confusion and feeling overwhelmed is the result.

The conjunction of Moon with Mercury also gives such a love of change that it can become disruptive to life at certain times, a trait intensified with the conjunction occurring in the 8th house. She is restless and high strung. Uranus most closely influences Mercury by conjunction. This plays up the themes of restlessness, but also gives originality and even certain genius. In many ways, Katy knows how to turn her deficiencies into financial opportunities.

Katy's Breakdown

At the time of her mental/emotional breakdown, the progressed Ascendant is in the last degree of Capricorn, ruled by Saturn, and her Saturn is square her progressed Sun. This aspect often reflects a disappointing and dismal period, when nothing seems to go right in professional or personal matters. This in turn leads to a pessimistic outlook or a depressed nature. Conflicts with authorities are common.

Connected to the same aspect, Katy had recently taken steps to separate from her stepfather, with whom she'd kept in contact for many years after he and her mother divorced. Her decision was due to what she says were sexual innuendos and perverted gestures she'd observed in him over the years. While he had acted as a benefactor to her in many ways and she wanted to remain friends with him, she felt that there were many inappropriate aspects to their relationship that made her ill when she was around him. For her healing, she felt she needed to cut him out of her life. These anxieties stem from her 8th house themes. Progressed Venus had come to square natal Moon, heightening emotional sensitivity.

The progressed Sun is semi-square its natal place, an aspect that occurs around the forty-fifth year, and which may combine with other factors to produce a crisis. Changes may be forced, and there are often separations within the family, or the health becomes a concern. In fact, issues with her mother had gone from bad to worse recently. It seems she cannot completely

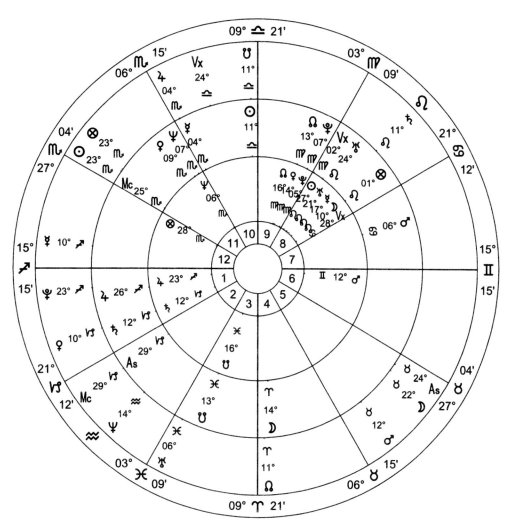

Figure 7d: Katy's Breakdown

Inner Wheel: Katy's Natal Chart: Aug. 20, 1960; 3:50 PM CDT; 93W06, 44N57
Middle Wheel: Progressed Chart: Nov. 15, 2005; 4:40 PM CDT; 93W06, 44N57
Outer Wheel: Transit Chart: Nov. 15, 2005; 4:40 PM CST; 93W06, 44N57

disconnect from her mom, no matter how much she wants to. She is repulsed by many of her mother's behaviors that stem from addictions to prescription drugs and alcohol, but Katy still feels a tie and a responsibility for her mother. The conjunction of natal Moon to Mercury suggests that this tie may be next to impossible to sever.

The previous months of frustrations at work are shown by the separating square from progressed Moon to natal and progressed Saturn, when efforts are not rewarded, leaving a feeling of inadequacy and sometimes melancholy. Progressed Moon is also separating from an opposition to the progressed Sun, often a critical and difficult period when compromise and cooperation are a must to avoid separations or serious confrontations.

Transiting Saturn is on Katy's natal Moon, often coincident with depression and troubling times.

Transiting Neptune opposes natal Moon and Mercury, reproducing an aspect from the natal chart that suggested an unreliable imagination and increased sensitivity. It can give a feeling of fear or dread. Incoming data is confusing or unclear and complicates relationships, both personal and business. Feelings may be misleading and strange moods come and go. There may be a world-weary need to escape. Difficulties within the home life, with the mother or another female relative, can undermine

self-confidence, complicating the way one deals with the outside world. We see that unresolved issues with her mom were a root factor that undermined Katy's ability to be objective in her other relationships, including her professional associations. This was a key aspect at the time of her breakdown.

Katy returned to work several weeks later, aware that many of her current anxieties and unexplainable fears could be attributed to transiting Neptune opposing her Moon and Mercury. Knowing that these were mostly groundless helped her cope. Eventually her relations with her superiors improved.

Case Similarities

Life Similarities: Both Dixie and Katy grew up with an alcoholic parent. Both were abused in childhood. Both suffered from eating disorders over prolonged periods. Both take antidepressant medications. Both were in the midst of trying to resolve conflicts rooted in early childhood, in particular, as these connected to their mother. Both were under pressure at work and felt they were treated unfairly. Both describe themselves as having clutter. Both are single. Katy never married, and Dixie has been single since her divorce from her first love in the mid-1980s.

Natal Astrology Similarities: Both have Saturn in the 1st house, giving a serious outlook and a deep sense of responsibility. Both Katy and Dixie have natal Moon and Mercury in hard aspect, with stressful aspects to the pair. Both have strong Neptunian/Pisces influences. Both have a strong Scorpio/8th house emphasis. Both have afflictions between Venus and Mars.

Progressed Similarities: Both had recent or current squares from progressed Venus to natal or progressed Moon, a time of increased sensitivity, when the feelings are easily hurt. Both had a luminary in square to natal Saturn, and both had hard aspects from transiting Saturn to the natal or progressed Moon, commonly a depressing period. Both were born near a New or Full Moon and had their breakdown during a major Moon phase—the reverse of the one they were born with. The major phases of the Moon, whether New or Full, have a strong influence over nervous, high strung, or sensitive people. Both women had hard aspects from transiting Neptune to the natal or progressed Moon. The common transiting aspect was an opposition between transiting Saturn and transiting Neptune. Taken at its core meaning, this is an aspect of fears stemming from the unconscious mind and past memories. Anxiety and mistrust stems from deep-rooted psychological problems. Institutionalization is one potential result of this combination and unfortunately, the tran-

siting planets tied in to an afflicted Moon in each case. The sensors were overloaded.

Panic Attacks Set Off by an Eclipse

Sara believes that an eclipse set off her long-lasting episode of frequent panic attacks. Born Feb. 7, 1955, 4:55 AM, 102W22/31N50, she wrote to ask if the astrology could offer understanding of what had happened. Sara gave her birth data, explaining that on May 10, 1994, there was a solar eclipse. She was working the desk at the downtown library at 10:30 in the morning when out of nowhere she started having a severe panic attack. She'd been having them since. She wanted to know if the eclipse triggered something inside her.

Her chart, with progressions and transits at the beginning of her first panic attack, is shown on the following page.

What is noticeable right away is that Sara was born near a Full Moon, an aspect of the luminaries that can give rise to tension and stress that might potentially escalate to panic under just the right conditions. Saturn, ruler of her natal chart, squares the luminaries, increasing such chances. The solar eclipse, falling in Taurus, happened to very closely square both her Sun and Moon as it also opposed her natal chart ruler Saturn. So, three of her

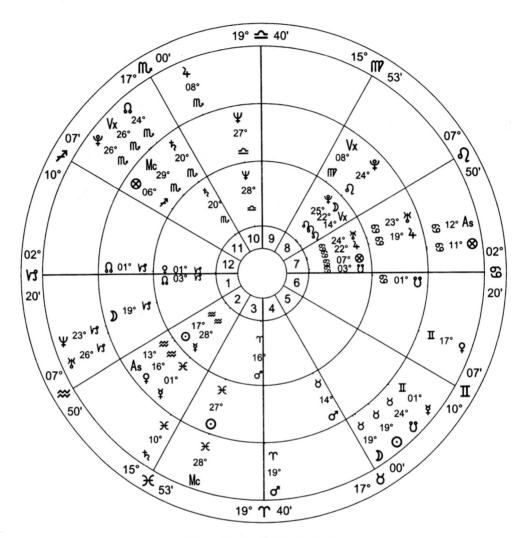

Figure 7e: Panic Attacks Begin

Inner Wheel: Sara's Natal Chart: Feb. 7, 1955; 4:55 AM CST; 102W22, 31N51

Middle Wheel: Progressed Chart: May 10, 1994; 10:30 AM CST; 102W22, 31N51

Outer Wheel: Transit Chart: May 10, 1994; 10:30 AM CDT; 102W22, 31N51 most personal planets were negatively impacted by the eclipse.

Sara also has a wide opposition between her Moon and Mercury in her natal chart, an aspect of potential mental confusion, that the eclipse also stimulated. Saturn and Pluto afflict this opposition in the natal chart, increasing worries, anxiety, and inhibitions. When the eclipse occurred, Mercury was Sara's co-ruler, with her progressed Ascendant in the second decan of Aquarius. Mercury was further afflicted, with her progressed Midheaven square natal Mercury. This brings the natal affliction into greater prominence, activating the potential. Transiting Pluto squares natal Mercury, creating difficulties in communication and intensifying the significance of daily interactions.

Transiting Neptune was opposing her progressed Uranus, producing confusion and particularly so, since Uranus is her main current ruler with her progressed Ascendant in Aquarius. Progressed Mars is square her progressed Ascendant, conducive to sudden health conditions, frequently more along the lines of a propensity for accidents. Transiting Mars square progressed Moon replays similar dangers. This combination of aspects appropriately reflects her statement that her panic attack started "out of nowhere." Transiting Mars also squared her progressed Jupiter from the cusp of the 4th house, near her natal Mars position.

There were likely tensions in her domestic life that were playing on her mind even while she was at work. (As it turns out, there was a divorce on the horizon.)

Panic Attacks Will Soon Subside

By the time Sara wrote, she'd been having the panic attacks for twelve years. Why was she still having them? Sara explained that what triggers the attacks is someone approaching her to ask a question or to watch her do something, like a social anxiety. The social anxiety seemed to particularly stem from natal Saturn square her Full Moon and Mercury that the eclipse stimulated. Charts for the time of Sara's inquiry are shown here.

Mars in its progression over the years had squared her progressed Ascendant, her natal Sun, opposed her Saturn, and finally squared natal Moon, now nearly exact. This revealed continued agitation, stress, and anxiety. During the interval that Venus was her co-ruler, her progressed Venus squared her Saturn, opposed her Moon, and moved over natal Mercury. Her progressed Ascendant was just leaving orb of conjunction to Mercury. These aspects kept the natal potential for mental anxiety stimulated.

But, it was only a matter of months before her progressed Ascendant would

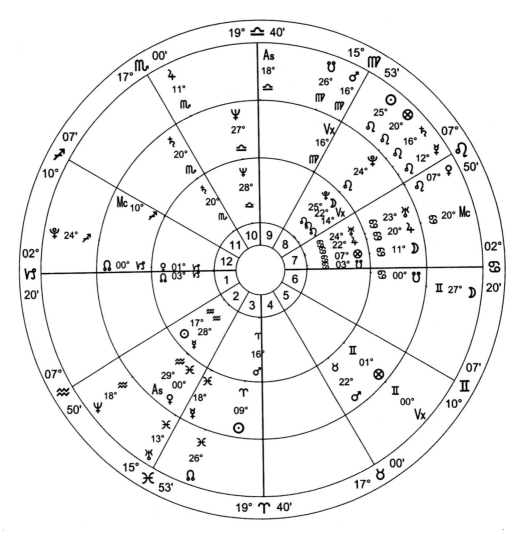

Figure 7f: Panic Attacks Will Soon Subside

Inner Wwheel: Sara's Natal Chart: Feb. 7, 1955; 4:55 AM CST; 102 W22, 31N51
Middle Wheel: Progressed Chart: Aug. 18, 2006; 11:30 PM CST; 102 W22, 31N51
Outer Wheel: Transit Chart: Aug. 18, 2006; 11:30 PM CDT; 102 W22, 31N51

change signs, moving out of Aquarius and into Pisces. This would give her new chart rulers; Neptune and Jupiter, considering that Neptune is the ruler of Pisces and Jupiter is the old ruler of the sign. With any luck at all, they and her progressed Ascendant would be involved in better aspects than her old rulers had been.

In fact, her natal Neptune is forming the closest aspect to her Mercury. This could bring some bright days ahead. Her Jupiter is sextile to progressed Mars while progressing Mercury in Pisces was coming to trine her progressed and then her natal Jupiter. It appeared that she might begin to feel calmer and more relaxed with her progressed Ascendant in Pisces and less anxious as when Uranus was ruling due to the natal squares it receives from Neptune and Mars while in the family sign Cancer. Sara was advised that happier days were ahead, an excellent chance her panic attacks would cease in 2007.

In following up a year and a half later, Sara reported that many changes had come about. She had done a considerable amount of traveling, starting in early 2007 (Neptune and Jupiter). She quit her library job and moved to New Orleans to be near her sister for a time. While there she worked at a veterinary clinic (Neptune). Then she moved to Oklahoma to get back with her ex-husband after an eleven-year separation following twenty-two years of marriage, and they are working things out. (These were the issues suggested by the earlier Mars aspects.) The first three months were rocky because of past issues that had to be discussed and dealt with, but they have come to a better meeting of minds. Mercury's nice aspects to her new rulers are especially helpful here, since Virgo is now on the progressed 7th house cusp so that Mercury now rules her progressed Descendant— her husband. They communicate much better and Sara says she is more open to discussing her feelings.

Sara's husband is a traveling nurse so much more travel is on the horizon just as her Mercury aspects to her new rulers suggest. She loves the sense of freedom, and extra trips are also planned to see her daughter graduate from college, then to her son's to visit a new grandson.

In early 2007, Sara allowed herself to be prescribed an anti-anxiety drug (Neptune) to help with the panic attacks, but not wanting to remain on them she quit taking the medications after five months. The panic attacks have not come back, and she has been free of them for a year! Sara was happy to share her story. It is a good illustration of how dramatically life can change based on the progressed Ascendant ruler. The ruler shows how life is going according to its aspects.

chapter eight

Accidents & Other Misfortunes

Accidents are generally shown by a combination of progressed and transiting aspects. These are likely to include afflictions involving Mars, both in the progressions and the transits. Mars is considered a malefic planet for good reason. When prominent and afflicted, it reflects potential for accidents, illness, and general conflicts.

Uranus is often a prominent planet when risk and danger are near. It is frequently involved in afflicting aspects when accidents occur, especially when they come out of the blue or unexpectedly. Uranus acts in lightning speed. Uranus in affliction with Mars is a most dangerous aspect, when trouble comes from unexpected directions. It is a fiery and explosive combination, suggesting accident-prone tendencies. The greatest caution is needed when handling fireworks, firearms, sharp tools, or machinery.

Depending on the factors involved in an accident, other afflictions would come from the particular area of involvement. Traffic accidents or problems with vehicles might have Mercury or the ruler of the 3rd house involved, probably in affliction to Mars. For a serious accident to occur, the natal Sun and the progressed angles of the chart would likely be seriously afflicted. The progressed Moon would also be involved in challenging aspects with natal, progressed, or transiting planets in the event of an accident.

The natal chart would show potential for the type of accident that might occur, and afflictions to Mars will generally be found. The progressions show when the potential might manifest.

An Exchange of Gunfire

The following chart belongs to Dan. After nearly twenty years on the police force, he answered a 911 call of an apparent domestic dispute. Unbeknown to Dan, a man who had just been shot by his son made the call. While the phone was still in his hand, the man's forty-five-year-old son fired again and killed him. The son then proceeded to kill his mother in her bed with another bullet, as she was begging him to stop. Neighbors say the threesome often had arguments over cigarettes, which may have been what started the incident.

The phone line went dead, and Dan left for the scene with another police officer following. Arriving at the home, they proceeded to the front door, knocking and making their presence known. In an instant, Dan saw the butt of a gun through the doorway, and then they were being fired upon. There was no place for concealment, and a third shot went through Dan's left thumb and into his upper right arm. He dropped his weapon, but recovered it as a third officer arrived at the scene.

An exchange of gunfire followed, and the crazed man was not subdued until he had been hit by three of the police officers' bullets. He survived the shooting.

A Police Officer's Nativity

In viewing Dan's natal chart, the Sun/Pluto conjunction on the Midheaven is evidence of his career as a police officer. The aspect signifies courage, leadership ability, and an ability to meet competition directly. Pluto rules the 1st house and at the Midheaven shows that Dan is attracted to public work. The Sun in the 10th house shows ambition to attain a position of authority. The conjunction of Pluto with the Sun, ruling the 1st and 10th houses, suggests there may be an element of danger associated with his job.

With this elevated pair (Sun/Pluto) in Leo, Dan's job is to provide protection. The Sun/Pluto conjunction is not afflicted, and the assisting aspects Pluto receives are evidence of many years of service without serious injury on the job. There would have to be other afflictions for serious personal danger to become a threat.

Going along with this theme is Jupiter in the 6th house, showing that Dan's work is service-oriented. This position of Jupiter offers him a measure of health protection as well as protection on the job. The ruler of the 6th house is Mars, another indication of his job as a police officer. Mars makes a sextile to Saturn, showing Dan's abilities to lead and command, and to accomplish what he sets out to do.

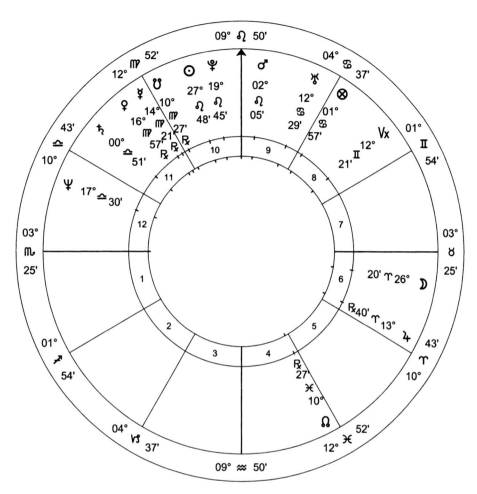

Figure 8a: Dan's Natal Chart
Aug. 21, 1951; 11:35 AM CDT; 85W40, 40N33

Mars squares the Ascendant, an aspect of potential danger, with Mars ruling Dan's 6th house of work. There is also a wide square to the Moon from Mars, and although it doesn't appear to be especially threatening, it will be found to be one of the stimulated factors at the time he was shot. The two are in complementary signs and are only widely square to each other. If the square had been closer, or the signs conflicting, the threat from this aspect would be more severe.

There is a square from Jupiter in the 6th house to Uranus, an aspect that increases in strength over the years as progressing Uranus moves forward. It is the major indicator of personal danger, and is quite a prominent factor at the time of the shooting incident. This shows surprising elements linked to his job. This could undermine or interrupt his safety on the job that is normally provided by Jupiter.

The Shooting

Uranus has progressed to a closer square to Jupiter, nearly exact now, emphasizing this affliction from Dan's natal chart. This is an important aspect because Jupiter is now Dan's ruler with his progressed Ascendant in Sagittarius. It is an aspect of potential unexpected trouble, with personal danger a possibility. Such danger

may come in the line of work, and travel might be involved.

Dan's progressed Sun and Jupiter are now in an opposition, an aspect of possible confrontation, as well as a potential physical risk. The latter theme is emphasized for Dan with Jupiter as his ruler.

Numerous afflictions can be seen in the progressed chart involving Mars. By progression, Mars is barely out of orb of a conjunction to the natal Sun while exactly squared by transiting Pluto. This square can carry a threat of danger and the inclusion of the natal Sun in the configuration increases the risks since Pluto in square to the Sun is also associated with dangers. Dan's natal Sun/Pluto conjunction is not afflicted. This repeating link between them signifies eventful times in connection with his profession. If these two had been afflicted in the natal chart, this incident might have been much more serious for Dan, possibly fatal. As it is, he escaped with relatively minor injuries. The square of transiting Pluto to progressed Mars is an important element in the timing of the altercation.

To intensify the forming theme, transiting Mars is conjunct natal Pluto while in square to the progressed Moon. This is a heated and potentially explosive combination. The angular position of transiting Mars and its aspect to Pluto helps

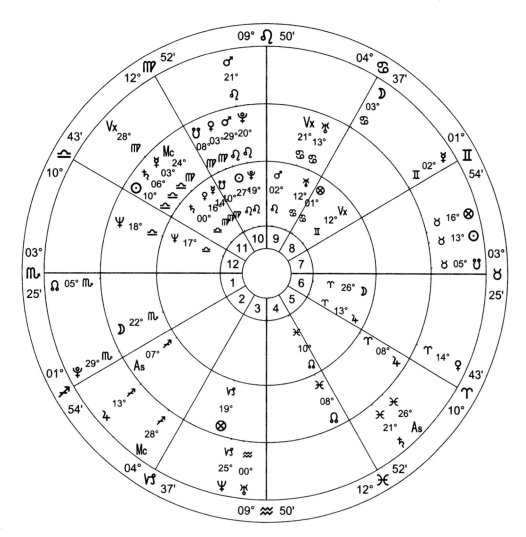

Figure 8b: The Shooting

Inner Wheel: Dan's Natal Chart: Aug. 21, 1951; 11:35 AM CDT; 85W40, 40N33

Middle Wheel: Progressed Chart: May 4, 1995; 3:47 AM CDT; 85W40, 40N33

Outer Wheel: Transit Chart: May 4, 1995; 3:47 AM EST; 85W40, 40N33

pinpoint the timing of the incident. The square from Mars to the progressed Moon repeats the natal affliction between Dan's Mars and the Moon. Squares between these two are often in evidence during physically threatening circumstances to an individual.

There are also two connections of Moon with Pluto. The progressed Moon is square progressed Pluto, and transiting Pluto is conjunct the progressed Moon. Afflicting aspects such as these are often in evidence at times of personal crisis brought about through a forced issue. Although there were no afflictions between the two at birth, the nature of Pluto must be considered a warning when afflicting a luminary. The fact that the aspect is repeated twice while other serious afflictions are present emphasizes such a warning.

Transiting Uranus is in opposition to natal Mars. This is an aspect of sudden and unexpected accidents, very explosive in nature. It can be far-reaching in its consequences, sometimes acting to break up existing circumstances. The transiting North Node is nearing Dan's natal Ascendant, often a time of important crossroads in life.

Transiting Neptune in the 3rd house is square Dan's natal Moon in the 6th house. This reflects some of the hidden factors involved in the incident. The mysterious 911 call in the middle of the night, and a

dead line before any information was relayed, is reflected in Neptune's position. Such an aspect is associated with weird experiences and deceptive elements. Dan's lack of awareness of the situation brought him into danger.

Other planetary features show the protection provided for Dan at this time. Progressed Jupiter is trine Dan's progressed Ascendant. It is always a help to have the ruler in good aspect to the progressed Ascendant, especially in this case due to the protective influence of Jupiter. Transiting Jupiter, widely conjunct the progressed Ascendant is in trine to Dan's natal 6th house Jupiter, also a protective theme.

Gains in life often coincide with beneficial aspects of transiting Saturn to the progressed Moon. Here, transiting Saturn is in trine to the progressed Moon, suggesting advancements. There are three other aspects that similarly signify an elevation of status. The progressed Moon is in sextile to the progressed Midheaven, progressed Saturn is sextile the progressed Ascendant, and the progressed Sun is sextile to the radical Midheaven. Progressed Venus in sextile to natal Ascendant also suggest gains and honors.

These aspects reflect the heroism Dan was recognized for, as well as his rise in status following the incident. A banquet was held in his honor, and he was presented with the Award for Valor, Citation for Valor, the Blue and Gold Citation, and the Blue and the Purple Heart.

The whole incident lasted just a few minutes. Both Dan and the man who shot him were rushed to the hospital and ended up next to each other in the emergency room. Despite two surgeries and several months of rehab, Dan will never have the physical abilities he did before the incident, but things could have been so much worse. Shortly after returning to work, he retired from the police force, but has continued to work in a security position.

The man who killed his parents and shot Dan was convicted of the crimes, but was found to be mentally unstable. He is serving more than a hundred years of prison time. While his birth data was unavailable, it is interesting that he was the same age as Dan, so his natal Pluto would also have been stimulated by the transit of Mars on that fateful night. There were likely to have been afflictions involving his radical or progressed Moon by this pair of malefics, and there would undoubtedly have been many ties between his chart and Dan's. There are frequently similar aspects in the charts of a victim and the perpetrator of a crime.

Dan's Wife, Sally

As can be imagined, Dan's wife of eighteen years was in shock about the whole incident for quite some time. The wife of a police officer would certainly dread such an incident, and such jolting news in the middle of the night would reinforce long-held fears. Pluto often works exactly this way, and it will be seen to be quite active in her chart at the time. She was born July 30, 1952, 10:59 AM, 85W39/40N33.

It would be expected that for such an event to occur, Sally's chart would show appropriate features. Her chart clearly shows alarming configurations for Dan at the time he was shot.

In Sally's birth chart, Mars rules her 7th house of partners. It is in a close conjunction to the natal Moon, suggesting that her husband will come before the public. In Scorpio, her Mars is descriptive of his role as a police officer, a uniformed worker, and an enforcer of the law. Her natal Mars is square the Sun, Venus, and Pluto, and is opposed by Jupiter, so these aspects show potential danger for him at some point.

Her progressed Ascendant at this time is within a conjunction to her radical Moon, and thus Mars is pulled onto the angle due to its close conjunction with the Moon. Mars on the angle indicates activity surrounding her husband. The natal potential for her husband to come before the public is emphasized by the present angular positions. At the time of the incident, the transiting Sun was opposing the

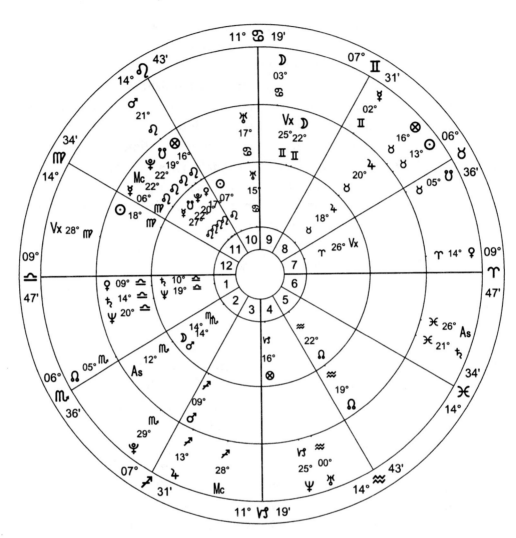

Figure 8c: Dan's Wife Sally

Inner Wheel: Sally's Natal Chart: July 30, 1952; 10:59 AM CDT; 85W39, 40N33

Middle Wheel: Progressed Chart: May 4, 1995; 3:47 AM EST; 85W39, 40N33

Outer Wheel: Transit Chart: May 4, 1995; 3:47 AM EST; 85W39, 40N33

Moon/Mars pair, while also opposing the progressed Ascendant. This puts more attention on her spouse and shows potential conflicts. The transiting Sun is one of the timers of Sally's husband Dan's dangerous encounter.

There is agreement elsewhere in the chart that trouble may come to her husband. Sally's progressed Venus is conjunct the radical Ascendant, bringing loved ones actively into the picture. With her progressed Ascendant now in Scorpio, she has Taurus on her progressed 7th house cusp. Venus rules Sally's progressed 7th house so its aspects signify conditions surrounding her husband. Venus is now in conjunction with natal Saturn, which often coincides with sorrows involving a loved one. Her husband might be facing restrictions. This aspect is repeated in the opposition of transiting Venus to the progressed Saturn. In square to Uranus, transiting Venus shows the sudden nature of her husband's ordeal.

Because the husband is also ruled by the Sun in a woman's chart, her progressed Sun with the transiting Saturn in opposition is showing possible threats to her husband as well. At the same time, transiting Saturn is in square to her progressed Moon, an unfavorable configuration, often showing illness, hard times, or other depressing events. (Refer to Chapter 16; Saturn Chasing the Moon.)

One of the most outstanding features among the progressions is the exact conjunction of progressed Pluto with the progressed Midheaven. Pluto on this angle sometimes coincides with the death of a close family member. These two in their progressions are conjunct the South Node of the natal chart. Such involvement of either of the nodes with either Pluto or Mars often signifies forceful events leading to turning points. Sometimes violence touches the life in some way. Transiting Mars was stimulating this threesome by conjunction in her chart when Sally's husband Dan was shot. Mars acted as a timer.

Car Wreck: Teeth Knocked Out

Jerry's chart shows that he has the planet Uranus in the 3rd house in his nativity. He was born Nov. 20, 1949; 4:04 PM, 97W31/35N28. The 3rd house is the house of short-distance travel, and Uranus is the planet of sudden surprises and unexpected happenings. Under just the right conditions, a car accident might result from this position of Uranus. Since his natal Uranus is semi-square Pluto, Jerry's risk of such an accident is slightly elevated. Pluto is in the 5th house of recreation and two other malefic planets accompany Pluto in the 5th house. He might be particularly at risk while pursuing recreational activities. Mercury rules his 3rd house. It is conjunct his Sun in Scorpio so he may have some intense experiences, but Mercury in close sextile to Jupiter lends him protection.

On the evening of Jerry's sixteenth birthday, on the first occasion he was of legal age to drive, he ended up in a bad car accident. He was having a little too much fun perhaps, partying a little too intensely, and driving a little too fast. He wrapped his vehicle around a tree and knocked his front teeth out.

In checking his progressions and transits for just past midnight when the accident occurred, there are a number of alarming aspects showing accident-prone conditions and personal danger.

His progressed Sun is in square to natal Mars at this point. As the life-giving planet, the Sun is always a vital factor, and an afflicting aspect to Mars is a potentially serious threat if agreement is found among other progressed and transiting aspects.

His progressed Mercury is square progressed Mars, an aspect specifically showing risk for a car accident since Mercury rules driving and Mars rules the mechanical components of a vehicle. His progressed Ascendant, near the end of Taurus now, has come into opposition to his natal Mercury, his natal 3rd house ruler. So we see that Mercury is a prominent feature in

the progressions now and it is under affliction.

With his progressed Ascendant in the third decan of Taurus, Jerry's main ruler is Venus, and his co-ruler is Saturn. It is fortunate that his progressed Venus is conjunct progressed Jupiter and that his natal Jupiter is now trine his progressed Ascendant, since these aspects offer a great deal of protection. However, his co-ruler Saturn in his 5th house receives harsh aspects from transiting planets. Pluto and Uranus are moving over his Saturn, equating to sudden blockages that will have personal consequences. Transiting Mercury is also square his progressed Saturn while transiting Saturn squares his natal Moon and progressed Sun. These aspects involving Saturn are connected to the loss of his front teeth.

The main timer in the event is transiting Mars opposing natal Uranus in the 3rd house. Accident conditions are present. Risky, impulsive actions can have sudden severe consequences. The Sun is a timer also as it swings in on his birthday to conjunct his natal Sun and Mercury and oppose his progressed Ascendant. Notice that his natal Mars is next to rise to the Horary Ascendant, denoting the accident.

Jerry recovered from the accident and got nice caps. He led an adventurous life, with more than one close scrape. Years later, around the age of forty-one, when

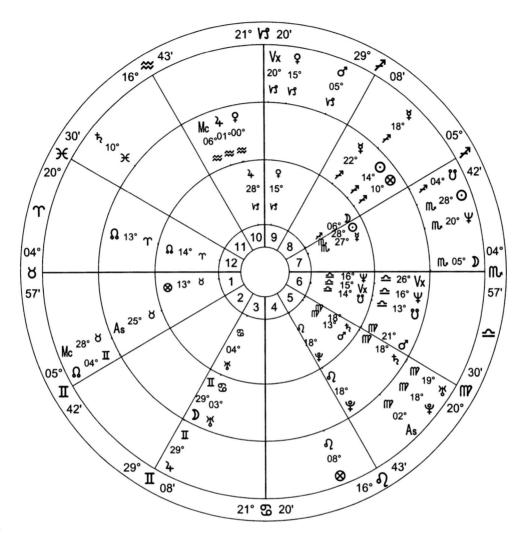

Figure 8d: Jerry's Car Wreck

Inner Wheel: Jerry's Natal Chart: Nov. 20, 1949; 4:04 PM CST; 97W31, 35N28
Middle Wheel: Progressed Chart: Nov. 21, 1965; 12:15 AM CST; 97W31, 35N28
Outer Wheel: Transit Chart: Nov. 21, 1965; 12:15 AM CST; 97W31, 35N28

Jerry's progressed Mars came into orb to square his progressed Uranus, which was progressing backward due to its natal retrograde motion, he experienced a long series of accidents, mishaps, and health crises. As progressed Mars moved through his natal 6th house, by the time it cleared the square to progressed Uranus, it came into square with natal Uranus, extending the period that he was exceptionally accident-prone. His back went out twice, incapacitating him for lengthy intervals so that his ability to work was affected (Mars afflicted in the 6th house). He was involved in a hunting accident, badly injuring his knee to the point he could hardly make it back to his vehicle to go for help. He had numerous problems with vehicles and most of his bad luck occurred when he was engaged in his favorite hobbies, camping and fishing.

So, this is something to keep an eye on. Mars moves only half as fast as the Sun by progression. When it comes into an affliction with an outer planet, the orb of influence could extend several years.

Sexual Abuse

Potential abuse issues will be shown by a combination of several severe afflictions. Venus as the goddess of love and Mars as god of physical sexual expression might be among the afflicted planets in a nativity that warns of such a possibility as sexual child abuse. These two are indicators of disharmony between the sexes when they afflict one another.

In a female's chart, there may be afflictions to both the Sun and Mars, since these planets represent the men surrounding her. With Venus involved, this would be the case if the abuse were coming from someone of the opposite sex. The Sun also rules authorities in general and could even signify abuse by someone of the same sex if they were in a position of authority. For a female to be abused by someone of the same sex, the Moon would also be involved in afflicting aspects. For an abuse situation, there would likely be testimony from the 7th or 8th houses, with afflicted planets in or ruling these houses.

All of the above holds true in Dixie's chart, used here for illustration. She was a victim of sexual child abuse from both a woman and a man, and both were relatives. An aunt, whom she'd temporarily been sent to stay with following her father's loss of his job, was responsible for a period of several months of severe mistreatment and sexual abuse. Dixie was only four at the time. When she finally did return home, the abuse continued, this time by an uncle who was staying with the family. This went on for another three years. Although the earlier experience was the most traumatic due to the extent of the accompanying mistreatment, Dixie says she felt preyed upon for several years.

In looking at her natal chart, the Moon is involved in several afflictions, showing that the mother and the other women may not have the best interests of the individual at heart. They may even be antagonistic and have a detrimental influence upon her. She is likely to feel unloved, and to be hurt often. These things are shown by her Sun and Moon in opposite signs, an opposition between her Moon and Venus, and by the Moon's square to Jupiter, all of which indicate family problems. The close opposition of Moon to Mercury emphasizes this and shows environmental problems as well as harsh handling by women and relatives. The square from the Moon to Mars shows that an aggressive or domineering personality within the home or family is a cause of conflict and upset.

The Moon reflects early childhood experiences directly related to the mother and/or parent. With severe afflictions, the mother may be poor, ill, or uneducated. Dixie's mother was mentally ill. The individual is prone to being a victim of circumstances, which will have quite an emotional impact. These events will begin to unfold at the time the afflicted aspects become exact through the progressions.

A conjunction of Sun and Venus in the 4th house is in square to Mars. The square from Mars to the Sun shows that the father may be ill or suffers straitened circumstances. The square of Mars and Venus indicates inharmonious conditions. Relations within the family are not satisfying, and painful feelings are the result. It is an aspect showing the potential to be used by another for sexual gratification—a key to the abuse. Venus rules the 12th house and is afflicted in Pisces, factors indicating possible secretive or deceptive elements. These aspects combined with the Sun and Moon in opposite signs show much discordance between the parents and many imbalances within the family unit that will tend to push Dixie into a position where she has no assistance.

Onset of Abuse

In the progressed chart for the beginning of the abuse, the natal potential is prominent in the progressed themes.

The square involving the Sun, Mars, and Venus is now exact, showing that conditions are ripe for the natal potential for harsh treatment to manifest. Her progressed Sun is conjunct her Venus, while both square Mars. This combination reflects domestic friction and very discordant conditions. There is trouble coming through her father. The Sun squaring Mars is doubly threatening since a bad aspect from Mars to the Sun is always a danger, and for Dixie, with Scorpio rising, Mars is one of her ruling planets as the traditional ruler of the sign.

Mercury turned retrograde soon after her birth, so instead of moving away from the opposition to her Moon, it has progressed back to form an exact opposition to the radical Moon. This increases the potential for sarcastic and harsh treatment, especially coming through a woman. It shows the timing of emotional experiences that are foreign to the senses, and the inability of the mind to grasp and assimilate such experiences into ready data for future use.

The progressed Moon and progressed Ascendant are conjunct and are approaching a conjunction to Saturn. Saturn conjunct the Ascendant suggests problems in connection with elderly persons and especially troubling times in family affairs. The Moon conjunct Saturn gives similar themes and shows sorrowful times, with unhappy experiences coming through those who are hard and unsympathetic. This aspect marks a critical stage for changes in the environment and general surroundings. The fact that the aspect occurs on the progressed Ascendant shows that these life experiences will leave an indelible mark on the individual.

The square from transiting Uranus to the progressed Moon is unfortunate, often signifying a time of great upset for an individual. The square to the progressed Ascendant from transiting Uranus in the 10th house underscores an unfavorable period, with stress in close relationships, relationships that may take an unconventional turn, and shows the timing of the upset brought about by her father's loss of his job. And, with Neptune transiting Dixie's natal Ascendant, it was a confusing, bewildering time for her.

Another important transit comes from Pluto, which is opposite her natal Sun. Such an aspect indicates a powerful force against the individual. Afflictions from transiting Pluto to the Sun are always potentially serious and especially in this case, since Pluto rules Dixie's Ascendant. The aspect is doubly threatening. Pluto is transiting the 10th house, a sign that any harm that might befall her (Sun) might come from someone whom she had been taught to respect. Pluto will soon oppose natal Venus and square natal Mars, again stimulating a discordant natal aspect. This particular link between Mars and Pluto sometimes shows danger or an actual attack to the individual. The opposition of Pluto to Venus is also one of forceful situations in relationships. The long duration of Pluto's afflicting aspects reflect the long spell that Dixie was abused. Neptune also remained in conjunction to her natal or progressed Ascendant for years. These aspects are behind her feeling of being preyed upon for several years.

The actual timing of the first incident in a series of abuse shows the transiting

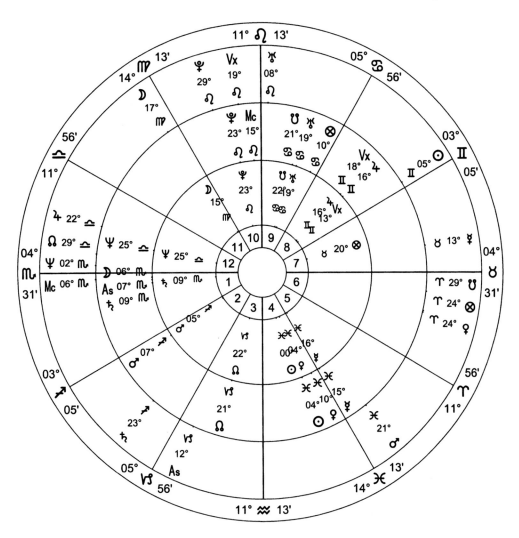

Figure 8e: Onset of Sexual Abuse

Inner Wheel: Dixie's Natal Chart: Feb. 18, 1954; 10:43 PM CST; 85W40; 40N33
Middle Wheel: Progressed Chart: May 26, 1958; 10:43 PM CST; 85W40; 40N33
Outer Wheel: Transit Chart: May 26, 1958; 10:43 PM CDT; 85W40; 40N33

Sun in the 8th house getting into the swing of afflictions as it squares natal Venus and opposes natal Mars, stimulating potential abuse aspects that appeared in the birth chart. The latter aspect is a repeating theme of the Pluto opposition Sun, indicating a potential physical attack. There are multiple transiting aspects with a similar theme, which, combined with the progressions in force at the time, could have foretold danger to the child.

The transiting Moon is now conjunct natal Moon, square Jupiter, and opposite Mercury, bringing several natal aspects to the fore that describe environmental and familial problems. Transiting Mars opposes the Moon, emphasizing potential conflicts. Transiting Venus opposes natal Neptune in the 12th house, and sums up the actual experience of secretive and perverted affections.

Dixie's Moon opposing Mercury signifies worry over her younger brother and sisters who were also recipients of abuse. They have also experienced problems as a result of the treatment they received as children. Her brother suffers from panic attacks, and has tried numerous forms of counseling. Her twin sisters have also been in therapy throughout most of their lives, and both suffer from mild schizophrenia.

Dixie may be the luckiest of them all. With Saturn on the Ascendant, she has learned to make positive use of her previous experiences. With Saturn trine Venus, she has a practical understanding of the needs of those less fortunate. Her great compassion for others is reflected in her Pisces traits. In discussing the abusive treatment she received as a child, Dixie still attributes her nightly panic attacks to the events during that time period. (See chapter 7.)

A Victim of Rape

The following chart belongs to a young woman named Cathy, born June 29, 1979; 12:55 AM, 96W47/31N36. When we met, she belonged to a group called American Community Services and was attempting to put her life back together following some unfortunate times with a rape, drugs, and related problems.

In checking for a potential rape situation, Cathy's chart shows that she has Pluto in the 7th house of other people. This shows that her life might be drastically altered through her associations with partners. Partners are often attracted who are strong-willed or domineering. There is a tendency to either dominate or to be dominated by others who are of a stronger will. Pluto is in a wide square to Cathy's Sun and in a close semi-square to her Moon, so that trouble may come through men who try to exercise control over her, and there may be strong disagreements, with intense or violent outbursts of temper.

Neptune rules her 1st house. Neptune is the most elevated planet in the chart and Venus opposes it. This aspect suggests that at certain times, deception, confusion, and intrigue are involved in the relationships that Cathy becomes involved in. There is danger of sexual seduction. Self-indulgent tendencies may bring about self-undoing through an involvement in drugs. With her ruling Neptune in the 9th house opposing Venus in the 3rd house, there are implications of harmful experiences during travels.

All of these factors are stimulated and part of the picture at the time of Cathy's attack. Natal Mars, as co-ruler of her natal 1st house, is square natal Moon, and this aspect is another one of potential danger. This affliction of the Moon and Mars will also be found to be heavily stimulated at the time of her attack.

In Cathy's chart, Saturn rules her 11th house of friends and group associations, and Saturn is also making a square to Mars, co-ruler of her natal 1st house. Saturn linked to Mars in such a way suggests that friendships can be an area where elements of repressed anger might one day erupt.

Attack by Rapist

On the morning of the attack, Cathy was living in a city far from her native home and had just made some new friends. She and one of these friends were riding around "slangin"—selling illegal substances.

Cathy and her friend James were doing some recreational drugs themselves at the time. Cathy was already taking Prozac, prescribed for her to combat depression. Saturn transiting her 1st house, in square to the natal Sun, shows her current tendency toward depression. Transiting Neptune opposes her progressed Sun, an important aspect with respect to her current involvement with drugs. It is behind her being too trusting and unaware. Dealings connected with illegal substances are sure routes to trouble.

Cathy and James were also smoking marijuana and doing crystal methamphetamine. While marijuana is not associated with violence when used alone, crystal meth is often associated with violence. A strong stimulant, it causes users to stay up for days at a time, without eating, thus depleting the body of nutrition and rest. Users become aggravated with slight provocation, and are highly explosive.

The evening before, a group of friends were with Cathy and James, and Cathy had gotten into a rift with James' girlfriend.

Now, during their cruise around town, the topic came up in conversation. The dialog between them soon turned into an argument. As the discussion became more heated, James became more antagonistic. He pulled over, saying that he needed a new fix and that he was going to get some drugs from the trunk. He went to the trunk and opened it. Cathy was sitting on the passenger side of the car, and before she knew what was happening, James had come around to her window and struck her violently in the head with a tire iron. Blood came gushing from her skull, and she was nearly knocked unconscious. Using her stunned response to gain the upper hand, James threw open her door and shoved her down on the seat. He was a huge guy, and Cathy was unable to get away or fight him off. With her head pinned under the steering wheel, he had his way and then dumped her at the side of the road and left her there. Stunned and bleeding, Cathy walked until she was picked up and taken to the hospital. James was jailed to await legal proceedings.

Cathy's progressed chart at this time shows a square between her progressed Sun and Moon. This aspect is associated with quarrels or differences with partners. For a female, there are often difficulties with men. At the same time, transiting Mars is conjunct her progressed Sun while square her progressed Moon, an aspect from her birth chart. These are close aspects and a timing element to the conflict.

Transiting Neptune in Cathy's 11th house opposes her progressed Sun while it squares her progressed Moon and progressed Ascendant. Neptune opposing the progressed Sun indicates that Cathy was not totally aware and was susceptible to being lead astray, both by her drug involvement and by forming of friendship with someone who turned out to be an enemy. Neptune's afflicting aspect to her progressed Moon is also a deceptive influence when problems may come from being too trusting with new acquaintances.

Both of Cathy's luminaries are afflicted at once, often a time of danger for an individual. There were several afflictions from the transiting planets to her Sun and Moon and to her rulers. Transiting Saturn was in square to her radical Sun while Jupiter opposed her Sun. Transiting Pluto was opposing her natal Mars while squaring her natal Moon, aspects that are quite descriptive of the violent events that took place. Her progressed Moon is in Aries, near her progressed Ascendant in Aries, which is closely squared by transiting Mars and Neptune, reflecting the bloody blows from the sneak attack.

Transiting Uranus is opposing her radical Mercury, ruler of her natal 7th house. It shows the sudden turn against her of an

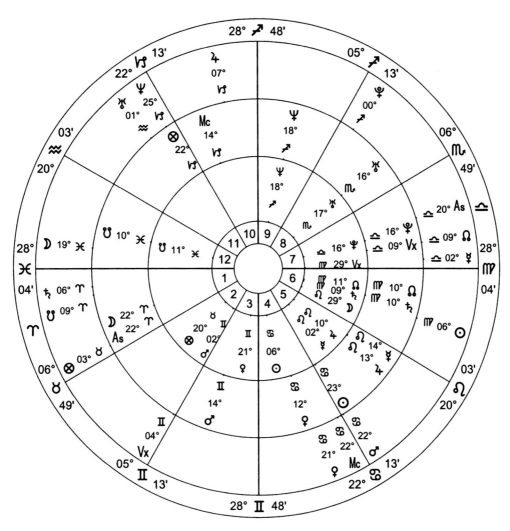

Figure 8f: Attack by Rapist

Inner Wheel: Cathy's Natal chart: June 29, 1979; 12:55 AM CDT; 96W47, 31N36

Middle Wheel: Progressed Chart: Aug. 29, 1996; 10:30 AM CDT; 96W47, 31N36

Outer Wheel: Transit Chart: Aug. 29, 1996; 10:30 AM CDT; 96W47, 31N36

enemy and suggests that something unexpected would take place in the course of travel. Uranus rules her 12th house, which is associated with drugs and with deception or illusions.

The natal opposition between Venus and Neptune is the basis upon which much of the events were able to manifest. The deceptive quality of this relationship is seen in the aspect as well as the drug involvement. Transiting Venus and Neptune are in opposition with one another, repeating the natal link. Even the transiting Moon forms a square to natal Neptune and Venus, emphasizing that natal aspect and showing the very personal violation connected with a deception.

Cathy feels she learned some valuable lessons, and she is determined to turn her life around.

chapter nine

Death & Bereavement

Although death is almost never predicted for someone else, there are numerous cases on record of astrologers accurately predicting their own deaths. Mark Twain predicted his death by the return of Haley's Comet, which he was also born under. Evangeline Adams is said to have predicted her death in 1932 based largely on a transit of the lunar nodes. Grant Lewi, famed astrology author, took out a large life insurance policy a few months before his death from a sudden cerebral hemorrhage at age forty-nine.

A natural death after a full lifespan should be anticipated unless there are significant indications to the contrary. The 8th house combined with the 6th house should be studied for information on death brought about by a natural decline of bodily functions over a lifetime. Physical health indicators are discussed in chapter 6.

The Ascendant gives information about longevity. Generally, a fire sign rising is strongest, followed by air, then earth, and then water. Cardinal signs and fixed signs have more staying power than mutable.

The luminaries also provide vital information. The Sun reflects much about vitality and longevity. When there are many beneficial aspects to the Sun, they will go a long way to offset harsh aspects among the other planets. When the Sun, Moon, Ascendant, and its ruler are all strong by sign and not afflicted, long life is probable. Length of life is judged based primarily on these four. When there's a fortunate aspect from Mars or from a benefic to any of the four, longevity is increased. The opposite is the likelihood when all four are badly afflicted and weak by sign. Harsh aspects to the Sun are more serious than to the Moon, and squares to either luminary by Mars or Saturn may shorten length of life. The Moon is significant in determining functional disorders while the Sun tells of hereditary or constitutional disorders.

Indications of a violent, accidental, or an unnatural death are found when the luminaries are both afflicted by malefic planets, and neither has the assistance of Venus or Jupiter. If either of the luminaries are afflicted by more than one malefic and there is no assistance from either benefic, or if each are afflicted by one or more malefic without assistance, then an unnatural death may be signified. A conjunction by Mars to either luminary may be considered an affliction if Mars is the elevated planet. Generally, afflictions of Mars are more threatening if it is the elevated planet. Malefic planets opposing one another from the angles is an aspect of warning, especially if from cardinal signs or from signs said to rule violence. The violent signs are traditionally said to be Aries, Scorpio, and Capricorn. The horoscope of the infant, Rita, illustrated in chapter 6, contained afflictions indicating an unnatural death.

While the 8th house gives clues to the cause of death, the 4th house gives clues to the circumstances in the final years of life. With afflictions to the 8th house, death may come by illness or accident. A planet that exactly aspects the cusp of the 8th house may be a factor involved in the individual's death. Difficult conditions in old age may be indicated by afflictions to the 4th house. It shows the end of life conditions.

The 8th house also tells of death and rebirth issues. Features of this house may signify the loss, through death, of someone the individual is close to.

Bereavement is found by a combination of multiple factors in the progressions and transits. The Sun may be afflicted by a malefic in the progressed chart and often by more than one. A malefic planet may afflict Venus when there is the loss of a loved one. Sometimes Jupiter afflicts Venus, denoting deep grief and sorrow. The signs Taurus and Scorpio may be prominent, with afflictions in these signs. The cusps of the 2nd or 8th houses, or planets in these houses, may be involved in afflictions. Pluto, as the planet of transformation, elimination, and death, may become particularly active at the time of bereavement.

When multiple aspects signify bereavement, it is often possible to determine the direction from where a loss will come. The death of a parent may be signified by afflictions involving Saturn or the Moon, with Saturn most significant of the father and the Moon most significant of the mother. Confirmation may come from afflictions involving the planetary ruler of the 4th house or the ruler of the 10th house.

The death of a husband will usually be shown by afflictions involving the Sun and Mars. The death of a wife may be shown by afflictions to Venus and the Moon. In addition, in the event of the loss of a spouse, the signs Aries and Libra may hold afflicted planets, or the 7th house ruler becomes involved in afflicting aspects. An afflicted Venus may show the loss of a sweetheart.

The death of a son will usually be signified by afflictions involving Mercury and Mars, while the death of a daughter would be shown by afflictions to Venus. In these cases, the 5th house, planets in the 5th house, or ruling it may also become involved in afflictions.

The death of a sibling may be indicated by afflictions involving Mercury, or by afflicted planets in or ruling the 3rd house. The death of a beloved pet may be preceded by afflictions to Mercury or involving the 6th house or its ruler.

In the event of bereavement from any direction, there will be multiple indications of a similar nature among the progressed aspects.

Sudden Illness & Death of Husband

For Donna, 2004 was a roller-coaster year, the worst year of her life. It was an emotional time, when many unexpected and troubling events occurred, ending with the sudden death of her husband.

Married for twenty-two years, Donna's husband Larry was seventeen years older than she. This was a second marriage for them both, and it had been a happy one. She felt lucky to have him. He was a good person, didn't have any bad habits, and was definitely a model spouse compared to her first husband of five years, who was an unemployed alcoholic. Donna and Larry had no children, only a nine-year-old dog, Angel, that Donna adored. Angel was the love of her life. Donna was born May 23, 1953; 1:14 PM, 72W56/41N18.

Larry, born July 19, 1935, 11:30 PM, 74W05/40N44, had recently retired from his job so that Donna now maintained the health benefits for the household. She worked a full-time job, a recently acquired position in a very structured company. But the position paid well and had excellent benefits.

As far as they knew at the beginning of 2004, Larry's health was fine, other than a chronic back problem. Life was more or less a routine. But, that was about to change. Their lives were about to take a drastic turn.

Her progressions and transits, shown here for the spring of 2004, reveal a number of troubling configurations. First of all, it is loaded with eclipses, including a recent one on her Midheaven, and another opposing her Sun, indicating turning points, with changes and transitions for the masculine benefactors in her life. Their fortunes could change in a way that impacted her life. These benefactors included her boss and her husband.

Donna's 2004 Progressions

Progressed Mars is conjunct progressed Sun and this pair is in square to her progressed Ascendant. Progressed Sun also squares her Neptune and Saturn on one side of the chart, while in square to her Venus on the other side. This creates a number of serious afflictions. Her Sun in square to Neptune and Saturn represents vulnerability and restrictions for her husband (Sun). Sun square Saturn suggests depressing developments. Sun square Venus is inharmonious, possibly sad. Mars repeats all of these squares through its association with the Sun and Mars is elevated over the Sun, increasing the danger for her husband. The Mars aspects multiply the potentially severe consequences surrounding Donna's husband Larry. Multiple aspects show danger, including progressed Uranus in conjunction with progressed Mars, which rules her progressed 7th house. The danger will come unexpectedly and sudden.

Her natal 7th house ruler, Neptune, is in conjunction with the progressed Ascendant, also indicating that her partner's interests are now in focus. The picture is troubling due to the afflicting aspects to Neptune, especially the opposition to Venus. That is a double threat since Venus naturally represents partners. Emphasizing this theme, an eclipse soon falls on Neptune.

The main theme that stands out is *potential health problems or accidents* for her husband and of extra responsibilities surrounding an elderly person. This comes chiefly through the afflictions involving the Sun and Mars, ruling her husband, through Neptune, ruling her natal 7th house of partners, and through Saturn. Neptune conjunct Saturn in her natal chart suggests that Donna would marry someone older. Saturn in conjunction with Neptune and their opposition to Venus also indicate testing times in relationships that would require her compassion and devotion. Saturn opposing Venus alludes to sorrow over a sweetheart.

Sun square Neptune can also show a time of uncertainty about life direction as one floats in limbo. A person may feel temporarily discouraged or inadequate.

Not only are things threatening for her husband, but the aspects also suggest potential health issues for her. Her progressed

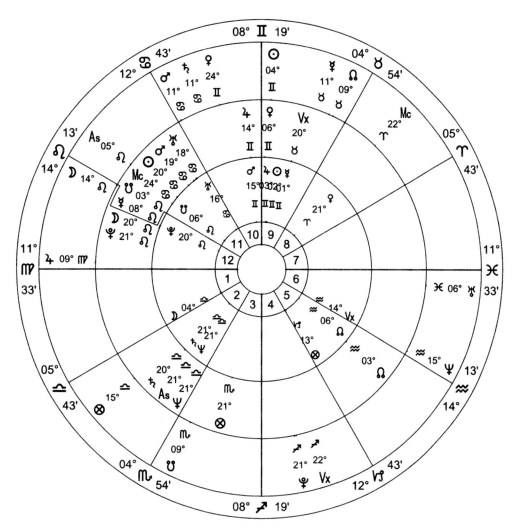

Figure 9a: Donna's 2004 Progressions

Inner Wheel: Donna's Natal Chart: May 23, 1953; 1:14 PM EDT; 72W56, 41N18
Middle Wheel: Progressed Chart: May 25, 2004; 10:00 AM EDT; 72W56, 41N18
Outer Wheel: Transit Chart: May 25, 2004; 10:00 AM EDT; 72W56, 41N18

Ascendant and her Sun are both afflicted, as well as Venus, her ruling planet.

In fact, this was the first manifestation of the aspects of 2004. In early spring Donna had a serious case of hives that put her under heavy doses of medications. Her body was covered with welts, including her lips and neck. The doctor believed it was stress related, and her case of hives occurred just as her progressing Moon moved into conjunction with her natal Pluto as transiting Mars squared them both. Fortunately, Mars passed quickly, and she was okay within a few days. Had it not been for the combined influence of progressed Saturn and Neptune in square to her progressed Sun at the same time, the afflicting transit from Mars to her Moon/Pluto pairing might have passed with much less trouble. As it was, both of her luminaries were under attack at the same time, elevating her potential to experience a health crisis. Mars to Moon afflictions can be most abrasive, apt to coincide with illness or accident. Of course Mars rules the head and is associated with rashes and fevers.

Soon after, Donna learned that her boss was taking an early retirement. This came as a major shock to her. She'd had no idea, even though the two were pretty close. He had to keep these developments quiet due to the high level exposure of his job. Very concerned for her, he was doing what he could to place Donna in another position. A short time later, she started her new position, with a female boss for the first time ever. These events were reflected in the eclipse on the Midheaven, showing that occupational changes were coming, while an afflicted Saturn suggested trouble for superiors.

In the meantime, another set of developments had begun to unfold. In April of 2004, Donna's husband was diagnosed thru an MRI with spinal stenosis, which is a narrowing of the space around the spinal cord. It affects balance, leg muscles, and causes general weakness. They met with a neurosurgeon to schedule surgery right away. Donna, who wanted to share her story with astrologers in the hopes that it would contribute to their studies, explains what happened next:

"On Tuesday, May 25th, 2004, my husband Larry was in the hospital for the scheduled spinal surgery. That surgery went well, and he was supposed to be released on Thursday, May 27th. However, his neurosurgeon wanted him to stay a couple days in rehabilitation to gain some strength. The night he was moved to rehab, I got a call around midnight saying my husband had a very bad attack (what they thought was a massive heart attack) and that he was moved to the intensive care unit. In fact, he did not have a heart attack but did have an aneurysm that burst in his abdomen, which caused very low blood pressure (60/30) and a near-death experience. He was stabilized until a general surgeon was brought in who decided to operate on him. It was then discovered that he had a major "bleed out" (internal bleeding throughout the stomach from the burst aneurysm, which caused them to remove half his pancreas, half his colon, and resulted in a major loss of blood). After five hours of major surgery and ten vials of new blood, this surgeon saved my husband's life. If he had come home on the original release date, he would have died at home. The percentage for surviving an aneurysm is 5 percent. After two weeks in ICU, he lost thirty pounds, went to rehab, and finally came home on June 30th."

The major progressed configurations that stand out in Donna's chart for this event includes the progressed Sun in square to Saturn, Neptune, Venus, and the progressed Ascendant. These show *dangers for her spouse*. The fact that Mars, as the other planetary ruler of a woman's husband, is also involved in multiple afflictions emphasizes the severity of the situation. Mars is the ruler of her progressed 7th house, *so conditions are very threatening*. The situation appears critical from many directions and progressed Uranus in conjunction with progressed Mars suggested *unexpected developments*.

Crucial transits that underscored the progressions included a close square from Uranus to progressed Venus near the natal Midheaven, indicating unexpected circumstances involving a loved one. The Sun, transiting across her progressed Venus and within orb of the Midheaven was the triggering planet. Combined with Uranus, the emergency situation was critical. Mars was approaching a conjunction to her progressed Uranus and progressed Mars pair. Because Mars carries such powerful initiating energies, it will often help to trigger developments even from a wide transiting orb if other conditions are prime.

Transiting Pluto is sextile her Neptune, trine progressed Moon and natal Venus. These reflect Donna's summary about the surgeon's (Pluto) miraculous works that saved Larry during what the doctors described as "one of the most catastrophic medical emergencies" they have ever had. Donna explains:

"It was unequivocally the *worst* time of my life. I have never felt so shocked, traumatized, depressed, not knowing how things would work. Seeing Larry every day for two full weeks in the ICU, I was torn between the hospital, a new job, and duties at home. I had a lot of support from my family and friends, which helped greatly. However, inside I felt so sick every day and I did not want to face life."

While she felt sick inside, she showed strength on the outside for Larry's sake. He had to relearn all his basic living skills, undergoing physical, occupational, and speech therapy. After three months of therapy and nurses in the home, Larry began doing better.

Another pair of eclipses falling in Donna's 2nd and 8th houses showed that financial matters would undergo transformations, especially those relating to insurance. Eclipses show where changes evolve and this manifested in the huge medical bills that began pouring in.

Larry's Final Surgery

Unfortunately, Larry still needed another surgical procedure (colon reversal) following the original surgery. This procedure was scheduled to take place shortly following the solar eclipse on Donna's Neptune, one of the original indicators of a transitional period for her partner.

The follow-up surgery, performed the morning of November 17th, was catastrophic. Larry had another major bleed out and was put in the critical care unit on life support. By dawn the next morning the surgeons had to go in again to try to stop the bleeding. Afterward Larry was put back on life support, with another operation planned for the next day, but Larry passed away that next morning. There

were too many complications, and the surgeons could not save him. Donna felt he was finally at peace, as he could never have recovered to live a normal life. She believes there was a problem with his blood flow that was long undetected.

Larry's time of birth is approximate, based on his mother's memory, so we are unable to do a complete delineation. However, his natal chart shows that his natal ruler Mars is square his 8th house ruler Pluto, while his Sun, ruling his 6th house, is also square Mars. Thus, there are indications *for an unnatural death, especially with these afflictions in cardinal signs. The square of Sun and Mars is behind his bleed outs and subsequent death, while the afflicted Sun predisposed his back problems.* His 6th house Venus and Neptune are opposed by Saturn, also indicative of consequential heath issues.

Larry's progressed chart at the time of his first surgery and near-death experience shows stress to his chart ruler, Mars, which has progressed into the 8th house of death and rebirth. Mars is square progressed Venus in the 6th house, showing dis-ease, while transiting Uranus afflicts both planets, indicating a disruptive and surprising set of developments. On the evening of Larry's first aneurysm, the transiting Sun in Gemini (shown in Donna's outer wheel) opposed his progressed Mars, stressing the natal affliction between them. This was

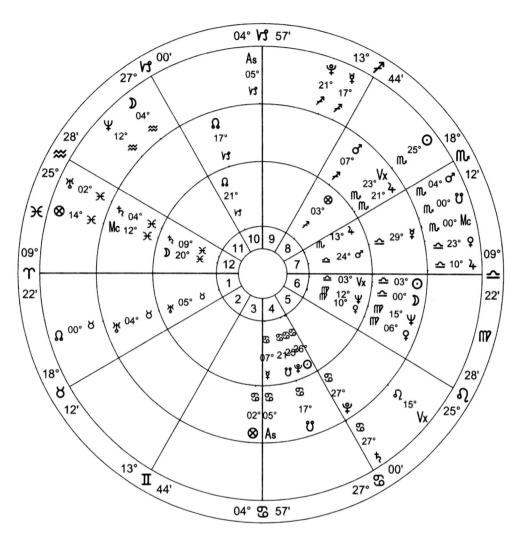

Figure 9b: Larry's Final Surgery

Inner Wheel: Larry's Natal Chart: July 19, 1935; 11:30 PM EDT; 74W05, 40N44

Middle Wheel: Progressed Chart: Nov. 17, 2004; 10:00 AM EDT; 74W05, 40N44

Outer Wheel: Transit Chart: Nov. 17, 2004; 10:00 AM EST; 74W05, 40N44

the event timer of his aneurysm. Transiting Pluto, moving back and forth due to retrograde motion, was square Larry's natal Moon. With his progressed Ascendant in Cancer, the Moon is his ruler. His progressed Sun is also in the 6th house in square to his progressed Ascendant.

There were many of the same progressed aspects in force for the time of his surgical repair procedure and subsequent death a few months later. Also at that time, transiting Saturn moved over his natal Sun and progressed Pluto and squared natal Mars, further stimulating that natal affliction involving his natal ruler, Mars, and the rulers of his 6th and 8th houses. With the natal Sun square Mars aspect so prominent and afflicted, it was a dangerous time for an operation. Mars rules incisions, the surgeon, and the surgery. There was danger of hemorrhage. An eclipse had fallen on his 1st house Uranus less than a month earlier and at the time of his death, transiting Mars was opposing his eclipsed Uranus. This was a major timer of the event of his death.

Now, in regard to surgical procedures, we can see some unfavorable features in the positions of the planets that contributed to the tragic outcome of both surgeries. The outer wheel of Donna's chart shows the planetary positions at the time of his first surgery, and Larry's outer wheel shows the position of the planets for the second surgery.

For Larry's first surgery, the transiting Moon was in Leo, the sign that rules the back and spine. One of the most important rules to follow when selecting the best time for an elective surgery is to avoid having the Moon in the sign ruling the body part to be operated on. (See chapter 6.)

For his second surgery, the transiting Moon was precisely square transiting Mars, something to avoid for an elective surgery. The Moon should be as free from impediment as possible—this is a particularly dangerous aspect. In this case, the surgery Moon and Mars also afflicted Larry's 1st house Uranus, making matters worse. With his progressed afflictions so prime for something to go wrong, and with his progressed aspects emphasizing a natal affliction, the complicating transits played right into the picture.

Soon after his death, a New Moon formed in Larry's 6th house, as the progressing Moon reached the place of his progressed Sun. The New Moon symbolizes new beginnings. As Donna said, he no longer had to suffer.

Loss of a Beloved Pet

For Donna, with so many stressful aspects among her progressed planets, the next couple of years were difficult, not only dealing with the loss of her husband, but in other areas of her life. Progressed Mars,

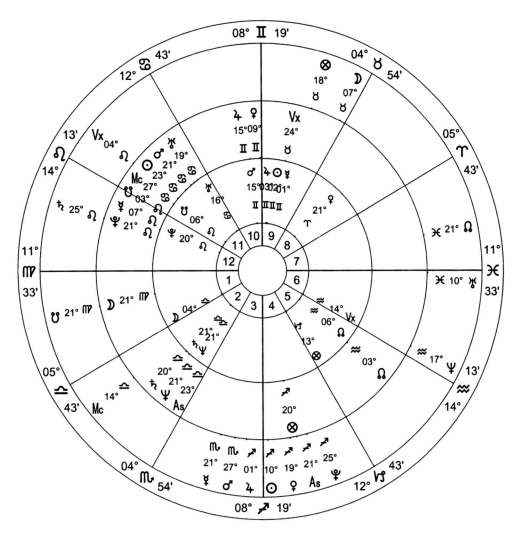

Figure 9c: Loss of Angel

Inner Wheel: Donna's Natal Chart: May 23, 1953; 1:14 PM EDT; 72W56, 41N18
Middle Wheel: Progressed Chart: Dec. 2, 2006; 8:00 AM EST; 72W56, 41N18
Outer Wheel: Transit Chart: Dec. 2, 2006; 8:00 AM EST; 72W56, 41N18

in troubling aspect to her personal planets for a few years, reflected the spell of challenging times.

In the spring of 2005 she got a grim result from her routine colonoscopy and had to undergo colon surgery. A gigantic polyp needed to be surgically removed by a specialist. Fortunately the biopsy results came back negative for cancer cells and the surgery went smoothly. Health issues were shown in her chart by the many afflictions to her progressed Sun, to her progressed Ascendant in Libra, and to her ruler Venus.

With her progressed Ascendant afflicted, reflecting the life experiences she was meeting up with, the next year and a half brought relationship upsets, storm damage to her home, deaths of some friends and family members, and disastrous results when she eventually started dating. Her aspects, with her Sun, Mars, and Venus afflicted, were not conducive for meeting a man she was compatible with. The one area that went well was her professional life. Progressed Venus on her Midheaven was a big help in that respect.

Then, in 2006, her beloved dog Angel began to develop various problems. Angel was twelve, eighty-four years old in dog years. There were multiple trips to the veterinarian that year. Angel was diagnosed with diabetes in August, with related kidney problems. By early December, Angel was doing worse and worse. Another trip

to the vet and a round of tests showed that she had fluid on her lungs and a heart murmur, in addition to failing kidneys. The evening following the results of the latest tests, Angel had a really bad night, and early the next morning Donna had to make the decision to have her put to sleep, as she couldn't bear to think of her in pain. It was a very sad day—a sad month. Angel was the most important thing left from Donna's life with Larry, who gave Angel to Donna as a Christmas gift eleven years earlier. Donna couldn't stop crying.

Her progressed chart for this event shows that progressed Neptune is exactly opposite natal Venus. With Pisces now on the cusp of her progressed 6th house, Neptune rules that house, the house that rules pets. The opposition of Venus to Neptune, with Venus as Donna's ruler, reflects the sad loss of her pet. Progressed Mars is square progressed Neptune, another close aspect that shows the ill health and subsequent death of her dog. As Donna put it, Angel was the love of her life. Other aspects emphasize this loss and her grief. The ruler of her natal 6th house is Uranus, and it is opposing her natal Ascendant, suggesting a separation. Transiting Neptune is moving through her natal 6th house, opposing her Pluto, showing Angel's vulnerability. As the natural ruler of pets, her natal Mercury is opposed by transiting Jupiter and by Mars. Her progressed Mercury is squared by transiting Moon, showing her worry and stress over Angel, while transiting Mercury was precisely square her progressed Pluto when Angel had to be put down.

A major indicator of this sad and difficult time, and the sad days ahead, is seen with the transiting South Node moving over Donna's progressed Moon. This is usually a melancholy time. Often there are personal, domestic, or family changes that bring an upset. Combined with her other aspects, it was an occasion of much grief and sorrow over her loss.

In due time, Donna got another little dog, which did give her something positive to turn her attention to, and the new puppy has helped ease her pain. Donna's aspects are slowly improving and she is positive and hopeful for the future, especially hopeful for eventually meeting someone nice to share the rest of her life with. She feels there are future good things to make up for the bad ones in the past.

PART TWO

The Return
Charts

chapter ten

Basics of the Return Charts

While the progressed chart will always have priority over any other predictive chart, the Solar and Lunar Returns are helpful in pinpointing the timing of major events that are in evidence in the progressions. Reading the return is similar to reading any other chart, but with more specific rules. In a natal chart, any planet on an angle is doing something. In a return chart, this is more emphasized. The angular planet represents particular activity for the time period of the return, whether it is a planet in the actual return chart or a planet from the natal chart that aligns with an angle of the return. In a Solar Return, events reflected by the planets on an angle will occur during the year; in a Lunar Return, during the four weeks following the return.

A Solar Return or Solar Revolution is calculated exactly as it sounds. Each year when the Sun returns to the exact degree it held in the nativity, a critical point in the life cycle is set in progress. Because of this, the configurations formed by the transiting planets at this time are more significant than ordinary transits. A chart calculated for this precise moment is predictive of the year to come.

The return of the Sun must be calculated to the degree, minute, and second of the natal Sun. The natal chart must be calculated for the exact time of birth in order for the subsequent returns to be accurate. This is not to say that a chart calculated for the day of the return will not offer valuable information for the year. It will, but to determine accurate timing of the events signified requires precise data.

Return charts are calculated for the city of residence of the individual at the time of the return. The Tropical zodiac and Placidus house system provide the best results and are used here.

The Question of Precession

With return charts, the question of whether or not to use the precessed method of calculation will arise. This has been a subject of much controversy among astrologers. While some insist on using the non-precessed method of calculation, just as many are adamant about using the precessed method. Most computer programs offer both methods of calculation. Ronald C. Davison's *Cycles of Destiny* outlines the calculations for doing them manually.[1]

A non-precessed chart, my longtime favorite, is one in which the return chart is calculated for the return of a planet or luminary to the exact degree and minute it held at birth. Precession of a chart takes into consideration the precession of the equinox since the time of birth, thus the luminaries advance very slightly as one's age progresses. The difference between the Sun's return to the first and the last position may be several hours, altering the resulting chart. The older one becomes, the greater the variance.

Trying to discover which method was best, I spent several years comparing the results of the two methods and have concluded that both charts are informative. It may be largely a matter of choice and familiarity. The major planetary aspects remain the same, which accounts for much of the information obtained from the return chart. Evidence suggests that the precessed chart patterns show events as they are experienced on a psychological level, while the non-precessed chart patterns present the way they are experienced on the material and earthly plane. In comparing the two methods objectively, it is sometimes the non-precessed chart that can be easily tuned in to, and other times it is the precessed. The patterns of the alternate chart reflect accurately upon the events taking place, but from an alternate perspective.

An optimum solution is to calculate and use both return charts, which are actually in agreement. It is as if one has the advantage of having two eyewitness accounts or two expert opinions on an issue. Sometimes, what may not be so accentuated in one account is highlighted in the other. Pay particular attention to planets (return or natal) that fall on the angles. Example delineation of charts in this section uses each method side by side, so you can judge for yourself.

Converse Returns

While the usual return goes forward in time to a birthday following birth, a method called converse goes backward in time the same number of years, and this chart also produces excellent results. There is absolutely no depreciation in the significance of these configurations due to the reverse calculations. Even though the angles and planets are in totally different positions, the overall theme of the chart will be similar to those in the chart resulting from the direct method calculations.

Reading the Returns

These methods give a total of four charts possible for one Solar Return. Any one of the four can be used alone, or they can be used in any combination for more detail. I utilized them as two sets of two, extracting the most significant themes from each and then blending these to produce a composite reading. The precessed direct motion and precessed converse charts comprised one set, and the non-precessed charts made up the second set. Each chart is then read in much the same way as a natal chart, keeping in mind that the effects are temporary. The return chart may be used in a bi-wheel with the natal planets in the outer wheel. Otherwise, note the natal planets on the single wheel return, near the inner circle.

The birth chart holds all the keys to what the individual attracts over a lifelong period. The ties made between the new Solar Return chart to the nativity is key in what will be brought to the surface in the year to follow. The house holding the Sun is particularly importance.

As the angles and cusps of the return chart line up with a specific natal planet, that planet is given a place to come to life, so to speak. First one and then another of the natal planets will also come into alignment with planets in the return chart, giving the opportunity for these two planets to mix elements. The result will manifest in the area represented by their house position in the return.

The same rules are applied to the Lunar Return chart, which is calculated for the exact time that the Moon returns to its natal position. This occurs approximately every twenty-eight days, and the resulting chart can be used to effectively forecast the four weeks following.

There is not much difference in reading the Solar or Lunar return charts, except the length of time covered. Obviously, configurations within the Solar Return chart will signify more intense and far-reaching potential than those in a Lunar Return, due to the length of time it is in force. With the Lunar Return chart, extensive detail can be extracted by referring to the previous Solar Return chart from which it extends. There are thirteen Lunar Returns within the Solar Return period.

If a predominance of planets happens to fall in the angular houses, important events should be forthcoming. If there are no planets near the angles, it will usually be a more or less routine period.

Another point to take into consideration in the preliminary stages of interpreting the return is hemispheric emphasis. If most of the planets are above the horizon, outward motivations are pursued. If below the horizon, it is a more subjective time when personal issues are handled. If most of the planets fall on the eastern side of the chart (left), one has personal control over events and will set these in motion. If on the western side (right), other people are in a position to influence the decisions of the individual.

If the planets are scattered throughout the chart and there is really no pronounced emphasis, there is a less obvious effect. Things may be fairly evenly balanced, or it may just be a time when it is hard to stick to a plan as the individual vacillates between several courses of action. The aspects will reveal which course.

Stelliums will bring a heavy accent to the return house and the sign they occupy. Any return house holding four or more planets will be an especially active area for the return period. The house of the natal chart that holds this group of planets will likewise be stimulated, and a connection of issues involving this natal house and the corresponding return house will result.

The Return Chart Ascendant

Since the time of the return varies, any sign can be found rising on the cusp of the 1st house. This shows how the individual will project him or herself to others. The sign ascending shows the characteristics of the individual's demeanor and personality, as well as the types of experiences attracted during the return period. This sign will lead the chart with its general characteristics.

As an initial step, the quality of the rising sign should be considered. The cardinal signs represent initiative, change, and activity. There are new projects, new beginnings, and action. Commanding would be an apt term to describe the cardinals. Libra commands that attention be given to relationships and cooperative ventures, with a need for diplomacy and balance. Aries commands attention to the self, and the individual may strike out on his or her own. Cancer commands that the home is a sensitive area deserving of attention, and family relationships have priority. Capricorn demands that responsibilities be met and even increased. If Capricorn is rising, the individual accepts or administers discipline and takes care of business.

Fixed signs usually indicate that conditions and events will help to bring about stability. The fixed signs are good for finishing, building, or bringing about concrete conditions. With Taurus, this may be in a material way. Scorpio is also concerned with finances, but here it is loans, taxes, insurance, and other joint property. With Scorpio rising, there may be a need, or it is time, for important and permanent changes. Leo, with the Sun as ruler, usually indicates some degree of progress, which can enrich the ego. Great strides are often made in pursuing a life direction and following a true purpose. The individual may acquire a position of leadership or authority, or improve his or her image. Aquarius may bring group activity and solid achievements of a humanitarian nature. Permanence and endurance is associated with the fixed signs.

The mutable signs rising show changing conditions and a need for adaptability. Transitions are at hand, and preparations are made. Fluctuations come about in Gemini through intellectual vacillation, mental breeziness, and versatility. The individual could become scattered. Mercury as ruler of Virgo signifies details to handle. The critical faculties are stimulated and the individual puts everything under analysis. With Sagittarius, there is exploration of new territories and a need to expand. Pisces shows a need to transcend the boundaries between the real and the fantastic. Dreams can come true for those who have the vision to see both sides. The mutable signs indicate restlessness and fluctuations of interests. Associated with the cadent houses, these signs often represent a certain amount of obscurity for the time, while the individual regroups by getting in touch with inner needs. Plans and strategies for the future are formulated.

The natal Ascendant must be blended with the rising sign of the return, because the individual still has his or her own original makeup and personality. If the return chart has a sign rising that is square the natal Ascendant, significant changes could be at hand, and there may be some difficulties adjusting.

In the event that the rising sign happens to be very close to the same degree as the Ascendant of the natal chart, it will be an extremely significant period for the individual. Interestingly, if the return Ascendant happens to be at about the same degree as the natal Descendant, it is also a significant time. In this case, rather than being in a position to control events, cooperation is a must. With the nativity thus turned upside down, the interests of others must be considered. If the 10th house of the nativity is rising, one becomes noticed in a public way. The individual is in a position to reap success for a job well done. However, mistakes made will not go unnoticed.

Usually there will be other indications in the chart that match, or agree with, the influences shown by the rising sign. This puts an even heavier emphasis on these sign characteristics for the return period. For example, with Virgo rising in the return and three of the return planets are in the 6th house, a great emphasis of Virgo issues will be noticed during the time period of the return. There might be issues involving co-workers or situations on the job, issues connected to pets, routine health checkups, or a diet.

Sometimes this emphasis comes from the way the natal planets fall into the houses of the return. If Cancer were rising in the return, then several natal planets in the sign of Libra would fall into the 4th house of the return, giving an added Cancer/Moon/4th house emphasis

Use the short list of keywords below to help define your return rising sign. Note the aspects formed by the planetary ruler of the Ascendant to see the kinds of experiences you'll attract, whether to go strongly forward, or whether to proceed with caution.

Aries: new ventures, action, self-interest, daring, passionate (ruled by Mars)

Taurus: money matters, creature comforts, artistic (ruled by Venus)

Gemini: busyness, mental stimulation, errands, communications (ruled by Mercury)

Cancer: home and family matters, changeable, emotional (ruled by the Moon)

Leo: taking center stage, honors, leadership potential, creative (ruled by the Sun)

Virgo: analytical, detail-oriented; practical, health, or work issues (ruled by Mercury)

Libra: partnerships, other people, relationships, cooperation (ruled by Venus)

Scorpio: time for change, transforming, intense, energy, willpower (ruled by Pluto)

Sagittarius: optimism, seeking distant goals, travel, education (ruled by Jupiter)

Capricorn: taking care of business, work, status, public reputation (ruled by Saturn)

Aquarius: friendships, groups, group ideals, hopes and wishes (ruled by Uranus)

Pisces: visionary, artistic, reflection, adaptability, sympathetic (ruled by Neptune)

First Natal Planet to Rise

When interpreting a return chart, I recommend a technique that provides clues to the overall trend for the upcoming time period. The more I read lunar returns, it became evident that the first natal planet to rise to the return Ascendant gave reliable indications of the types of events that soon transpired. This would be the first natal planet counterclockwise from the Ascendant of the return chart.

This is similar to a technique practiced by Evangeline Adams, which incorporated traditional Horary rules with that of the nativity of a client. She would quickly refer to tables to find the degree rising at the moment a client entered her office. From that she would determine which of her client's natal planets would be the first to rise. This gave an indication to the types of events that her client would encounter in the immediate future, and she relied on this technique no matter what question was on the mind of her client.[2]

This method works especially well with the Lunar Return chart, because of the temporal nature of the chart. The nature of the first natal planet to rise can also be revealing about the speed with which events begin to transpire. Saturn brings delays to personal plans, Mars acts quickly, and so on.

The distance away this planet is from the return Ascendant may also be informative. The closer the natal planet is to the ascending degree of the return, the more quickly events signified by the planet may

begin to transpire. Using the same two planets for illustration, natal Mars just two degrees below the return Ascendant might indicate a new project to be undertaken immediately by the individual. Natal Saturn as first to rise, but in the 3rd house of the return might show worries over a sibling or news of a serious nature that takes place well into the return period. The rest of the chart and prevailing trends reveal how these indicators should be read. The return house in which this natal planet falls shows the area where the planetary energy will manifest.

Following are some general guidelines on what to expect in regard to each of the natal planets rising. As always, the condition of the natal planet must be considered. A natal Jupiter making several stressful aspects may not be counted on to bring all of the fortune implied and may indicate the squandering or loss of resources instead. In the same way, a well-aspected natal Mars rising is nothing to worry about and will generally reflect new ventures or activities initiated by the individual.

Jupiter

If natal Jupiter is first to rise to the return Ascendant, things go very well and there is a measure of luck. Jupiter implies expansion, protection, and beneficiaries. If natal Jupiter forms nice aspects in the birth chart, or receives helpful aspects by return planets, the benefits or beneficiaries associated with Jupiter will begin to make themselves known right away. One feels lucky, and there are things to be thankful for. Good fortune or gifts come to the individual. Material increase is associated with Jupiter, and if it falls in the 2nd house of the return, this can often be anticipated. Because Jupiter is expansive, the good fortune may be spread out over the time period, with benefits coming steadily. As the Greater Fortune, Jupiter is a strong influence for good when first to rise.

Mars

If a return chart shows Mars to be the next natal planet to rise, arguments or conflicts may be forthcoming unless Mars is free from afflicting aspects. This is based on the nature of Mars. One of the best descriptions of the type of events associated with Mars comes from the name of the planet: to "mar," which means to blemish, damage, spoil, or harm. There is often a need to take a stand and confront an issue. Sometimes a conflict comes in the form of an accident or an illness, and in rare cases surgery might be required. If Mars is free of unfortunate aspects and instead receives favorable aspects, the individual may undertake a personal project or new venture with resulting success. Mars corresponds to masculine types, who may play

a significant role in the events in the immediate future.

Uranus

Uranus acts abruptly and out of the blue. Events occur that were not anticipated, and plans will often need to be altered. Disruptions occur, flexibility is required, and caution is advised in making commitments to a new project. Some unusual circumstance is likely to interfere with the smooth flow anticipated. It can be a disruptive period unless Uranus is involved in very good aspects, in which case the surprises occurring may be advantageous in the long run. Uranus signifies new ideas, scientific interests, astrology, and those connected with these topics. Significant activities or dealings may be related to these. Uranus also rules electronics, computers, the very old, and the very new. Very sporadic in nature, Uranus as first to rise symbolizes events occurring abruptly at any time during the return.

Sun

The Sun, as the giver of life, works very similarly to Jupiter, and usually brings benefits when first to rise. Benefactors play an important role at this time, and the individual may receive gifts or favors. Strong male figures and leader types are associated with the Sun—there may be assistance from such types. It may show opportunities arising that are important in the overall life direction, purpose, or destiny of the individual. The aspects to the Sun will reveal whether things are flowing smoothly or if any challenges will have to be met, but this is overall a strong and helpful influence. The Sun usually acts dynamically, so benefits often begin to accrue shortly after the onset of the return.

Neptune

Neptune, being the natal planet and the first to rise, most often indicates the surfacing of an issue of some confusion, illusion, or mystery. This may come about through an acquaintance or the individual may be deceiving him or herself on some issue, and should refrain from making important decisions unless very sure that all the facts are known. They probably aren't. Neptune is subtle, and situations may be brewing without the knowledge of the individual other than a feeling. There is often delay associated with Neptune before the individual has all the facts brought out into the light for examination. If Neptune forms unfavorable aspects, there may be fears or paranoia or other confusing feelings. It's often a time to wait things out and try not to worry too much. If Neptune is favorably aspected, it may be a time of inspiration.

Venus

Venus is the Lesser Fortune. If Venus is the first natal planet to rise, safety and happiness are insured unless Venus is severely afflicted. Venus attracts gifts and favors. Venus is the prime indicator of love, attractions, marriage, and romance. Venus signifies young women, all things feminine, art, and social events. Any of these may play a more prominent role in life.

Saturn

If Saturn is the first natal planet to rise, then worries or delays may be in store, and this may be in regard to the plans most important to the individual. It is a time when patience is called for. It signifies the disciplining of one's self, and is good for taking responsibility. Saturn usually tends to delay matters throughout the return period. The aspects that Saturn is involved in will reveal how frustrating or disagreeable the period will be, or if patience will be rewarded. An authority figure or an older person may be of special significance in events that take place. Saturn can also signify business issues, which the individual will be involved in.

Pluto

Pluto, as the first natal planet to rise, often indicates financial issues or changes to handle. Reorganization might be related to either an increase or a decrease in available funds or due to the exposure of new facts. Pluto is favorable for projects of reorganization in general, and, if the aspects are good, it is an excellent time to initiate or follow through on important projects. Similar to Mars, Pluto is sometimes active when a conflict arises. Occasionally it signifies sexual issues. Pluto can usually be anticipated to bring profound changes one way or the other, sometimes in the form of psychological insights. There may be an encounter with someone who acts as a catalyst to needed changes. Much depends on how the individual responds to Pluto, shown in the natal chart, and by the current trends.

Mercury

Mercury as the first natal planet to rise indicates a busy period with many interactions, communications, and appointments. The individual will probably receive some news that will alter plans. There is an emphasis on scheduling and making plans for the future, and if Mercury receives unfavorable aspects, one may feel stretched thin. Mercury is associated with traveling and travelers, and one of these may be of primary interest to the individual. It also governs contracts, paperwork, agreements, transport, writing, media, and interviews, any of which may be highlighted during the return.

Moon

The natal Moon being the first to rise shows that the individual will be making changes, often related to travel plans or a move. It is associated with domestic issues and concerns, which center on women, especially the mother. If the Moon forms favorable aspects, it is an excellent time to make changes.

If more than one chart is used, say a converse and a direct motion, then the first natal planet to rise in each chart will offer information for the time to come.

The preceding descriptions may also be applied to a return planet conjunct the return Ascendant.

1. Ronald C. Davison, *Cycles of Destiny* (London: Aquarian Press, 1990), p 35.
2. Evangeline Adams, *The Bowl of Heaven* (New York: Dodd, Mead, 1926, first printing by Sun Books: Santa Fe, NM, 1995), p 9.

chapter eleven

Fine-tuning the Returns

The house of the natal chart that is rising in the return is most important for predicting what area of life predominates in the coming time period. The activities ruled by this house are being given an outlet by moving to the Ascendant and will require the attention of the individual for the return period.

The Ascendant is like the front door, allowing an opening where these issues can surface. The natal promise linked to this house comes into prominence. If the Ascendant degree happens to fall a few degrees just before a natal house cusp, it will usually bring about issues involving that next house.

The natal house in which the return ruler falls should be considered. If the return ruler is Mars, its new placement in the natal chart shows where assistance will be found for the coming time period. Similarly, the ruler of the natal chart shows where assistance can be found in achieving an important goal during the upcoming period, according to its house placement in the return chart.

The planets from the natal chart should be inserted into the return chart, or in a wheel around the return chart. This is an important step and is very revealing. If a natal planet happens to fall exactly on one of the return house cusps, a simple description gives large returns on what to expect in connection with that house. For example, natal Mars on the cusp of the 5th house brings increased activity to the area ruling children, creative activities, and romantic affairs. The aspects made to Mars and other 5th house significators determine the type of activity. If a natal planet falls on one of the return planets, the two are combined in a similar fashion. The natal and the return house positions determine where their combined influences will play out.

Any planet that is prominent in the natal chart due to position or aspects should be given special attention. This includes the ruler of the nativity, the Sun, the ruler of a stellium, and the Moon. Of course, when working with a Solar Return, the Sun will always be exact or nearly exact its natal degree, depending on whether the non-precessed or the precessed chart is used. But it will be in a different house each year and will aspect the other return planets differently.

As with any other chart reading, we are looking for a theme to appear. Consideration should be given to any grouping of planets from the natal chart that falls into one house in the return chart. This will show a heavy accent on affairs ruled by that house. Which house in the return is most accentuated by planets from the natal chart? This will be blended with the house holding those same planets in the nativity.

Just as in the progressed chart, whenever planetary links are made in the return chart that reconnects planets in aspect at birth, those aspects are of exceptional significance. The nature of the aspect is not as important as the fact that the same planets are once again linked together.

At this point, it should be noted that the condition of a planet in the nativity predetermines its capacity to be of help or hindrance in the return. In other words, a strong, well-placed, well-aspected planet in the natal chart is not likely to cause severe problems, even with challenging aspects in the return chart. On the other hand, a very weak planet in the nativity cannot bring a disproportionate amount of benefits, even if well-aspected or situated in the return. A planet that is not well-integrated in the natal chart may be difficult to substantiate in the return. In particular, the outer planets may show little unless they are prominent in the natal chart by proximity to an angle or in close contact to the personal planets.

Always start with simple descriptions, giving plenty of latitude for the charts to lead. Do not underestimate the amount of information possible by keeping the interpretation simple. It is more likely to overlook indications by attempting too much.

The Angles and Aspects

The angles cannot be overemphasized. Any planets very close to an angle (and to a lesser degree, planets in angular houses) get extra attention. Several planets in the angular houses indicate an extremely eventful period. Look at what types of aspects are made between these angular planets to planets in the natal chart. Consider any return planet that falls on an angle of the natal chart as well.

Usually, if the return planets are in favorable aspects among themselves, a favorable period can be anticipated. The aspects made by the Sun in the return chart are especially important in this regard. Many other stresses can be handled successfully with a well-aspected Sun. However, if several return planets are squaring one point in the natal chart, then stress is indicated. This is especially likely if the targeted planet is one of the luminaries. The stress will come about in connection with the planet and house of the natal chart in which it is found, and will be linked to its position in the return. The afflicting planets provide more detail based on their position in both the return and natal chart.

Benefics on the Angles

When there are benefic planets on the angles of a return chart, a favorable period can usually be anticipated. These are the traditional Jupiter and Venus, the Greater and Lesser Fortunes, and also the Sun. If any one of these is on an angle and making easy aspects to other return planets, a joyful and auspicious return period can usually be looked forward to. These three bodies can generally provide health, wealth, and good times, in amounts according to the summary of the chart.

If, however, there are badly afflicted benefics on the angles, it can show all kinds of upsetting circumstances, quite often indicating a health problem, distress, or grief. Having an angular benefic afflicted by malefic planets is most difficult and emotionally disturbing if Venus is the afflicted benefic. A benefic planet on an angle represents ease and harmony unless afflicted. A square or opposition to the angular benefic represents dis-ease. Venus against Jupiter may indicate grief if combined with other similar indicators. Venus against Jupiter without other major afflictions often shows excess of some sort, added expenses, or financial losses. Mars afflicting Jupiter may show accidents, carelessness, extravagance, or going overboard in general. Distressing aspects from malefic planets to an angular Sun may indicate a health crisis.

Malefics on the Angles

Malefics on the angles generally correspond with challenges, these becoming more serious if they are afflicting the other return or natal planets. Mars and Saturn are the traditional malefics although Uranus, Neptune, and Pluto can likewise be an indication of trouble. Afflictions to the Sun are the most serious. When angular malefics are in bad aspect to other malefics in the chart, challenges may be great. Malefics forming hard aspects to the angles of the return are likewise difficult, especially if the stressful aspect is to the return Midheaven. A well-aspected Mars, Saturn, Uranus, or Pluto on an angle is nothing to dread. As a matter of fact, it may correspond with great strides and achievements. Neptune on an angle usually means the direction is unclear. On the Midheaven, the profession may be in limbo or transition. On the Ascendant, the individual may be confused, deluded, or deceived. The descriptions of aspects in chapter 14 may be applied to the return charts.

Planets in the Return

The following brief descriptions should be helpful. In the case of the slower-moving planets, there is a description of the natal planet in the return chart and a description of the return planet in the return chart. There are subtle differences. The natal planet in the return shows what the individual has brought into the new period. The return planet in the return chart indicates issues and situations that originate more from external circumstances. As always, if an angular house is involved, the planetary energies involved have an ideal environment in which to manifest.

Pluto

The house position of natal Pluto in the return chart indicates where strength may be required, but where it is also available. It is a subtle strength and one that may be taken for granted until the period is over. Initially, significant people or situations may force the individual into an unfamiliar set of conditions. Then, in the course of adapting to life's new situation, he or she taps into an inner source of strength and pulls through.

Pluto in the return chart indicates new ventures or changes. On an angle, this is more emphasized. For example, Pluto on the cusp of the 10th house often indicates a new or transformed status. Pluto shows where there are transforming qualities present and an opportunity to upgrade or improve a situation. Circumstances seemingly out of the individual's control may force him or her to make a declaration that results in bringing about major changes. There may have been vague inclinations regarding the issue beforehand. The actions brought about by Pluto cannot be undone, and the individual often finds that his or her stronger foothold and improved circumstances were well worth any initial discomfort.

Breaks that come about have finality, and there is no looking back. Whatever is rebuilt upon these ruins will have a more solid foundation than the old situation. The energies of Pluto are always to be desired in the long run, as there is purification of some element that had become stagnant. The house in the return chart that Pluto rules may furnish additional information as to the source of Plutonian changes.

Uranus

The house position of natal Uranus in the return chart is an area in which to expect some surprises. There are unanticipated developments in regard to these house matters. Whether the surprises will be appreciated will be shown by the overall indications and by the response of the individual to Uranus as shown in the nativity.

Uranus is the most unpredictable of planets. The house position of return Uranus shows where new or unusual elements or people enter the life. They may act as a catalyst to the individual, who becomes involved in new and exciting interests as a result of the association. The people associated with the house occupied by Uranus may act out in surprising ways, or the affairs ruled by the house take unexpected turns. Sometimes there are unexpected upsets and separations. Some degree of flexibility is usually required in the area where Uranus resides in the return chart. The return house ruled by Uranus may show the root of Uranian energies.

Saturn

Saturn is the teacher. It shows where discipline and responsibility are necessary. If the individual has Saturn prominently placed in the birth chart or if the twenty-eighth birthday has been reached, then Saturn is more integrated into the life so that natal Saturn's house position in the return chart can be looked to for rewards of a Saturnian nature. There may be more responsibility or authority in this area. Respect and slow steady progress come about as a result of determination of purpose. If the individual does not take well to such things as authorities, discipline, or responsibility, then Saturn's position may indicate restrictions, or blocks to the self-determinism from this area.

The return Saturn shows where a lesson may be learned. To the unresponsive student, the lesson may seem severe. Rather than fight Saturn, it is best in most cases to accept the limitations imposed and make whatever adjustments are necessary until the period is over. Many times, Saturn just means to slow down and practice patience while incorporating a needed disciplinary measure into a structure. The house in the return which Saturn rules will be helpful in determining what these responsibilities are linked to.

Neptune

Natal Neptune's house position in the return chart is often an area of some mystery, uncertainty, or confusion to the individual. Problems in this area may be more difficult to resolve because all of the factors involved are not exposed for the analysis of the individual. Something in this area may be subject to deterioration or disintegration. If forming favorable aspects, Neptune may show ideal circumstances, blissful conditions, and dreams that come true. Inspiration flows, and intuition is reliable.

The return Neptune's position in the return chart shows an area where deception might occur. This can be either someone deceiving the individual or vice versa. Something remains hidden or out of sight. Confusion or unclear elements reside here. Neptune can also be indicative of drugs, alcohol, and other forms of taking leave of reality. These include daydreaming, fantasizing, or excessive sleep. Confusion or deceptions may attach to the people of the house occupied by Neptune. Dissolving conditions may be taking place in this house that will lead to new entanglements or conditions. At its best, Neptune signifies an idealistic attitude, where compassion may be given or received. Sometimes it provides peace and tranquillity. The house governed by Neptune in the return offers a link to the Neptunian energies.

Jupiter

The house position of natal Jupiter in the return chart is an area where an element of protection exists for the individual. At some point during the period, benefits will come from someone represented by this house. Qualities of faith, goodwill, and an optimistic attitude attract the same back to the individual.

Jupiter's return position shows where expansion takes place. This is the Greater Fortune, so Jupiter can bring money, luck, happiness, and social occasions. A return with Jupiter on an angle and receiving assisting aspects is one to look forward to. This is where the individual reaches out to embrace more. Depending on other factors, it can also show excess, overindulgence, or taking on more than one can handle. Occasionally this can be quite literal, and if Jupiter is found in the 1st house and ruling the 6th house, the body may expand from overeating. The house ruled by Jupiter shows a link to this expansion factor, or what might bring it about.

Mars

The position of natal Mars in the return shows where a self-serving attitude may lie. Disregard for the rights of others in the area may stem from the individual feeling he or she must have immediate gratification. Aggressiveness, initiative, temper, are all indicated by Mars. If it receives good aspects in the natal chart, or by return planets, it may mean successful new enterprises in the matters of the house it occupies. It may show inner strength, initiative, and resourcefulness. Mars is similar to Pluto in this respect.

The house of return Mars indicates an area of action, energy, and eventful situations. There is always a great deal of activity in the matters of the house occupied by Mars. Mars is where adrenaline is felt, so this can create very exciting or very aggravating situations. Efforts are put forth, and there may be some excitability in connection with this house. The aspects show application of the will and strength. Mars shows an area where the individual becomes involved in new ventures. In the better aspects much can be accomplished, and a good deal of personal credit will result. Mars is physical in nature, and it sometimes reflects accidents, illness, or confrontations. It might show an illness involving the people ruled by its house position, or it may show conflicts there. The action of Mars will be in connection with the house it rules.

Venus

Venus is the Lesser Fortune and usually represents pleasant circumstances wherever it falls. Venus shows what things the individual is attracted to, or where the affections are strongest. Happiness is found by participating in the activities governed by Venus' house position. This can be an area where social activities play a large part during the period. Favors, gifts, or kindnesses are likely to come from someone ruled by the house of Venus' occupancy.

Mercury

Mercury indicates activity involving communications and agreements as well as movement and travel. There may be excessive errands, much coming and going, or various concerns surrounding the matters of the house occupied by Mercury. What the individual has on his or her mind are shown by Mercury's location. Since Mercury is a neutral planet and is so easily influenced by planets in aspect, note the planet forming the closest aspect to find its influence. Depending on the aspects, it might show where nerves get frazzled or worries arise. If the pace becomes too fast, the individual feels the pressure. Movement, and many daily activities involve those things signified by Mercury's house position.

Moon

The Moon rules the family and the domestic situation, so the Moon's placement and condition in the return offer valuable information about events that are likely to occur during the period of the return.

Fluctuations abound in the matters of the house occupied by the Moon. The emotions and sense of balance are closely attached to the affairs of this house. This shows the focus of the emotions and the things that occupy the awareness. The placement of the Moon shows sensitive areas that are prone to changes. The sign position is just as important as the house position. Between them they show emotional qualities, the tenor and tone of the environment, and the daily conditions. (chapter 13 describes the Solar Return Moon by house and sign.)

Sun

The Sun's position in the return chart is most significant. The house holding the Sun in the return chart is where the individual attempts growth and progress. The ego, ruled by the Sun, is only able to fulfill itself by meeting the conditions of the house it occupies. This house defines the kinds of experience through which an individual must resolve his or her purpose and destiny. To evolve spiritually, the individual must gain a command over this area. Success or failure is measured by the degree to which the individual is able to meet the requirements defined by this house. Great efforts are put forth in handling these matters, and an aggressive quality is often noticeable. The aspects show the degree of difficulty in the things attempted. Under good conditions, great confidence, authority, and leadership abilities are demonstrated in handling the issues of this house. An easier period lies ahead if the aspects to the Sun are beneficial ones.

House Emphasis

There are a few ways to have a house emphasized. First of all, the house affairs naturally corresponding with the return rising sign become activated. If there are many planets in a house, then the affairs ruled by that house are more emphasized during the return period. The house holding the Sun is particularly emphasized, showing where much personal effort is put forth. The issues relating to the house of the natal chart that holds the rising degree of the return will be brought to the attention of the individual. Following are brief summaries of each house. They can be referred to for any type of house emphasis.

1st House

With an active 1st house, situations call for an accurate appraisal of self-worth. The individual is in a causative position, with confidence and self-reliance at high levels. Energy, initiative, and new beginnings of a personal nature are some of the things signified by an active 1st house. The appearance and qualities of attraction, as well as physical energy and vitality, may be of support in making a statement. The individual may need to demand earned rewards or be forthcoming without much effort.

2nd House

With a 2nd house emphasis, the focus is on financial assets and resources. Heavy gains or expenditures are likely. Larger or more expensive items or services may be purchased. The individual may feel either a need to consolidate resources or a need to own more luxurious items. There could be either an increase or a decline in income, depending on aspects into the 2nd house.

3rd House

An active 3rd house shows an increase in activity relating to communication and transport. There is a need to express ideas in some form. The daily tempo increases, and there may be more involvement with those in the immediate environment, such as neighbors or relatives. Vehicles may be an area of concern. The 3rd house also symbolizes youth and their education. The aspects made to planets in the 3rd house show whether the area will be smooth or if conflicts are likely.

4th House

When the 4th house becomes active, it is often a time of reappraisal of the individual's basic securities. The subjective self and foundations found within the home and family are the focus. The individual may prefer solitude while undergoing some type of self-analysis. During this time there is an extra emphasis on the home and/or family members, often including one of the parents. The 4th house governs the domestic conditions and activities as well as real estate. Look to the aspects into the 4th house.

5th House

Activities involving children, creative projects, and romance are the rulership of the 5th house. One or the other, or all three, depending on the individual's circumstances, will most certainly be stimulated during an active 5th house period. Matters surrounding children become highlighted. Talents in a creative area may blossom. There is a strong urge to put something concrete out into the physical universe that reflects individuality. He or she may fall in love. The 5th house also rules sports, games, and gambling—any of which may become activated. Aspects into the 5th house show ease or challenges in the area.

6th House

An active 6th house means the individual may get more gratification than usual from his or her job, but this gratification is more likely to be personal than monetary. Involvement with co-workers may pick up, and changes take place in schedules and personnel on the job scene. This may coincide with a time of various routine health checkups, or attention to diet and exercise. Areas of health and work may go hand in hand, calling for balance. Overwork can bring about stress, which affects the health. Activity may also involve pets. Look to the nature of the planet in or ruling this house and its aspects to judge these matters.

7th House

Important relationships may be established when the 7th house is stimulated, including marriage or business partnerships. The marriage partner may be a source of concern. Confrontations may arise, as well as the breakup of close associations. The aspects into the 7th house will show conflicts or the reverse. Legal activity may become necessary in extreme cases. Cooperation and balance may need to be restored, which calls for the advice or counsel of an expert in some field.

8th House

The usual issues to arise with an active 8th house are those involving finances. Joint financial matters or money from outside sources are especially active areas. Increases are just as likely as a decrease. The aspects into the 8th house will show this. Taxes, loans, or insurance matters usually need to be handled at this time. Sexual issues may arise. The sexual urges might decline or may become more active. This house also signifies recovering from loss and could coincide with the death of someone close. Usually, however, it is more likely the death and rebirth of a situation that takes place, passing from one condition to another. There may be talent for restoring life to something left for dead, or rejuvenating others.

9th House

Long-distance travel may involve either the individual or someone close with many planets in the 9th house. Increased interaction with in-laws is a possibility. There is more interest in abstract or philosophical subjects, and the individual may enroll in an educational course or study on an informal level. Teachers or professors could have an important impact on the beliefs of the individual. A conclusion regarding a personal belief or religious issue might occur. Publishing and the promotion of ideas might be areas of interest. The 9th house also signifies the law, so a legal issue might require attention.

10th House

The 10th house shows that ambition, career, vocation, and overall life direction of an individual are areas of great focus and activity. Issues will require attention, putting the individual's reputation under scrutiny. He or she will undoubtedly be given a fair amount of attention, and advantage can be taken of this. The attention may come from an authority or from the public. An elevation or decline in status will show through the aspects made into the 10th house. A parent may play a more important role during this period or be a source of concern.

11th House

An emphasis in the 11th house represents activity in connection with friendships, groups, clubs, and associations, possibly as an extension of the profession or career. Satisfaction and rewards may come through these associations. The individual may be elected to speak on the collective goals of the group. Hopes and aspirations are shared with many others and may be pursued with more intensity. With stressful aspects into the 11th house, there may be conflicts with friends or within a group

to which the individual belongs. Separations or misunderstandings may take place.

12th House

With an active 12th house, the individual may spend more time alone, possibly on a research project, where seclusion is preferred. Overcoming some long-held fear or other important breakthroughs into the psyche may take place. Self-undoing is also ruled by the 12th house, and the judgment of the individual might be questioned if there are many afflicted planets in the 12th house. It might not be a good time to make important decisions, but more a time to take in information and wait for a more propitious time. The 12th house rules over institutions of all kinds, and is active when hospitalization or recovery time takes place for the individual or for someone close to him or her.

House Polarities

Because the house polarities are more emphasized in return charts, it will sometimes be found that the issues of the opposite house will be stimulated. Opposing houses represent similar issues. For example, the 2nd house represents money the individual earns for himself or herself. The 8th represents the money earned in cooperation with another or others. A heavily tenanted 2nd house is sometimes also indicative of joint financial issues. Because of this polarity factor, it is often helpful to consider the issues of the opposing house when assessing the return charts.

Working with Eclipses & the Nodes in Return Charts

Working with eclipses can be tedious and time-consuming in the beginning. However the rewards are worth the extra effort. If an eclipse occurs on a house cusp of a return chart, watch for events involving that house for the remainder of the return period. Changes attach to the matters of the house where an eclipse falls. The same is noted if an eclipse falls on a planet in the return. In this case the planet, house, sign position, and aspects of the planet should be considered.

The Moon's nodes should not be overlooked. They exert extreme energy in the return chart, especially if close to another planet. They bring out and emphasize the particular nature of the planet they are with, so they are valuable tools for predicting. They provide excellent information when forming a conjunction to another planet.

The nodes are considered karmic in nature. Traveling backward through the zodiac they reconnect one with things of the past. They symbolize give and take, learning life lessons, playing by the laws of the universe, reaping karmic rewards, and paying karmic debts. The North Node is more representative of opportunities and good tidings, while the South Node represents trials and tribulations. They show karmic occurrences and reflection on destiny issues. The return node or the natal node on an angle may indicate a significant and possibly karmic occurrence during the period of the return. On a non-angular house cusp effects are similar but less profound and in connection with those house matters.

If the North Node happens to exactly conjunct a house cusp in the Solar Return, then events linked to that house will occur throughout the year when there is stimulation to that degree. This is even more spectacular if another planet was near the same degree in the return.

The nodes travel quickly enough that they have an effect similar to that of an outer planet as they make contacts. In the year following a Solar Return, the nodes travel backward about nineteen degrees, making major aspects to many planets in the return and to natal planets at important places in the return. This brings out the potential of the planet. Chapter 15 is dedicated to eclipse and nodal activity.

Special Points

Other points to consider include any planet or angle at the zero degree of a cardinal sign. Such a planet holds an elevated status and significance. The Pleiades, a group of stars in the last degree of Taurus, is associated with the weeping sisters and is significant of potentially unfortunate situations if a planet occupies its degree. The Vertex, a point of fate, is informative if conjunct a planet. Chapter 16 expands on each of these special points.

Using the Solar & Lunar Returns Together

To complete the yearly cycle and narrow down the timing of events shown in the Solar Return, a set of thirteen Lunar Returns should be calculated. These charts are then interpreted with the Solar Return chart as a base. It is advised to calculate these charts along with the Solar Return. They can be tagged for several features all at once.

When a Lunar Return chart appears to closely match the Solar Return, it often signifies important developments for that month. An important event may occur that is shown in the yearly chart. There will usually be a similarity between the house cusps of the Lunar Return and those of the Solar Return. Repeating aspects are significant

as well, and show the time when they will manifest.

If a planet from the Solar Return appears on an angle of the Lunar Return, something in connection with that planet will occur in the affairs governed by the Lunar Return house. If the planet was prominent in the Solar Return, it is more significant.

If the Lunar Return holds a planet in a degree closely matching an angle of the Solar Return, it will become particularly prominent during the four weeks to follow. Activity associated with the planet will be observed in the house it holds in the Lunar Return, and in the house it occupies in the Solar Return. There may be multiple significant developments and this represents an important time.

By watching the transit of the Sun through the Solar Return houses, it is possible to gauge when certain types of events will take place. This is done easily by comparing the Lunar Return's Sun position to the Solar Return and finding which house of the Solar Return the Sun now occupies. Just as the various areas of life are stimulated by the transit of the Sun through the corresponding natal house, the same formulas apply as the Sun transits through the Solar Return houses over the course of the year. The Solar Return acts like an auxiliary natal chart for the year. Events associated with each house will correspond with the time the Sun transits the house. This gives the astrologer an edge on predicting events.

For instance, if marriage is promised in the Solar Return, it will most likely take place when the Lunar Return Sun falls in the Solar Return 7th house—or, more simply, when the Sun is transiting the 7th house of the Solar Return chart. The most important events for the year are likely to take place when the Sun transits the angles of the Solar Return. The readings are done exactly as they would be if the natal chart were being considered, and can be blended with the natal house in which the Sun is transiting to provide more detail.

The other planets can also be used in this manner to show the timing of events. The Lunar Return can be compared to the Solar Return to find the house activated by each planet. As the planets transit the houses of the Solar Return, developments associated with the planet will take place in those house matters.

Planetary Transits to the Return Angles

Just as the most important events for the year are likely to take place when the Sun transits across the angles of the Solar Return, the Lunar Return period will often produce the most dynamic events when the Moon transits across an angle of that chart. These Moon transits bring an urge for stimulation, for changes and movement. Actions that are initiated often produce events or new developments.

In fact, if any planet crosses one of the return angles, the nature of that planet and the things it represents will rule the day.

Mercury produces mental stimulation, and there may be many communications or errands. With the Sun, there may be a burst of energy, or involvements with authorities and masculine types. With Venus, there may be compliments, gifts, or money, or just a lift in mood and increased interest in appearance. With Mars, there may be challenges or demands to meet, and it is a time when one is more easily irritated. Accidents or mishaps might occur. The aspects formed by this transiting planet to other transiting planets are influential in how matters signified by the planet will go.

With the outer planets, they would have to be near an angle in the return in order to have the opportunity to cross it. This is a powerful position for an outer planet to hold in the return, and its influences will be quite noticeable for the period of the return. The effects will become stronger yet if it transits the angle. And, with the outer planets, it may spend several days on the angle.

With Jupiter crossing an angle, there are opportunities for expansion and growth unless it forms very unfavorable aspects, in which case losses may occur. With Saturn, there are responsibilities or burdens, and this may feel like a testing phase. With Uranus, there are surprising turns of events or excitement in the air, and unusual people to meet. With Neptune, there may be confusion in the air and various uncertainties, on top of which a person may feel tired or weary. With Pluto, new facts emerge that require immediate action. This may lead to a face-off or to very important changes.

To help judge probable effects, check the aspects to this transiting planet from other transiting planets. The next section gives more insight to the particular energy associated with each planet.

Retrograde Planets in the Solar Return

This is one of the most fail-proof systems for predicting events using the Solar Return. Make a note of the sign and degree of planets that are retrograde on the birthday or will go retrograde shortly after the birthday. At the time they return to the degree they held in the return chart, there is a release of energy associated with the nature of that planet. Significant events take place

as indicated by the planet and its placement in the chart.

If a planet goes retrograde after the birthday, it will pass over the degree it held in the Solar Return twice more within the return period, and events signified by the planet might manifest on one or both of these days. Usually, the direct transit is the more eventful of the two, but not always. Occasionally events happen on both days, and are frequently in connection with the same issue. This is especially likely if an ongoing project is underway or if there is an important issue to be handled.

Frequently, the first pass of a retrograde planet to its Solar Return position signifies an opportunity to solve an issue and coincides with a climactic point concerning the issue. If actions taken then do not resolve the problem, then the second transit of the planet across its Solar Return degree will coincide with a second climax and a final opportunity to take care of the problem. The more serious the nature of the situation, the more turbulent this transit might be. By the time the second transit comes along, the individual may be more or less forced to take action. If a project is concerned, the first transit will coincide with important activity related to the project, while the final transit produces the fruit of previous efforts. If the individual has taken an improper path on his or her life journey, these transits may coincide with barriers to the success of the efforts taken. The individual may become resigned to the failure of the enterprise on the final passage.

The prominence of the planet in the return will show whether the event will be of major or minor importance. Following are some general guidelines for each of the planets as they return to the degree held in the return.

Mercury

If Mercury is retrograde in the Solar Return or turns retrograde soon after the birthday, it will pass over the degree it held in the return one or two more times. Generally, there will be news or some communication that will alter original plans. Sometimes it brings an emphasis to events involving vehicles and transportation issues, or the more common associations with contracts and agreements. The most likely activity to take place can be traced to Mercury's house position in the Solar Return, combined with its return position in the natal house. Aspects made to Mercury in the return will show the nature of the news or travel situation along with the people who might be involved.

Venus

Venus returning to its Solar Return position generally brings a pleasant social oc-

casion. This might be fairly significant, and the individual could meet a romantic partner or form an important relationship. Frequently there are gifts, favors, or money received at this time. Planning a social activity for the day would be appropriate. The passage of Venus over its Solar Return degree shortly after the birthday is the one to track rather than the transit that may occur nearly a year later. However, this later transit of Venus (near the next birthday) may be significant as well.

Mars

Mars passage over its degree in the Solar Return brings a release of energy and usually calls for decisive action to be taken by the individual. Sometimes a needed confrontation brings a sense of relief. Mars often signifies aggravation or a conflict, so the use of self-restraint may be good advice for the day. However, it's better to let the steam out than to hold back and inadvertently become the victim of Mars' energies. In this case irritations or minor accidents may be noted on the day that Mars returns to the degree it held in the Solar Return.

Jupiter

Jupiter's return to its Solar Return degree can usually be anticipated for the benefits it brings. Like Venus, it often coincides with social occasions. Favors or gifts may be received, and it usually brings money or some other form of good fortune. Pay raises are common, or some stroke of good luck may present an opportunity for expansion. A friend received a one thousand dollar bonus check exactly on the day Jupiter retrograded across its Solar Return degree. Although she was looking forward to the day it made its final passage, nothing of significance occurred on that day, except for her abundant enthusiasm for life! Traveling for pleasure is another likely possibility with Jupiter's return to its Solar Return degree.

Saturn

Saturn returning to the degree it held in the Solar Return generally brings up issues of responsibility and/or interaction with authorities. Saturn issues often deal with business situations, and long-term efforts toward achievement. There may be limitations or restricting circumstances, often imposed by authority figures or older people. Delays are generally in evidence and patience is required. In many instances the circumstances of reality are not as serious or depressing as the individual perceives them to be. Things have a way of settling out once the transit passes. However, be wary of opportunities that are presented on this day, since they may turn out to be a disappointment. It is usually not advis-

able to make final commitments on new projects.

Uranus

Uranus returning to its Solar Return degree brings about an eruption that may seem untimely or out of control. Sometimes the events associated with Uranus are out of the blue and unexpected. In other cases the individual may be forced to deal with some long overdue issue that has been brewing. There may be a sense that things are going to pieces. As a result of Uranus activity, the air is cleared and in most cases the new conditions will usher in needed experiences.

Neptune

Neptune has two quite different sides. It often reflects deceptions or the surfacing of confusing issues. The individual may be fearful or unsure regarding a situation, and if decisions are made without having all the facts at hand, it can bring about setbacks for the individual. On the more positive side, an opportunity to use the intuitive faculties may appear and coincide with an instinctual decision that opens doors to the future. In this regard, Neptune's return to the Solar Return degree sometimes brings the materialization of dreams. Much depends on the response of the individual to Neptune, in general, shown primarily in the natal chart, as well as by Neptune's aspects in the return chart.

Pluto

On the day that Pluto returns to the position held in the return chart, an issue that one has put off or even dreaded may finally be confronted. The individual either realizes that time has run out and is forced to finally make a move, or becomes tired of avoiding the situation and now has the energy to deal with it. This may be a relatively minor issue, but occasionally the transit will signal a time of overcoming some larger obstacle. A sense of personal power and control will usually aid the individual in expert handling of the issues that evolve.

chapter twelve

The Return Techniques in Practice

In the following delineation of return charts, many of the techniques outlined in the previous chapters are seen in action.

This set of return charts belong to Dan, the police officer who was shot and wounded in the line of duty. Dan's progressed charts, having already been assessed, provide a solid background for accurately reading his returns. The progressions offer the plot of a story, showing the kinds of events that are ripe to occur when stimulated by transits. His progressed aspects were discussed at length in chapter 8.

To briefly review, Dan's natal chart showed his potential to become an officer of the law, and the fact that he served in this public capacity for twenty years without injury was depicted in his chart by many safety-insuring aspects. His natal chart did, however, hold a couple of aspects denoting potential danger on the job. By his forty-third year, those aspects were becoming prominent in his progressions, joined by other alarming aspects.

The main aspect of risk came from natal Uranus in square to his 6th house Jupiter. By progression, Uranus moved into a closer square with Jupiter. At the same time, Mars became involved in numerous afflictions in his progressions. In a close square to his Ascendant in the natal chart, it was another aspect that indicated potential personal danger and risk. His progressed Moon also began forming aspects indicating a personal crisis. While Jupiter formed some aspects of protection, the major theme of his progressed aspects leaned toward danger, confrontation, unexpected accidents, and potential physical health risks. Life transitions were at hand.

Of course all these things transpired within a short period. Working in the wee hours on the morning of May 4, 1995, Dan responded to a fateful 911 call. Unbeknown to Dan, it was a domestic dispute between a mentally unstable adult male and his parents. The father made the call after his son shot and wounded him. But, with the phone still in the father's hand, his son fired another shot, killing him. The deranged man then proceeded to shoot and kill his mother. As the phone line went dead, Dan left for the scene with another officer following. Unaware of the severity of the situation at hand, Dan also became a victim.

A Year of Major Crossroads

Dan's Solar Return charts prior to this life-transforming incident are presented first with a short commentary. They show how the dangerous implications in his progressed aspects are repeated in his returns. They are also useful to illustrate the repeating themes and connections between the Solar Returns to the subsequent Lunar Returns during times of important developments.

Dan's Precessed Solar Return closely matches his natal chart, indicating an important year for personal developments. Scorpio is rising in the Solar Return, so it is a time for changes. Significant events are forthcoming with several planets in angular houses. Certainly the year did bring huge changes for Dan.

Ruling Pluto is in the 1st house while square the Sun. Pluto with the North Node is a dynamic force. This implies a degree of danger, physical in nature, and doubly so with his chart ruler and the Sun involved in an afflicting aspect. The aspect suggests struggle and problems may stem from an underestimation of efforts required to do a job. Carelessness or unnecessary risk may bring serious consequences. North Node in the 1st house suggests events that may seem particularly karmic in nature.

There is a lot of activity in the 10th house, showing a focus on vocation and status. The Sun in the 10th forms an opposition to the Moon, suggesting culminations. The Full Moon is a tension-producing aspect. It sometimes calls for yielding to another or making compromises and often brings separations. Dan's natal Pluto is on the return Midheaven, another emphasis toward status changes. As a result of his injuries and loss of function in his arm, Dan was forced to leave the police department and his career of twenty years.

Neptune and Uranus in the 3rd house show mysterious or foggy conditions and disruptive influences in the environment and in the case of travel. Neptune squares his natal Moon in the Solar Return 6th house, representing misleading influences.

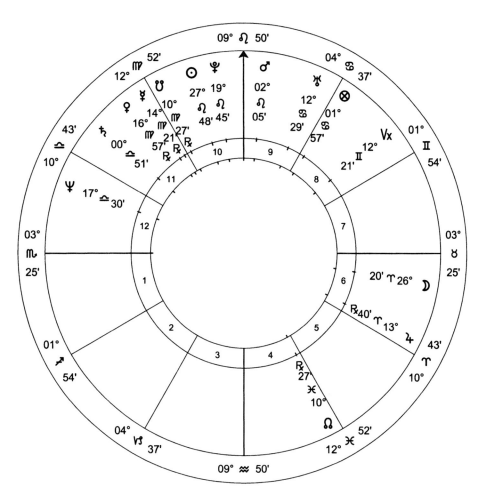

Figure 12a: Dan's Natal Chart
Aug. 21, 1951; 11:35 AM CDT; 85W40, 40N33

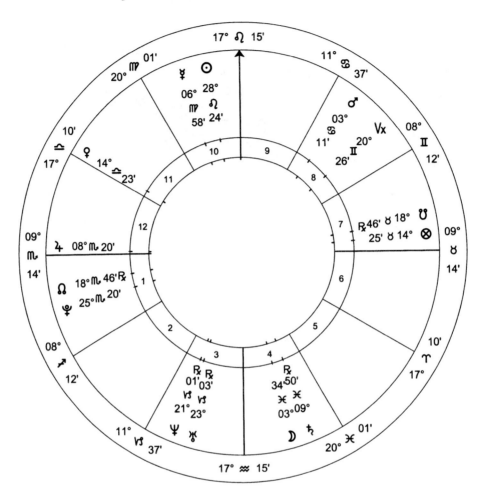

Figure 12b: Dan's Precessed Solar Return
Aug. 21, 1994; 12:02 PM EST; 85W39, 40N33

Fluctuations occur in work with the natal Moon here, and Aries on the cusp indicates increased activity. Uranus is also square natal Moon in the Solar Return 6th house, a disruptive influence.

Saturn with the Moon in the 4th house shows involvements in difficult family relations. In opposition to the Sun and Mercury, there are possible confrontations or conflicts. With Sun and Mercury in the 10th house, opposed by the Moon and Saturn, there are also difficult decisions to make in vocational matters.

Jupiter on the Ascendant is of mixed influence. Good aspects from the Moon, Saturn, Mars, and Mercury serve as protection from severe harm. Honors or ceremonies may be forthcoming. However, return Jupiter is square his natal Mars at 2° Leo, a risk factor. Jupiter on an angle and square his Mars represents risks and possible losses. Fortunately, Solar Return Sun is sextile return Mars, a helpful influence that saved him from more tragic consequences. Things could have gone much worse.

Using Mars as the chart ruler, its placement in the 8th house suggests moving through doors, transitioning from one condition to another. This played out in many ways, from his fateful experience and close brush with death, to his surgery, his rehabilitation, and subsequent leave from his job after twenty years.

Pluto and the Sun are the strongest angular influences in this chart, with Pluto most emphasized. The precessed return chart shows personal danger, important decisions, and permanent changes.

Dan's non-precessed Solar Return repeats the same themes. Aries is rising so there is action and new ventures in the year ahead. Ruling Mars is angular in the chart and squaring Dan's Solar Return Ascendant, so there is a potential conflict at hand. This aspect is a repetition of Dan's natal square of Mars to his Ascendant, an aspect of danger. He may be dealing with aggressive forces.

This is his natal 6th house rising, bringing an emphasis to job, work, and health. The return Sun and Mercury occupy the 6th house, bringing more focus to job and health-related affairs. The Sun in the 6th house is opposing the Moon, a tension-producing aspect. The Sun is square Pluto, also troubling for the health and in work-related matters. There may be danger on the job. Mercury in the 6th house is opposing Saturn, also pointing to work or health-related problems and worries.

The return also shows Neptune in the 10th house, often coinciding with a phase of transition in professional affairs. As ruler of the 10th house, Saturn is opposing Mercury, but gets a trine from Jupiter, so while there are vocational worries and

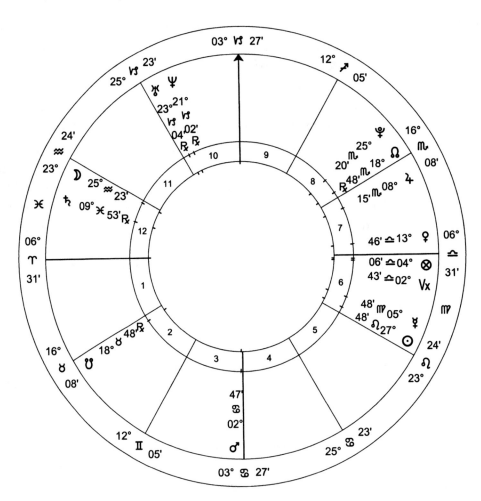

Figure 12c: Dan's Non-precessed Solar Return
Aug. 20, 1994; 2:00 PM EST; 85W40, 40N33

restrictions, there may also be professional honors.

Venus in the 7th house is square two outer planets, Uranus and Neptune—and by a wide orb, Venus is also square Mars. In other words, Venus is an afflicted benefic on an angle, so there is a disturbance to the usual harmony. When the natal planets are inserted, Solar Return Venus opposes natal Jupiter in the return 1st house, another indication of dis-ease and possible losses. Though natal Jupiter is first to rise, the opposition from Solar Return Venus adds to the indications that suggest disturbances to harmony.

As ruler of the Solar Return, Mars is on the cusp of the 4th house and in Cancer, so there is personal involvement in a family conflict or a domestic dispute. This theme is repeated in many ways. His natal Uranus falls in the Solar Return 4th house, combined with Solar Return Mars, so the family issues may come up suddenly, unexpectedly, or in surprising ways. This is a dangerous combination, often coinciding with accidents. Solar Return Mars and natal Uranus are the most angular planets in the return chart. His Solar Return Moon is in a close square to return Pluto. The Moon rules the Solar Return 4th house, an indication of intense or violent emotional outbursts in family relations. Of course it was a domestic dispute he was responding to in the line of duty when the perpetrator shot him, so these are very telling configurations.

Solar Return Neptune is square Dan's natal Moon in the Solar Return 1st house, a time when misleading influences can lead one astray—it is a time to be very alert, especially with strangers. This is the aspect that became his downfall. He was unaware of what a dangerous situation he was entering into when he left the station to investigate the 911 call. Living in a small, normally quiet community, murders didn't happen. At least he was unprepared for the attack on his life.

The non-precessed Solar Return shows important changes, personal danger, and health risks, similar to the themes suggested by the precessed Solar Return.

Both Solar Returns show at least one serious affliction involving the chart ruler. Both show afflictions to the Sun. Both show a heavy emphasis on job, work, and vocational affairs, with changes ahead. Both show health dangers with potential accidents. Both returns suggest involvement in a domestic altercation.

The theme of the charts played out. While his life was spared and Dan received awards and citations at a banquet held in his honor, he was forced to leave his post and seek another job, due to his inability to perform certain tasks as a result of his injuries from the shot that pierced his right arm.

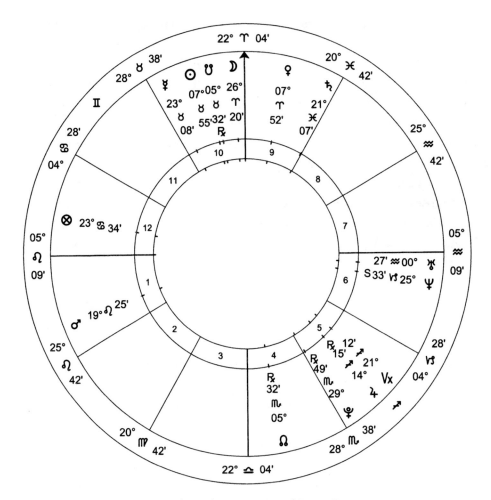

Figure 12d: Dan's Non-precessed Lunar Return
Apr. 28, 1995; 11:39 AM EST; 85W40, 40N33

While a great deal more detail can be found in the Solar Return charts, the above should suffice for purposes of illustration. We'll next take a look at Dan's Lunar Returns just before he was taken unaware. The Lunar Return offers more detail and helps pinpoint the timing of events suggested in the Solar Return.

A Fateful Encounter

Here are Dan's Lunar Returns preceding his close brush with death.

Dan's non-precessed Lunar Return just prior to the fateful 911 call and his subsequent injury, shows that return Mars occupies the Lunar Return 1st house. This suggests dynamic personal action. The closest aspect of Mars is a square to Mercury, so there is some dispute or conflict. This Lunar Return Mars is conjunct Dan's natal Pluto, implying the possibility for personal danger as the aspect sometimes coincides with violence. In fact, his natal Mars at 2° Leo is conjunct the Lunar Return Ascendant, representing that a conflict is at hand that should be forthcoming very soon. Dan may be dealing with very aggressive forces.

The Lunar Return ruler is the Sun, with Leo rising. The Sun is conjunct the South Node in an angular house, and it is square Uranus. The Sun is also square his natal Mars on the return Ascendant, and by wide orb, the Sun is applying to square return Mars and natal Pluto. This brings the Sun into the category of an afflicted benefic on an angle. There are inharmonious influences present. Some event will upset the status quo. Losses may occur, and with the South Node conjunct the chart ruler, there are potential vulnerabilities and health dangers for Dan. This Lunar Return Sun opposes the Solar Return Jupiter as well, an aspect of meeting with opposing forces. The Lunar Return Sun actually falls on the 7th house cusp of the precessed Solar Return, also pointing to important and potentially difficult encounters with others.

The Lunar Return Ascendant is square his natal Ascendant, so this may mean significant changes with difficulties adjusting. Leo is a fixed sign. With such a sign rising, permanent changes are made. With Leo, this may involve life direction and purpose.

This is Dan's natal 10th house rising in the Lunar Return so this brings an emphasis to career, status, and vocational affairs. This theme is repeated with much planetary activity in the Lunar Return 10th house. The Moon there shows fluctuations, but the Sun with South Node suggests unwanted developments, especially with the many afflictions into the 10th house by Neptune, Uranus, and Mars.

This Lunar Return repeats many themes from the precessed Solar Return.

Neptune and Uranus in the Lunar Return 6th house indicate that some illusive and surprising elements may arise in the line of work. They square his Moon in the 10th house, and Neptune is square the Moon within a one-degree orb. There are some deceptive influences. This is an aspect from Dan's Solar Return chart that *has now come closer*. It is very revealing of the events that came to pass in the middle of that fateful night. It was just a few days into the Lunar Return period when the altercation took place. This was just as the transiting Moon came to the cusp of the 12th house.

Dan's precessed Lunar Return shows return Mars precisely conjunct the Ascendant. This replays a familiar theme of conflicts, especially since Mars is square return Mercury and Pluto, and conjunct his natal Sun and Pluto. The chart suggests personal confrontations and aggressive forces. The themes of danger shown in the Solar Return charts are now repeated and emphasized in the Lunar Returns.

His first natal planet to rise is Pluto. It is closely conjunct the Lunar Return Ascendant. Combined and compounded by return Mars and its influences, this also suggests personal danger and that he may be dealing with aggressive forces. The danger may come suddenly, and it is not far away. With natal Pluto first to rise, it is time for developments leading to permanent changes.

This is Dan's 10th house rising, bringing professional concerns into focus. This emphasis on the 10th house is repeated with planetary activity in and near the 10th house cusp.

The Sun is again on the Midheaven, now conjunct the 10th house cusp within three degrees, and the Sun is conjunct the South Node. With the Sun ruling the Leo Ascendant, this shows vulnerabilities for Dan, and there are possible health connotations. The Sun is an afflicted benefic on an angle, representing dis-ease and upsets to harmony. This Lunar Return Sun is closely opposing Solar Return Jupiter, reflecting opposing forces. This Lunar Return Sun is conjunct the precessed Solar Return 7th house cusp. This suggests important developments in the coming four weeks. It also emphasizes dealings with others.

With the Sun conjunct South Node on the Midheaven, there may be sacrifices in connection with vocation.

Neptune and Uranus are once again in the 6th house, indicating mystery, illusions, and unexpected elements in Dan's job-related affairs. His health may also be prone to the same kinds of influences. There are vulnerabilities and surprise elements. Neptune is in a close square to

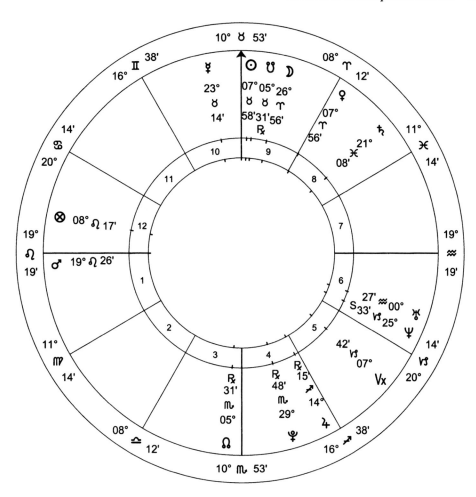

Figure 12e: Dan's Precessed Lunar Return
Apr. 28, 1995; 12:51 PM EST; 85W39, 40N33

his natal Moon, symbolizing strange influences and a liability to deceptions. It brings weird experiences and represents a time to be most careful in all dealings with other people. For Dan, with Lunar Return Neptune in his 6th house, these influences are apt to play out in his line of work. His natal Neptune falls in the Lunar Return 3rd house, an indication that mysterious influences might be met during travel in the near vicinity. This repeats a theme from his precessed Solar Return, which had return Neptune in the 3rd house.

Pluto occupies the 4th house of this Lunar Return, and is afflicted in opposition with return Mercury. This also represents a potential conflict or confrontation in the course of travel (Mercury). This return Pluto in the 4th house also shows involvement in potential domestic disputes. It is closely square his natal Sun in the 1st house of the return.

With the return showing personal danger and possible violence, and with an emphasis on encounters with others, and with the 6th and 10th houses of work and vocation so in focus, Dan would have been advised to be especially cautious on the job. In his line of work as a police officer, the warnings were clear. Had he known these things beforehand, he could have been more prepared and could have averted the danger.

Timely Transits to the Return Charts

On the night of the frightful 911 call, the transiting Moon was transiting the precessed Solar Return 8th house, and, at the time of the shooting, it was exactly conjunct Solar Return Mars. The combination of the Moon with Mars is very combustible, and it is frequently in evidence in a major aspect at the moment of accidents, injuries, or ill health.

The transiting Moon was conjunct non-precessed Solar Return Mars on the 4th house cusp at the moment he was shot after responding to the 911 call of a domestic altercation. This was an important event timer when combined with the other dangerous indicators for the time period. Such an aspect between the Moon and Mars often coincides with conflicts.

Many other important ties are seen between the event transits and the return charts, with the triggering planets, Mars and the Sun, becoming angular in the precessed returns.

These charts show that no matter which chart method is used, non-precessed or precessed, there will be similar themes, and there will be important links between the Solar Return and a subsequent Lunar Return when major events for the year take place. The Lunar Return will emphasize

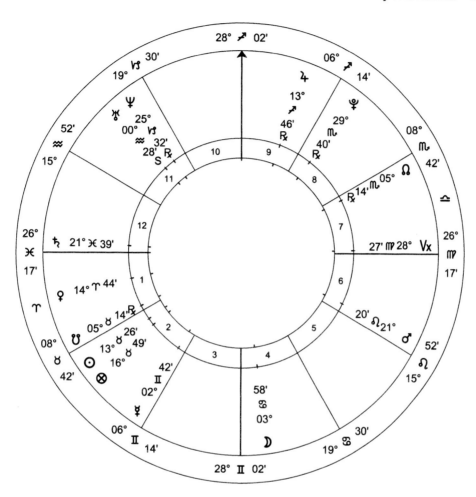

Figure 12f: Event Transit Chart
May 4, 1995; 3:47 AM EST; 85W39, 40N33

themes shown in the Solar Return when such events are about to occur. The Lunar Return provides details and timing.

The Progressed Solar Return Moon

Since the Solar Return Moon progresses at the rate of one degree per month, it offers insights throughout the Solar Return year as it forms aspects to other return or natal planets. At the time of Dan's dangerous encounter and injury, the non-precessed Solar Return Moon had progressed nearly nine degrees, coming to an opposition with Solar Return Mercury. The aspect suggests trouble while traveling, and it often means a person over-reaches in some way. There are often oppositions with others. It is also an aspect of job-related worries and concerns. Similarly, the precessed Solar Return Moon had progressed forward almost nine degrees and came to an opposition with Dan's natal Mercury, echoing the same concerns.

chapter thirteen

The Solar Return Moon

The natal Moon is an important indicator of personality and disposition, and shows the kind of domestic environment we attract over a lifetime. The Moon also reflects on land and property matters, and it describes the important women in our lives. The Solar Return Moon provides these details for the coming year, acting as a gauge to reflect minute fluctuations within the environment and revealing the current conditions and tempo within the home. It further points to the personal concerns and indicates the response we evoke from others. The yearly Moon allows one to experience new emotional qualities. The sign of the Solar Return Moon indicates one's current sensibilities. For example, the Moon in Taurus inclines to emotional stability, whereas an Aries or Gemini Moon tends to be high-strung. The house position indicates an area of emotional stimulation and sensitivity. If the Moon is on an angle, domestic and family issues will be of special importance for the year. If it makes contact to a planet that it also aspects in the natal chart, it shows a time in which that potential will have an opportunity to express. The new aspect is not as important as the reconnecting link.

If the Solar Return Moon is conjunct a natal planet, the nature of the two will combine, either harmoniously or otherwise. If the return Moon is in square to many of the natal planets, especially to the natal Moon or Ascendant, there is a need for personal adjustments in order to appreciate the current potential. Such a necessity is usually apparent near the onset of the return. If making a fortunate aspect to its natal position, environmental circumstances do not require as much adjustment at an emotional level. The natal house occupied by the return Moon shows an area subject to fluctuations.

The Moon's Sign

The qualities of the signs will reveal quite a bit as a preliminary measure in assessing the Moon. In the fixed signs of Taurus, Scorpio, Aquarius, or Leo, the Moon takes on the elements of stability. The emotions are calm and stable, but may also be somewhat inflexible. In the mutable signs of Sagittarius, Gemini, Virgo, or Pisces, the emotions are in a state of flux, as a response to changing conditions. With the Moon in the cardinal signs of Aries, Cancer, Libra, or Capricorn, the emotions are ambitious and ready to initiate changes.

Aries

When the Moon is in Aries, changes are made, often involving the career or the start of a new enterprise. Ambitions are stimulated. With Aries being the pioneer sign, a streak of individualism and self-initiated action is noticed. It is an exciting period. Decisions made are based on the emotions and acted on immediately. With a need to have one's way, advice from others may not be taken. There is often a new element involving the home and domestic life. The position might occur in the chart of someone setting up housekeeping for the first time. It might be a year when a new home is built, or it could signify a move into a new home. There is also usu-ally a masculine element involved. Important women in the life are self-reliant.

Taurus

In Taurus, the Moon indicates material and financial concerns. The actions of another person may influence financial decisions. There are new purchases for the home, and comforts are usually more plentiful, unless there are disagreeable aspects. A security factor links the emotions to the abundance or lack of material resources. Taurus signifies peaceful tranquillity and luxurious surroundings. This is considered to be the best position for the Moon. The senses like gratification here, and there may be a tendency to over-indulge or become lazy and out of shape. A Taurus Moon is conservative and content with the status quo. Important women in the life are grounded and practical.

Gemini

The pace picks up with a Gemini Moon. The domestic environment is full of comings and goings, errands, and things to do. Calls and plans need to be made, correspondence and paperwork become part of the daily routine, and there may be increased involvement with neighbors, young people, or close relatives. Gemini, light and airy, skips around from one thing to another. It may be hard to complete projects or live up to commitments because of frequent changes of mood and focus. Depending on aspects to the Moon, stress can result from this position because of the high levels of randomness. There may be a tendency to gossip. Important women in the life tend to be intellectual or talkative types.

Cancer

All domestic and family affairs are highlighted with a Cancer Moon. There is an attachment to home and family. Ambitions must somehow coexist with family schedules and priorities. All things concerning motherhood are highlighted. Becoming a mother, or having the responsibilities of motherhood emphasized, is common. One's own mother may be a source of concern or someone of a protective nature may play a significant role in life. This does not necessarily have to be a woman, although in many cases it is. Property matters may be in focus. Emotional satisfaction comes from domestic interests and homemaking activities. The personality may be somewhat passive. Important women in the life are warm, maternal types.

Leo

Leo is a nice placement for the Moon. Children, hobbies, romance, and recreational activities come into focus. There's a need to love and be loved. A Leo Moon in the return often corresponds with a time when someone becomes a central figure to the individual. More meaning and satisfaction enters the life of the individual through this association, and he or she may tend to revolve around this person. Other times it is the individual who becomes a central hub to someone else. The position inclines to leadership and independence, and indicates confidence and ease in expressing the emotions. The personality is generous and the outlook positive. This position of the Moon sometimes occurs when there is an emphasis on the "provider" of the home. Important women in the life are dignified and generous.

Virgo

A Virgo Moon brings work conditions into focus. Job or schedule changes or increased dealings with co-workers are highlighted. Others make demands, often the boss, expecting extra service. There could be a situation where no one else seems to be qualified to properly tend to details except the individual. The daily routine can become tedious. There may be a tendency to be overly critical, or to have someone nearby that is. There is a love of analyzing and an enjoyment in the details of life. Getting organized and cleaning out the nooks and crannies of the home often coincide with the placement. Becoming more health conscious, there may be health-related changes, such as visits to the dentist, or taking up a new diet or exercise regimen. Important women in the life are practical and methodical.

Libra

The Moon in Libra seeks balance and harmony in relationships and in the environment. A common result of this position is redecoration of the home. The domestic scene is harmonious unless the Moon is afflicted. A love of decor of any kind is prominent with this position, including one's personal appearance. There is an increase of interest in all forms of beauty, and new activities related to art or music are common. The social life picks up, and the individual enjoys entertaining at home. There is keen sensitivity to the attitudes and reactions of others, especially marriage or business partners. With this position of the Moon, an important relationship may develop, possibly leading to marriage. In an afflicted chart, some adjustment in a relationship might be required. Important women in the life are impartial and attractive.

Scorpio

With a Scorpio Moon, joint finances come into focus. Mortgages, loans, insurance, taxes, or matters surrounding the property of the deceased become central issues. Activity may involve investments to en-

hance future savings. Some aspect of the domestic scene undergoes a transformation. Some physical part of the home itself could break down, requiring major repairs or a series of smaller repairs. Or, some new element may affect the domestic scene. It might be a person who enters or leaves the household. Changes made tend to be permanent. A great deal of willpower and self-control is exhibited. It is a good time to eliminate bad habits. An afflicted Moon here, in combination with corroborating indications, could coincide with divorce, or someone close might require surgery. Important women in the life are passionate and determined.

Sagittarius

With a Sagittarius Moon, educational activities are often highlighted. Classes may be undertaken, or a family member may be taking up new studies or going off to college. Travel is in focus. Long-distance trips might involve a member of the household, or the family might make an important trip. There may be increased involvement with in-laws or dealing with matters at a distance. Religion, legal matters, or publications are other subjects that may become the focus of attention. Since this is a mutable sign, there may be changes in habits, environment, job, or health. In an afflicted chart, unemployment may be drawn, or circumstances may be such that the domestic environment is in a state of flux, with an unclear picture of what lies ahead. Important women in the life are refined and gentle.

Capricorn

With a Capricorn Moon, there are increased responsibilities. This position of the Moon often occurs during a year of important achievements. Gaining prestige and success becomes important, and it is a good time to plan carefully and lay a strong foundation for future advancement. There are more connections to business people in general. This can come from a rise in status or from increased recognition. Issues surrounding the father or a family member are accentuated, with increased responsibilities. If the Moon is afflicted, the individual might feel pressured, restricted, or beset by delays. Health-wise, there is a tendency to catch colds or there may be a need to have dental work done. Important women in the life are practical and cool.

Aquarius

With an Aquarius Moon, the social life intensifies. There are involvements in committees, clubs, forming new friendships, and acquaintances. Affiliations in organizations and associations become more important. One may become connected to a group through the professional arena, possibly becoming a spokesperson. Some new circumstance might considerably alter the lifestyle. Changes may come about abruptly or in unexpected ways. This is an unpredictable period that calls for flexibility. Plans may be altered by last-minute interventions and it may seem difficult to get things to settle. This can be a most exhilarating year. It is important to select friends with care. Important women in the life are intelligent and idealistic.

Pisces

Changes are in store with the Moon in Pisces. Old conditions dissolve and are replaced by new conditions. This is often a period of transition, sometimes a difficult and vulnerable time, when other people may take advantage. One should not be overly trusting. There may be contact with someone who is undergoing physical, mental, or emotional problems. They may have an illness that is hard to define, or they can't tolerate the drugs prescribed to them. If not someone hospitalized, it may be someone who has a drug or alcohol problem with whom there is close contact. There may be a desire for drugs or alcohol as a way to escape the harsh realities of life, though with the Moon in Pisces, there is increased sensitivity to drugs and chemicals, including prescription medications. Important women in the life are trusting and sympathetic.

The House Position of the Solar Return Moon

The house position of the Moon is very revealing. The house position indicates areas of emotional focus and attachment. A person reacts unconsciously to outer stimuli and other people in the department of life governed by the Moon's house position. There are mixed emotions, with frequent changes in mood and attitude toward the people and matters of the Moon's house. This house reveals the kinds of concerns and activities that dominate the domestic life. The Moon indicates fluctuations, so where it lies in the chart shows an area subject to instability or changes.

1st House

With a 1st house Moon, an individual bases decisions on personal preferences as opposed to giving in to others. Even so, there is increased personal sensitivity to others and to environmental factors. Impressionable and nervous, outer elements and the actions of others have a pronounced effect on the individual, who may have frequent mood changes as a response to minute stimuli. Significant changes occur at a personal level. The individual initiates new ventures and may change vocation or location. Others may overly influence the individual, depend-

ing on other factors. There is a tendency to take things personally. Confrontations could arise.

2nd House

The 2nd house Moon shows fluctuations in material resources. There may be an increase or a decrease in the amount of money the individual is able to earn. The emotional focus is drawn to income sources or to problems surrounding possessions. The individual is likely to feel that he or she must build up resources or get property affairs in order. Increased expenditures should be expected. Profitable activities may be those that deal with public interests or with women's affairs. This house represents personal values generally, and emotionally based decisions may reflect changing values.

3rd House

A 3rd house Moon is associated with all forms of communication. It is a very busy time when one takes on and tries to balance several projects and activities. The mind is sensitive, impressionable, and intuitive. There may be a knack for saying what the public wants to hear, making this a favorable time for dealing with clients and customers. Activities related to transportation, shopping, and interaction in the community are more pronounced. There may be more interchange with siblings, relatives, or young people. Moving is usually indicated by either a 3rd house or a 9th house Moon, depending on other factors.

4th House

A 4th house Moon usually shows a close emotional involvement with family members and the home, and one or both may require more attention. This area of the chart relates to how secure an individual feels in terms of foundations and family roots. The emotions are quite sensitive regarding heritage and family background. The position may coincide with a time of subjectivity while a reassessment of these foundations is taking place within the individual. This position signifies parental concerns, with many changes in and around the home and family. The sale or purchase of a home would be appropriate during the year.

5th House

The 5th house Moon signifies a busy social schedule. Parties and pleasurable activities with friends and acquaintances are frequent. There's an accent on children and their training. The birth of a child might occur with this Moon position. Romance may be signified, and the individual might fall head over heels. If the Moon is afflicted, there could be dependency issues, tension, or moodiness. The sense of creativity is pronounced. Hobbies, sports, games, and all kinds of activities that bring pleasure are notable possibilities. For those who are creative in any of the arts, this may be a year of exceptional progress.

6th House

The 6th house Moon coincides with fluctuations on the job. This includes changes in personnel or superiors, changes in schedules, or in the duties of the job. Duties and health matters are the area of emotional focus, subject to nervous reactions. A new interest in health matters is common with this position, and the individual may learn about vitamin supplements or turn over a new leaf in the area of health maintenance. All of those routine tasks necessary to keep life running smoothly seem to command a greater degree of attention than usual. There's a natural sympathy and response to those needing help.

7th House

With the Moon in the 7th house, an individual is supersensitive to the reactions of other people. Changes occur in the individual's important relationships. An engagement or marriage might take place, or another important relationship may be formed. In some cases, there may be a dependency issue or tension connected with a mate or someone else close to the individual.

This position may reflect a confrontation or a break in a relationship if the Moon is afflicted. Open enemies could also be a source of conflict if the Moon is afflicted. There is active participation and cooperation with the public in some way.

8th House

An 8th house Moon commonly emphasizes financial concerns. Activities involving shared resources, budgets, loans, taxes, insurance, wills, or investments are focal issues for the year. There may be an increase in sexual activity or some problem in this area, with partners out of sync. There may be preoccupation with these matters. A fear may be faced or recovery from a loss may coincide with this placement, as it is good for dealing calmly with emergencies or crisis. There may be the death of some situation or condition, followed by a rebirth. If other indications concur, surgery is a possibility.

9th House

The 9th house Moon may indicate a move or travel. There is a longing for faraway places. Trips (or planning for such) and visits from relatives are likely. Fluctuations and changes occur in affiliations. New associations formed with someone from a great distance may prove to be of special significance to the individual. Activities of a legal nature may need tending to. Ceremonies such as weddings, or any ceremony that legalizes an event, may involve a close family member. Educational activities, religion, and involvement with any of the people associated with these may be indicated with this Moon position.

10th House

A 10th house Moon often brings one into the limelight in a personal way. Some amount of publicity is promised, and there is a degree of fluctuation regarding the reputation or status of the individual. A career change might be made. A rise to a position of increased responsibility or authority might mean that the individual must maintain an unusual amount of emotional control in the decision-making processes. Being in the public eye may cause some nervousness, but it also appeals to the individual. Even a wedding could occur at such a time because of the change in status, attendance of guests, and the publicity of the event.

11th House

The 11th house Moon highlights connections with friends and associates. There may be changes involving one's relationship within a certain group or organization. New acquaintances may be met, or an important person may enter the life through a mutual friend. New affiliations come about. The individual is sympathetic to community or group interests, and excited to join with others of similar sentiments. There may be an increased interest in astrology or another scientific field. Resources available to one as a result of career efforts, such as fringe benefits or connections with influential people, have special significance.

12th House

The 12th house Moon usually finds the individual spending time behind the scenes, requiring more solitude. There is an emotional focus on the deeper meaning of life and sympathy for the less fortunate. There may be contacts with hospitals or rehabilitation institutions. Someone closely associated may have a drug or alcohol problem. Situations involving secretive information may be dealt with. The 12th house also rules self-undoing, and an afflicted Moon here may be an indication that the individual becomes his or her own worst enemy. The judgment may be fuzzy, and it is best to carefully consider all possible ramifications before following through on an emotionally based course of action.

Return Moon Aspects

The Moon is so sensitive that it is easily influenced by planets that it aspects. The Moon's aspects in the Solar Return describe influences for the year. If the Moon

forms favorable aspects, the personality is pleasing, the public image is good, and one's home life is in harmony. A favorable Moon is even beneficial for the health, especially for a woman. If the aspects to the Moon are unfavorable, there may be problems in any of these areas and relationships with women may be stressful. If the return has Cancer rising, the lunar aspects are most important. Each of the Moon's aspects is revealing.

Lunar aspects to the Sun reflect the general degree of domestic harmony. They signify the degree of balance between the emotions and the ego. Highly driven, ambitious, and often successful, the hard aspects indicate inner tension. The conjunction, a New Moon, reveals new beginnings relating to the return and natal house position. Sometimes a surge of energy is experienced in connection with the return house in which a New Moon falls. A square indicates domestic friction or emotional tension. An opposition, or Full Moon, indicates completions. Sometimes separations occur with the Full Moon. Even though outer success may come, there may be a search for emotional satisfaction.

Lunar aspects to Mercury reveal the quality of communication between the mind and the senses, influencing speech, memory, concentration, and objectivity. If afflicted, criticism can be damaging.

Links to Venus show an affectionate and loving nature. Domestic harmony and happiness result from the good aspects. Stressful aspects may indicate a need to overcome emotional wounds.

Contacts to Mars reflect public image. Individuality is stimulated, and passion provides a strong start to new projects. Discipline may be required to bring about a completion. Stressful aspects may indicate family conflicts or a health issue.

Aspects to Jupiter reflect harmony in the larger family unit, and opportunities to improve these ties. In positive aspects, generosity, prudence, and cordiality inspire confidence in others. Stressful aspects reflect an excessive or impractical personality.

Lunar contacts to Saturn show a tendency to concentrate on the serious aspects of life. Positive links reflect a sense of responsibility and loyalty that impresses others. Stressful aspects may indicate self-centeredness. A tendency toward dental problems or colds may require precautionary measures.

Aspects to Uranus indicate unforeseen elements influencing home and family. With stressful contacts, reversals may occur as a result of unconscious longing for adventure or a streak of rebelliousness. With positive aspects, a magnetic personality naturally attracts, and original ideas abound.

Contacts to Neptune indicate increased sensitivity. Others are inspired by an idealist approach. In unfavorable aspect, there's a tendency toward confusion and impracticality in setting or reaching goals.

With Pluto, a strong desire to change existing conditions leads to constructive action or destructive maneuvers. In fortunate aspect, one has the ability to energize visions to bring about the desired result. Adverse aspects show a tendency to be pushy, forceful, or impatient with others.

The Solar Return Moon progresses one degree per month, advancing forward twelve degrees over the course of the year. It may form aspects to other returns or natal planets as it progresses. Each aspect formed by this progressing Moon is descriptive of influences during the month of the contact. (Chapter 14 deals more extensively with each planetary aspect.)

PART THREE

The Planets & Other Points

chapter fourteen

Activity & Aspects of the Planets

The aspects rule! The strongest aspects are those involving an angle. The angles are extremely sensitive points, and when a planet connects to an angle, the angle provides an opening through which the planet potential finds maximum expression. The next strongest aspects are those involving the Sun. The Sun enlivens and vitalizes a planet it contacts, enabling it to express. Solar aspects are nearly as potent as aspects involving an angle. One could tabulate the major events in life using only the progressed aspects involving the angles and the Sun.

When major events are forthcoming, the progressed aspects will include angular contacts, or aspects involving the Sun. The return charts will also include close aspects of planets to the angles or to the Sun prior to important events. There are often both types of aspects in the progressions and the returns prior to very significant events in life. Only relatively minor happenings can occur without aspects involving the angles or the Sun. These developments are described by a summary of the planetary aspects in play at any given time.

The planetary aspects supply important details. The nature of a planet describes the realm of likely events to come, and the things it symbolizes will be more evident in life. This is more emphasized if one particular planet becomes prominent due to being involved in multiple aspects. The matters of the house ruled by a planet in aspect become active, influenced by the nature of the aspects. For any one major event to occur, it will need to be shown by more than one aspect.

The aspects involving the Ascendant ruler are consequential and informative. In the progressed and the return chart, these aspects show the kinds of experiences a person attracts.

The strongest progressed planetary aspects are those that reconnect two planets that were in aspect at birth. At times of important events, there will often be an exceptional number of aspects that repeat a planetary link from the natal chart. These are useful in describing the nature of events likely to take place. The natal aspect determines the degree of helpfulness or hindrance from the current contact. The current contact allows the natal potential to manifest. There may be an opportunity to master some lifelong issue or a chance to capitalize on inherent talent. These aspects may form in a number of ways, often in combination throughout the charts when a life-changing event occurs. These repeating links may begin with an aspect between a natal and a progressed planet, or between a progressed and another progressed planet, and then fortification may come from a transiting planet to a natal planet, from a transiting to a progressed planet, and even from a transiting to a transiting planet. This feature of repeating natal links also occurs in the return charts prior to important events.

At the most important junctures in life, natal links will be in evidence, solar aspects will be prominent, and there will be aspects involving the angles.

The progressing Moon often acts to set off events as it forms aspects of reinforcement. For example, if there is an aspect between a planet and an angle and the progressing Moon moves over the angle while the aspect is in orb, this will act as a trigger, bringing about the effects of the aspect. Or, if two planets are in progressed aspect and the progressing Moon aspects either of them, this will often hasten the full effects of the planetary aspect.

Following are the influences of the luminaries, each planet, and their aspects. These will aid the interpretation of planetary prominence and aspects in any chart.

The Sun

The Sun indicates the real purpose in life. The cosmic life work is found in the placement of the Sun, and it rules the individuality and dominant instincts. It represents willpower, leadership, and creativity. It shows the conscious aim and gives the urge to achieve. One seeks spiritual growth in the area of the Sun's sign and house placement. This is where the individual can shine, and where he or she feels alive, working toward achieving expertise. Unusual amounts of strength and potential for success are shown by this placement.

In these dealings, an individual often expresses a masculine attitude.

The Sun provides the energy, vitality, and drive in life. In the birth chart, it gives clues to health and length of life. It signifies power, honor, and glory. Vocation will often be found to coincide with the professions ruled by the Sun sign. As a masculine planet, the Sun also represents important masculine figures. It signifies the father, and in a female horoscope, the husband.

When prominent in the natal chart, the Sun shows one who is dignified and of noble character, or conceited and prideful, depending on its overall condition and aspects.

When the Sun becomes active in the progressions, it represents important times, especially when in aspect with an angle. These aspects stimulate the will to achieve and give increased determination. When prominent, the Sun vitalizes the creative abilities, gives power of leadership, and a sense of independence and enterprise. Unless the natal Sun is very afflicted and unable to bring good tidings, even a square may represent opportunities for advancements. When the Sun is prominent and the aspects are favorable, there is general success and a rise in life. These times coincide with remarkable progress in the life direction and purpose. Honors

may be received, or one is thrown into the limelight. There are opportunities for prosperity and achievements. It is a time to reap rewards and cultivate new opportunities through connections with those of honorable character. Help often comes from superiors or through masculine associations.

In a woman's chart, progressed aspects of the Sun to an angle may indicate marriage. When the Sun forms fortunate aspects in the progressed chart, success and benefits come more easily for the important men in her life. For a man, things go well for his father and for the other important masculine benefactors in his life. Heavy afflictions to the Sun show times of hardship for the masculine benefactors. Their health or fortunes may suffer, impacting negatively in the life of the individual. The progressed aspects of the Sun also tell of the individual's vitality. An afflicted Sun may indicate ill health.

When the aspects of the Sun are unfavorable, obstacles create challenges to progress. There are risks of loss of prestige, or damage to property due to misfortune, improper choices, or false pride. The challenges are to help a person overcome excessive pride or egotism, to develop independence, or to make him or her consciously aware of the real self. The afflicting planets show the source of challenges.

Sun/Moon Aspects

These aspects stimulate a desire for harmonious achievements. There are new attachments and changes. Favorable aspects give the ability to communicate easily and to get along well with others. The ego and the feelings are in harmony, and advancement comes from an expanding consciousness. The Sun increases the recuperative powers and promotes general health. With hard aspects, there are inner conflicts and difficulties in relationships with the opposite sex. There may be ill-advised changes, domestic and family problems, or unpopularity. An opposition may result in inner tension—however this may drive one to attain material success. The emotional state may react negatively on the physical body.

Sun/Mercury Aspects

These aspects stimulate mental activity. The easy aspects enable an easy expression of ideas. These bring opportunities for travel, gains through communication or literary work, and prosperity for siblings. Hard aspects could bring problems through paying insufficient attention to detail, setbacks due to gossip, restlessness, or unwise changes.

Sun/Venus Aspects

These aspects stimulate the affections. Easy aspects bring success in artistic and social affairs. There are new attachments, possible engagement or marriage, and pleasurable activities. A woman with this aspect may have a father or husband who spoils her, as she is the recipient of many gifts and favors. Hard aspects incline to disappointment in matters of the affections. There are difficulties relating to others.

Sun/Mars Aspects

These aspects stimulate the passions and energy. Favorable aspects give confidence and a dynamic disposition. Opportunities to advance personal interests come through energetic action, independent plans, or enterprise. The overall health and vitality improves, and the individual has the energy to tackle whatever is required in order to pursue life goals. Hard aspects may denote conflicts with authorities and career setbacks due to impulsive or rash actions. Losses may occur due to carelessness. These interfere with health, signaling accidents, inflammation, fever, overwork, or strain on the heart. A conjunction may operate either positively or negatively, depending on aspects to the pair.

Sun/Jupiter Aspects

These aspects stimulate the desire to expand materially or experientially. Favorable aspects bring opportunities to gain distinction or honor, often through the help of an influential benefactor. There may be financial rewards, promotion, travel opportunities, or an increase in social standing. Wealth may also increase. Vitality increases and the health is robust, often due to freedom from worry. With hard aspects, the individual may be wasteful, boastful, or have questionable philosophies. Damage to prestige may be due to errors in judgment or overconfidence. It is an unfavorable time to be involved in a lawsuit. Extravagance or self-indulgence may bring financial losses. The same behaviors may negatively impact health.

Sun/Saturn Aspects

These aspects stimulate ambitions. With a favorable aspect, rewards for past hard work come in the form of promotion, often through the help and interest of an older or more experienced associate. Authorities are of assistance. There may be the beginning of a new, long-term venture. There's a readiness to accept responsibility as the power of self-reliance and devotion to duty is strong. With hard aspects there may be heavy responsibilities, hardships, tests, and sacrifices. Delays, restrictions, interference to plans, or reversals for superiors could bring a fall from power. Financial or property losses might occur. There may be trouble for the father, or for the husband in the case of a female. The individual's own health might suffer, and there's a tendency toward depression.

Sun/Uranus Aspects

These aspects stimulate creative energy. With favorable aspects, the individual is spontaneous and has a magnetic quality that attracts and inspires confidence in others. New experiences come through unusual or chance contacts. These aspects denote a change of consciousness and an exciting new chapter in life. There may be connections with groups, societies, or large corporations. The father, or an important man in the life, may be an inspiration, and an original thinker. Adverse aspects incline to eccentric ways, revolutionary tendencies, or rebellious behavior that repels others or makes it hard to fit in. The individual may be prone to reversals or unforeseen misfortune. The father, or another masculine benefactor, may experience a setback, or behaves in unconventional and unpredictable ways. A relationship may break apart, or the health may suffer, sometimes from nervous complaints.

Sun/Neptune Aspects

These aspects stimulate the sympathies. Favorable aspects increase the intuitive faculties and expand the vision and foresight. There are opportunities for enlightenment, and the flow of inspiration is strong. Dreams may materialize. The individual is inspired by mystical forces of a high order, and may find an outlet in artistic pursuits or the occult. The father, or another important man in the life, may be charming and a source of inspiration. The hard aspects may bring a period of confusion. The judgment may be cloudy, leading to unwise associations, activities, or self-betrayal. The individual may be self-deluded, impractical, or have an inflated wish for importance. Connections with drugs, alcohol, or escapist tendencies may cause setbacks. One may fall victim to deceptive practices. Vitality is low and there may be sensitivity to medications. The father or another important man might have a drug addiction or a medical issue.

Sun/Pluto Aspects

These aspects stimulate self-determination. Self-assertive qualities are strong. Favorable aspects provide drive and power to achieve the goals of the ego. The individual is confident of his or her personal power, and is able to mold an image of their choosing. There may be new undertakings or creative changes. There are tremendous inner resources and enormous endurance, strength, and staying power. Any aspect may bring contact with those with whom there is a karmic bond. One might meet with destiny, or enter a new plane of consciousness. With adverse aspects, there may be changes or setbacks due to forces beyond the individual's control. There may

be demanding or disrespectful behaviors, or compulsive tendencies that attract opposition from others. The individual often runs into one conflict after another and does not properly gauge the efforts needed to get the desired effects. There may be an illness or the death of an important masculine figure.

The Moon

The Moon rules the domestic urges, and, just as the Sun rules individuality, the Moon rules personality. The Moon represents the feelings, memory, the senses, and instincts. It represents the domestic impulses and the protective and cherishing impulses. When prominent and in fortunate aspect, the Moon gives sensitivity, adaptability, and sympathy. If afflicted, an individual is moody and passive. The Moon rules women in general, the wife in a male horoscope, and the mother. Relationships with these women are shown by the condition of the natal Moon.

The condition of the Moon also shows how the public reacts to an individual. If it forms nice aspects in the natal chart, other people are favorably impressed. Such a person tends to be kind and even-tempered. With many aspects, fame is a possibility and much public popularity comes to those with a prominent and fortunate Moon. The opposite is true with an afflicted Moon, and such people are un-popular and prone to bad publicity. The sympathies tend to be directed inward, resulting in relationship difficulties. They may be inconsiderate, careless, lazy, or mentally dull. An afflicted Moon might lead to alcohol addiction. Severe natal afflictions might show danger of drowning.

When the natal Moon becomes involved in an aspect with a progressed angle, the sympathetic urges are stimulated. The impulse to nurture and protect becomes strong. There is an increased reaction to sensation, and an urge to enter into new experiences and make changes. With fortunate aspects, there are favorable happenings on the domestic scene in connection with the important women in the life, especially the mother, and there are opportunities for favorable publicity. When the aspects are poor, there may be vocational setbacks or unpopularity, family and domestic problems, or health issues. Functional disorders may result from an afflicted Moon, depending on the natal potential. Aspects involving the natal Moon are longer lasting, and thus a great deal more significant than aspects formed by the progressed Moon.

Aspects formed by the progressed Moon are fleeting, but important. Progressing at the rate of about a degree per month, the Moon acts as a gauge to activity occurring within the domestic scene.

It is especially tied in with such things as childbirth, marriage, and other personal and domestic changes.

The progressing Moon often acts to set off events as it forms aspects of reinforcement to major themes. For example, if two planets are in aspect in the progressions, and the progressing Moon forms an aspect to either planet, this will often hasten the full effects of the planetary aspect. Or, if there is an aspect between a planet and an angle, and the progressing Moon moves over the angle while the aspect is in orb, this will act as a trigger, bringing about the effects of the aspect.

The lunar aspects are more vital in significance when they coincide with the nature of the overall aspects in force. Otherwise they are indicative of likely events and are of a somewhat uncertain influence. If, let's say, Mercury is actively involved in progressed aspects and the progressed Moon passes through the 3rd house, the aspects that it forms from that house are likely to be especially fruitful. Effects would be similar if planets in Gemini were involved in aspects during the progressed Moon's travel through the 3rd house.

If the progressing Moon forms an aspect to a planet and there are no major progressed aspects reaching the peak of their orb to counteract it, the lunar aspect will be quite influential for a couple of months.

When the lunar aspects are adverse, they represent tests to help a person gain improved control of his or her feelings, responding appropriately to instinctual prompting, and to respect the feelings of others.

As the progressed Moon passes through the houses, it brings to the fore the matters associated with that house. This is an area that is susceptible to fluctuations. It is informative to note the natal house and the progressed house occupied by the progressed Moon. As the progressed Moon passes through the signs, it brings focus to matters governed by the sign. When the progressing Moon changes house or sign, there is a noticeable change. The descriptions of the Moon's sign and house position provided in chapter 13 can be applied to the progressed Moon. Following are the influences of the Moon's aspects.

Moon/Mercury Aspects

These aspects stimulate a desire to be active. The mind easily influences feelings. With an easy aspect, the memory is excellent and the individual is fluent in speech and expression. There are opportunities to make new acquaintances and advantageous changes. Activities may involve communication, speaking, literature, scholastics, or travel. There may be pleasant dealings with relatives, siblings, neighbors, or young people. The mother and other women are helpful. In any aspect, domestic or business changes may require careful attention to detail. With poor aspects, the individual may be forgetful and confused in his or her thinking processes. The person may talk glibly, never considering the listener, resulting in disfavor. Adverse changes may result from restlessness. Trouble may arise in connection with travel or education. Other women may be harsh toward the individual. It's a good time to take care in dealing with relatives. There's a tendency to worry, and the health may suffer due to nervous or mental instabilities.

Moon/Venus Aspects

These aspects stimulate a desire for comforts and pleasure. They awaken the artistic inclinations, the impulse for harmony, and the seeking of social contacts. Favorable aspects show good social manners and ease in communications. There are opportunities for domestic happiness, for financial increase, and for achieving social success and popularity. Plans proceed smoothly. There may be special emotional attachments formed (especially for a man) and pleasant occasions surrounding the important women in the life. The poor aspects tend to reverse the foregoing themes. The individual may be lazy, careless, or sloppy. There may be an overeagerness to make attachments or to bestow the affections, resulting in hurt feelings and emotional disappointments. Or, the person may be insensitive to the needs of others, with no real feelings for anyone, therefore being unpopular. It is not the best time to form attachments. Health may suffer from a rich diet.

Moon/Mars Aspects

These aspects stimulate a desire for change and new experiences. There's an urge for adventure and a tendency to take decisive action. With favorable aspects, there are opportunities for advancement through the use of personal drive and initiative. The important women in the life are vivacious and supportive. The individual makes a good presentation and maintains a good public image. A bad public image and attacks on the reputation may result with unfavorable aspects. Setbacks may result from argumentativeness, lack of discretion or tact, or because of impulsive and rash conduct. Unpopularity or making enemies may result. There may be discord in the domestic life, trouble or illness for the wife or another important woman in the life. There is susceptibility toward accident or illness. Impulsive action is often the source of troubles. In extremely rare cases, death in a public place could result, if other aspects supported such.

Moon/Jupiter Aspects

These aspects stimulate the generous and expansive urges. Favorable aspects bring opportunities to form beneficial social contacts and gain prestige, often due to an optimistic outlook. Others have confidence in the individual. There may be an increase of wealth, opportunities to travel, or to increase education. This may bring a very smooth period in the domestic life, with benefits through females. The health improves or becomes more buoyant due to a lack of worries. With unfavorable aspects, there are frequently domestic and family upsets and women may be a source of debt. There is a danger of losses due to bad judgment or extravagance. The reputation may suffer because of overconfidence or arrogant behavior, or due to the disfavor of some woman. Self-indulgence may lead to health issues.

Moon/Saturn Aspects

These aspects stimulate a sense of orderliness and cautious tendencies, and awaken the powers of perseverance. With favorable aspects, the feelings are stable and the individual has good emotional control, but may appear cool and detached. There are opportunities to make progress through a steady application of efforts toward whatever task is at hand. There is a tendency to be focused and undistracted by outside stimuli. The individual is apt to forego outside interests in the pursuit of goals. The home life is stable, and women may be particularly helpful and supportive. With hard aspects, disappointments, lack of prospects, and loneliness may result from an overly cautious, fearful, depressed, or pessimistic outlook and demeanor. Potentially helpful people may be repelled. The domestic life may lack congeniality, or there may be hardships or illness affecting the mother, or the wife if a man. Burdens may be imposed through an association with some woman. Depression may lower resistance to illness.

Moon/Uranus Aspects

These aspects stimulate the powers of originality and bring an urge for self-expression. There is a desire for change and independence. Favorable aspects bring opportunities for advancement due to an eagerness to try new methods. There may be a rise in popularity or fortunate publicity. New contacts are made, and there's an enthusiasm for entering into novel experiences. Domestic improvements may result from a lack of hesitation to initiate changes. Important women in the life are sparkling, effervescent, and helpful. With poor aspects, adverse publicity may result from erratic behavior. Unpopular-

ity or attacks to the character may occur. Unsettling changes may occur suddenly in the domestic sphere. Relationships with women tend to be problematic. The important women in the life may be unstable or inconsistent. Estrangements, separations, or breakups might occur. Nervous tension may affect health adversely.

Moon/Neptune Aspects

These aspects stimulate the sympathies and sense impressions. The imagination is activated. With favorable aspects, there are opportunities to achieve artistic success for those with talent. The individual is intuitive, imaginative, sensitive, and inspired. Emotional response is heightened. There is a charming manner and a mysterious quality leading to favor and popularity. An opportunity to travel may arise. The important women in the life are charming and a source of inspiration. With adverse aspects, the individual may be confused, or a daydreamer who never realizes his or her fantasies. Disappointments may come from investing in relationships with the wrong people. There is danger of being deceived. Or, there may be escapist tendencies, with a general refusal to face the realities of life. Cravings for sensation may lead to drug abuse. The women surrounding one may be irresponsible, confused, or deceitful. Health may suffer from weariness or lack of stamina.

Moon/Pluto Aspects

These aspects stimulate domestic instincts and intensity of emotions. There is a desire for change and adventure, and a desire to take the lead in a group effort. Favorable aspects lead to improvements in the domestic sphere and in family relationships. There's a strong desire to remold the domestic scene to a more perfected state. Opportunities for new contacts and experiences may come through an ability to arouse the emotions of others in a positive way. There may be prophetic tendencies. Hard aspects suggest upsetting changes. Restlessness or compulsive urges may cause setbacks. Stubborn, controlling, or vengeful behavior may arouse the antagonism of other people. Circumstances may throw the domestic scene into one of imbalance and unwanted changes. Trouble may surround the mother or another important woman in the life. There may be digestive problems.

Mercury

Mercury, as the planet of communication, rules the intellectual urges. Mercury gives the power to express thoughts, and shows what a person thinks about and talks about. Mercury is often an indicator of occupation. Mercury represents interpretation, reason, self-expression, and adaptability to the environment.

Mercury is a neutral planet, easily influenced by the sign in which it is placed and by planets making a close aspect. Mercury's manner of functioning can be determined by considering the planet it aspects most closely. Without aspects, Mercury takes on the characteristics of the sign occupied. It is essential to consider Mercury's natal condition and strength before judging its progressed aspects.

When Mercury becomes active through progressed aspects, things ruled by Mercury become prominent. This stimulates the powers of comprehension and perceptions. Activities involving the assimilation of detail and the ability to communicate come to the fore. Important decisions need to be made and it is a busy time in general. The powers of adaptability are tested. Travel, movement, detailed work involving reading, writing, and the communication of ideas, are some of the activities that occupy the mind. There are fleeting contacts with a variety of people. Mercury signifies writers, travelers, speakers, students, teachers, editors, clerks, agents, messengers, young people, neighbors, siblings, and close relatives.

When prominent and forming fortunate aspects, Mercury gives ingenuity, adaptability, and a quick wit. The memory is good, and learning comes easily. It is easy to keep pace while handling many details. There are opportunities for self-expression, for advancing the education, for receiving honors, and general progress as a result of intelligent forethought. If afflicted, Mercury may show a poor memory or learning difficulties. It may show a nervous temperament, or someone who may be superficial and indecisive. Setbacks may occur in the area of vocation or in the family, often due to a lack of forethought or attention to details, or because of petty gossip or restlessness. Excessive worry may affect the health negatively. There is a tendency for the mind to become anxious and overactive.

Adverse aspects of Mercury represent tests to help develop flexibility and versatility on the mental plane, or to overcome carelessness and indecision.

Mercury/Venus Aspects

These aspects stimulate a desire for pleasure and an appreciation for peace and harmony. Easy aspects promote social activities, giving good social manners and ease in communications. Goodwill and the help of other people are attracted due to a cheerful attitude. Progress may be made in artistic fields, or success in matters dealing with communication or travel. Life events tend to promote peace of mind. With hard aspects, slight upsets may result from placing too much attention on pleasures, or due to minor problems with women. Travel may bring a separation between friends.

Mercury/Mars Aspects

These aspects stimulate the mental processes and promote a spirit of enterprise. Easy aspects bring opportunities for progress and advancement as a result of demonstrating initiative. Success may come from activities involving communications, literature, study, travel, or transport. It is a busy time, but the individual is capable of handling extra work, as there is a desire to be doing something constructive. With hard aspects, danger of setbacks or reversals come from unwise judgment, often as a result of overexcitability and impulsive reactions. The individual may be sarcastic in speech, prone to arguments, or to arousing anger in others. Caution is needed in matters relating to agreements, communications, transport, and in dealing with relatives and neighbors. Health issues may result from strain or excessive work.

Mercury/Jupiter Aspects

These aspects stimulate expansive ideas. Favorable aspects promote an optimistic outlook, attracting the interest and help of authorities. Opportunities may lie in the areas of travel, writing, publishing, or education. The individual has sound ideas, and is able to put his or her knowledge to practical use. These show good judgment and a knack for saying the right thing at the right time. There may be success in litigation. With adverse aspects, losses or setbacks may occur due to mistakes in judgment, carelessness, overenthusiasm, or extravagance. Litigation is not favored.

Mercury/Saturn Aspects

These aspects stimulate mental focus and concentration, and they tend toward concerns of a serious nature. Any aspect tends to stabilize the mental processes, and the good aspects are excellent for assisting powers of concentration on deep subject matters. There are opportunities for success in connection with communications, writing, or education as a result of attention to detail, the ability to focus for long periods, or by increasing knowledge. Arduous tasks requiring solitude or exceptional mental stamina may be undertaken. With hard aspects, disappointments may come as a result of a pessimistic attitude or fear of failure. There may be a self-centered focus that repels those who could be of assistance. Delays or difficulties may occur in connection with travel, study, or literary activities, often as the result of flawed

details. Trouble may arise with neighbors or relatives. Health may be affected by a depressed state of mind.

Mercury/Uranus Aspects

These aspects stimulate inventiveness and a broadening mental perspective. They increase boldness and determination. Favorable aspects are excellent for success in connection with communications, publications, travel, and transport. There are opportunities to exercise originality and for accessing new ideas. There are flashes of insight or new insights to facts already known. The individual is witty. Positive changes may involve relatives or neighbors. With hard aspects, setbacks may be connected with communications, literature, study, or travel. Reversals may result from an inflexible adherence to wrong ideas, or by rebelling against a system he or she regards as unfair. There may be abruptness in speech. Nervous tension may result in health or mental problems.

Mercury/Neptune Aspects

These aspects stimulate the powers of the imagination and encourage mental sensitivity. With favorable aspects, the mind is receptive and sensitive, promoting a fine intuition for truth. The individual has a charming, graceful, pleasing manner in speech and writing. Opportunities occur for achieving success in creative work, in connection with communications, literary work, education, or travel. Fresh prospects may open up as a result of contact with new ideas. With hard aspects, the individual may be confused in his or her thinking. Setbacks may come as a result of a lack of purpose and drive, because of vague plans, or due to errors of judgment based on a tendency to self-deception. Reversals may occur due to gossip, deceptions by others, or vague and listless longings for the unattainable. In extreme cases there may be delusions. The health may be impacted negatively by low vitality or an overactive nervous system. A relative may be ill.

Mercury/Pluto Aspects

These aspects stimulate problem-solving tendencies, especially an urge to study hidden elements. The favorable aspect fosters the ability to investigate and get to the truth of matters in order to find the underlying cause of problems. There are good research abilities and resourcefulness in problem solving. These favor study, speaking, and activities in connection with communications, travel, or transport. Adverse aspects bring danger of setbacks or reversals due to wrong ideas, by inner compulsions or obsessive plans to carry out a deed at any cost. There may be tendencies to use manipulation, devious practices, blackmail, or foul means to ob-

tain the object of the desires. In rare cases, there may be the death of a child or near relative. Health risks come from a susceptibility to infections, particularly the lungs, or nervous disorders.

Venus

Venus rules social urges and that which one is instinctively attracted to, whether an object or a person. The center of the affections is shown by Venus' placement in the chart. It shows where and how one seeks happiness. Venus as the Lesser Fortune brings many of the good things in life, such as love, comforts, gifts, protection, and ease. If very afflicted, these things might be denied.

The function of Venus is to harmonize, beautify, soften, enhance, and pacify. Venus signifies florists, cosmetologists, beauty consultants, those who follow an artistic career, or who cater to those pursuing pleasure. It signifies the wife in a male horoscope, and young women in general.

If prominent, Venus gives an affectionate, sympathetic nature, and an attractive personality. In favorable aspect, Venus signifies a person with good taste and one who is likely to be artistic. Such people are easygoing and congenial, and may live a life of comfort and ease. They are popular and well received by others, always making for good company. A prominent Venus, especially in the 1st house, may show physical attractiveness or beauty. Individuals with Venus in favorable aspects receive gifts and have a love of adornment, especially jewelry. If very afflicted, it produces a narcissistic, flirtatious, lazy, and irresponsible disposition. An individual with an afflicted Venus may never truly love, or else their love is not returned except on temporary occasions. They may have poor taste, dressing outlandishly and wearing heavy makeup. Some may be extremely self-indulgent. Absent good morals, they may bring about their undoing. The condition of natal Venus is a strong determining factor when judging Venus' progressed aspects.

When Venus is active in the progressed chart, things signified by Venus become more prominent in the life. These aspects stimulate the emotional affections and a desire to form harmonious relationships. They also stimulate artistic appreciation. Venus is usually prominent and in good aspect at the time of a blooming romance, marriage, childbirth, and other happy occasions. It is often active when gifts or money are received, and when life is merry. An accent on artistic pursuits, decorating, or connections with young women will also find Venus active. When the aspects are unfavorable, there may be misplaced affections leading to separations, disap-

pointments, or losses in love. There's a tendency toward oversensitivity and to let emotional disappointments have too great an effect. There may be an inability to get along with others. An extravagant or lazy nature may bring financial setbacks. A diet of rich and sugary foods may have a negative impact on the health. Adverse aspects of Venus represent tests to help curtail self-indulgence, to curb pleasure seeking, to overcome idleness, and to develop an appreciation for the right use of relaxation.

Venus/Mars Aspects

These aspects stimulate the social and passionate urges, and give a desire for harmony in relationships. The easy aspects give passion and sex appeal, and an ability to get along well with the opposite sex. Relationships are harmonious in general. There are opportunities to form social contacts, to engage in pleasurable activities and to make peace with enemies. With adverse aspects, the individual may still be passionate, but is over-ardent and conflicts may result. There's a need to control the desires.

Venus/Jupiter Aspects

These aspects expand the affections and stimulate a love of ease and comfort. Favorable aspects bring opportunities for gains, honors, professional advancement, and improved finances. This may be the result of increased sociability, or gaining the notice of influential persons. Such individuals enjoy the finer things in life and much happiness. There might be an opportunity to meet a mate of good social standing. Adverse aspects may bring setbacks caused by carelessness, lethargy, poor taste, or sloppy work. There are disadvantages in the social life. Emotional upsets may occur due to a lack of discrimination in the target of the affections. Problems may arise from tendencies to be impractical, snobbish, or boring. Self-indulgence may react negatively on the health.

Venus/Saturn Aspects

These aspects stimulate a tendency to control the emotions. With favorable aspects, advancement opportunities come as a result of sober, steady efforts. Connections with those who are older are often advantageous, an avenue for gaining wisdom. Enduring friendships are established with reliable and steadfast individuals. The individual is steady in his or her affections. The financial situation may improve through long-term investing. The father may come into a prosperous period. With adverse aspects, the emotions may be cold. The individual may be selfish or unsympathetic to others, resulting in disappointments in relationships. There may be an illness in the close family. The health may be adversely affected due to emotional frustrations, a depressed state of mind, or lowered resistance to disease.

Venus/Uranus Aspects

These aspects stimulate the artistic tendencies and raise emotional tension. With favorable aspects, a good imagination and artistic tendencies may bring opportunities for honors and distinction. There is a spontaneity in the personality that makes such people exciting company. The individual is lively, entertaining, and magnetic. Gains may come in sudden or unexpected ways, often through new contacts or from spontaneous transactions. There may be a new love interest. With hard aspects there may be sudden unexpected developments causing emotional distress. The individual is prone to upsets in love, or may be attracted to bad company. Such people may be in love today and indifferent tomorrow. There's a tendency for discordant relationships and sudden interference to settled conditions. Upsets are often a result of difficulty controlling the emotions.

Venus/Neptune Aspects

These aspects stimulate the aesthetic sensibilities, the idealistic urges, and arouse charitable instincts. Favorable aspects bring happy emotional experiences and inner joy. Illumination or enlightenment may come in the form of visions. Artistic, creative inspiration flows easily and there may be an interest in decorating. Financial gains may result from a large-scale venture. Opportunities for increased popularity may come through female associations. There may be a sweet romantic attachment of ideal proportions. In any aspect, there may be a tendency to put those they love on a pedestal. With adverse aspects, there may be misfortunes in affairs of the heart. There may be temporary or permanent separations or misplaced affections may lead to rejection, deception, and strange experiences in love affairs. A desire to make easy money or taking shortcuts to achievements may bring reversals. Too great a desire for personal gratification and self-indulgence brings unpleasant repercussions.

Venus/Pluto Aspects

These aspects stimulate the emotional responses and artistic awareness. With favorable aspects, the mind is cheerful and there are opportunities to make friendships. Latent artistic or creative talents can be developed. These may bring a romantic attraction of karmic proportions. Strong feelings are stimulated in love relationships, sometimes of a very high and pure order. There might be a platonic love, or feelings that a love is fated. With hard aspects, setbacks may occur as a result of an inability to get along with others—judging

others too harshly, or trying to push loved ones into making commitments. There may be disappointments or heartbreak in love. Feelings may not be reciprocated, or disappointments in love may occur due to a connection with someone with immoral tendencies. Faithlessness may be experienced. In rare cases, there could be an illness or death of a loved one. Emotional distress lowers resistance to illness.

Mars

Mars represents the instinctive urge to survive as an individual. It signifies aggression and the urge to start something new. It is a planet of energy and passion. As the ruler of war, in the individual chart Mars indicates the "front line" in life or where one meets and overcomes opposition. It is a point where the individual experiences an instinctive opposition. Mars' energy may be most appropriate when facing danger because Mars' energy is similar to that provided by adrenaline. It gives the urge to flee or fight when facing opposition. Its action is to stimulate, energize, or aggravate.

A well-aspected Mars promotes self-confidence, even fearlessness. It gives good coordination, passion, and initiative, and these people enjoy competition and chances to show their courage. Those who are overly aggressive and combative often have an afflicted Mars, causing a violent temperament. They just can't resist a fight. The individual's actions stir up opposition, and this often works out to his or her disadvantage. The difficult aspects of Mars may indicate a susceptibility to accidents, illness, or conflicts in general. It is essential to consider the natal condition and strength of Mars before judging its progressed aspects.

When Mars becomes active in the progressions, the things ruled by Mars become more prominent in the life. These aspects stimulate drive and energy. Mars arouses passion and the urge to initiate action. There may be dealings or encounters with people in occupations ruled by Mars. It signifies athletes, soldiers, firemen, iron and steel workers, policemen, surgeons, those who carry a weapon, or who work with sharp tools or instruments. It rules men in general, and signifies the husband in a woman's chart.

When Mars is prominent and in favorable aspect there are opportunities to gain success through an energetic application of personal efforts. Successful new undertakings are signified. Energy and initiative is controlled and applied in a way that others do not feel threatened, often leading to an increase of power. In a woman's chart, it may show an opportunity to marry, or it brings the interests of her husband to the fore, with things going well. There may be activity surrounding a male child

or grandchild. These aspects replenish the energy stores, promoting good health. With hard aspects there may be a danger of setbacks due to haste, impulsive actions, or by arousing opposition in others. The actions may be foolhardy or hotheaded. The hard aspects test one's ability to utilize energy in constructive ways, to learn to control the passionate impulses, and to overcome bad temper or aggressiveness. If Mars becomes involved in several hard aspects, serious confrontations or danger may lie ahead. There may be ruin or damage to home or property, sometimes by fire. The important men in the life may fall ill or face problems. Or, there may be personal health issues, from overwork, depletion of energy, feverish complaints, inflammation, or accidents.

Mars/Jupiter Aspects

These aspects stimulate an enthusiastic desire for enterprise and self-expression. Easy aspects bring opportunities for recognition and advancement. They encourage good money-making abilities, and the individual is able to bring in an excess of what he or she can spend. Resources expand. A love of adventure and travel accompany the positive aspects, often with opportunities to undertake successful journeys. A woman with this aspect may marry. Physical energy is increased, and there is good coordination for participation in sports. There may be the birth of a son, or a son may be enjoying a beneficial period. With adverse aspects, the previous themes are reversed. The individual is likely to rush into projects without due consideration and may find him or herself overextended, either financially or in promises made. Legal difficulties, or problems through travel may arise. There is a need to handle resources wisely. It is an unwise time to lend or borrow money.

Mars/Saturn Aspects

These aspects stimulate ambition and determinism. Favorable aspects give willpower, stamina, and staying power. There are opportunities to realize goals and make steady progress through an application of constructive efforts. There are leadership abilities and the individual effectively commands and takes charge of others. With any aspect there may be the undertaking of hard or laborious work. The willpower is tested. Hard aspects may bring disputes as a result of a bad temper, or there may be constant blocks to achievement, sometimes due to stubborn or dictatorial behavior. Trouble may come as a result of overly aggressive tactics. There may be strained relationships with authorities, superiors, or the father. An important man in the life may suffer misfortune. Sometimes there are lost opportunities due to a lack of initiative. The health may suffer from a deple-

tion of energy, excessive physical strain, or accidents.

Mars/Uranus Aspects

These aspects stimulate the forceful inclinations, the creative and innovative instincts. The easy aspects may show genius in some field, and dynamic action involving new concepts or techniques. There may be inventive or mechanical ability, or the use of original methods. There is sufficient willpower, and plans are carried out easily. Success may come swiftly due to a sudden burst of purposeful action. New fields of activity may open up as a result of the breakup of old conditions. In any aspect there may be sudden or unexpected developments. Adverse aspects may show irritability, temper, or badly planned actions that result in setbacks. There's a tendency toward carelessness. Losses may result from entering into ventures that are too novel in nature. For a woman, there may be thorny or complex situations with the opposite sex. Health-wise, there are accident-prone tendencies.

Mars/Neptune Aspects

These aspects stimulate inspirational action based on idealistic desires. Favorable aspects foster a buoyant enthusiasm that appeals to others, often resulting in opportunities. There may be dedication to a cause or acts of kindness. It is easy to persuade others and to enlist their cooperation. Good intuition assists the actions of these individuals. There may be opportunities to travel. An adverse aspect may cause confused actions, often as a result of emotional impulses. There are tendencies toward self-deception and impracticality. The passions and desires for gratification of the senses require control to avoid encounters with unsavory people or situations. There may be bizarre circumstances, treacherous acquaintances, or trouble involving drugs. Health may be affected by a depletion of energy or by exposure to contaminants.

Mars/Pluto Aspects

These aspects stimulate passions and desires. There may be the undertaking of an arduous task. The favorable aspects give extraordinary physical strength and tireless determination to reach goals. Such individuals are courageous and will fight for what is right. There are opportunities to enlist the help of others. By demonstrating confidence and leadership, others are instilled with the same fighting courage and will help clear the way for constructive action. Hard aspects can bring setbacks through acting too forcefully, with disregard for others. An enemy may become particularly vengeful. A jealous nature may attract unpleasant developments in relationships with the opposite sex. Accidents are possible, or

an encounter with violence or danger in some form. There may be health issues or the need for surgery.

Jupiter

Jupiter rules the religious urges. It is representative of the higher mind, wisdom, enthusiasm, expansiveness, optimism, spontaneity, and benevolence. Jupiter's chart position provides information about a person's beliefs. It also shows how a person shares his or her generosity with others. Jupiter's function is to expand, multiply, or bring increase. It is a point of material supply, and the elements of affluence and accumulation are connected with Jupiter. It opens doors, and its chart position indicates the source and method used to attain wealth. A person is positive and optimistic in the department of life represented by Jupiter's house position, thus reaping rewards. Expansiveness is noted in Jupiter's sign position. Jupiter signifies those connected with the law, church, universities, publishing, philanthropy, or big business.

If in fortunate aspect in the natal chart, Jupiter gives generosity, enthusiasm, and wisdom-seeking tendencies. Such a person is fair-minded and good-humored. If afflicted, wasteful, gluttonous, selfish, and overexpansive tendencies may predominate. Overconfidence, self-indulgence, laziness, or an exaggerated sense of self-importance can lead to losses.

When Jupiter becomes active in the progressed chart, it stimulates the powers of growth. There are opportunities to expand on many levels: increasing wisdom, and multiplying possessions or social connections. It brings one into contact with those of a professional class and others ruled by Jupiter.

When Jupiter is prominent and favorably aspected, there are notable increases and expansion, often in the form of financial gains, honors, or advancement. Opportunities result from good judgment and an honest application of effort. Optimism inspires the support of others. Jupiter points to connections with influential people who may be of wise counsel. There may be opportunities to study, to broaden the education, or to travel. There may be increases of joy as the result of happy domestic and family circumstances. Legal ceremonies may take place. With adverse aspects there may be major setbacks as a result of faulty judgment. The reputation may suffer as a result of carelessness or from acting on bad advice. Material losses may result from overoptimism. Trouble may come through legal, educational, religious, or publishing affairs. The health might be adversely affected by an over-indulgent or rich diet. Adverse aspects of Jupiter help the individual learn to control tendencies toward carelessness, mistakes in judgment, extravagance, and overexuberance. They encourage a more philosophical view of life.

Jupiter/Saturn Aspects

These aspects stimulate the power to put resources in order, to develop wisdom and judgment. With favorable aspects the individual is willing to take on increased responsibility as a means of developing judgment and a good business sense. This leads to a gradual expansion of resources. It is favorable for acquiring property and lasting wealth due to the ability to balance the concepts of conservatism and expansion. With hard aspects, there may be missed opportunities due to a lack of initiative or a wish to avoid responsibility. There may be financial struggles or setbacks because of extravagant tastes, and it is unwise to lend money or take financial risks. If the conservative tendencies are stronger, missed opportunities may be the result of a fearful or pessimistic outlook. Actions may be ill-timed due to an overly cautious nature. There may be a gradual depletion of resources. The father may suffer from failing fortunes.

Jupiter/Uranus Aspects

These aspects stimulate the wish for independence. There is a love of freedom, adventure, and travel. The religious instincts may be aroused. With favorable aspects, there are opportunities for success in connection with travel, publishing, religion, law, or education. Financial advances may come from invention or through connections with large corporations or organizations. Progress may be made in the study of occult or unusual subjects. The new and untried are favorable areas to explore. Unexpected happenings tend to work out favorably, sometimes resulting in wealth. Marriage may occur. Adverse aspects give tendencies to take chances that ultimately backfire. Setbacks may occur from entering into an unprofitable commitment during a sudden spurt of enthusiasm. There may be religious disputes or problems involving litigation, publishing, or travel. Debt may be the result of unexpected circumstances.

Jupiter/Neptune Aspects

These aspects stimulate the impulse of generosity, and religious urges. Favorable aspects may bring an increase of status or prestige due to involvement in a charitable enterprise. Sizable financial increases may result from investment in large-scale enterprises, especially if connected to overseas transport or oil. This is the millionaire aspect and the judgment is assisted by good intuition, sometimes revealing a remarkable talent for speculation and for handling financial affairs generally. Gainful opportunities may come through an involvement in religion, law, publishing, travel, or education. The affairs of the house with Pisces on the cusp are strongly accented. Hard aspects may bring difficulties due to impracticality. Financial reverses may arise from relying on unsound hunches or faulty information. Losses may result from connections with dishonest associates. There may be an inflated sense of personal capabilities.

Jupiter/Pluto Aspects

These aspects stimulate the tendencies of expansion and a desire for independence. Favorable aspects bring opportunities for success through an attitude of self-assurance that attracts the confidence and support of higher-ups. Advances or progress may come from an involvement in matters connected with education, religion, travel, law, or publishing. There may be gains through inheritance. With hard aspects there may be a tendency to be wasteful with resources. Setbacks may come from extravagance or from gambling. Impulsiveness may lead to financial problems. Litigation may turn out badly. The illness or death of a friend or family member may result in expenses. Dispersed energy may affect the health adversely.

Saturn

Saturn's presence in the horoscope indicates the urge for safety and security. It is the planet of necessity or lack. What one needs most in life or where there is an awareness of deficiency is shown by the placement of Saturn. For instance, in the 2nd house of finances, it would indicate a lack or loss of, and great need for money. The person might be quite wealthy (if Jupiter is well placed), but would feel the necessity of making every penny count.

Saturn functions to perfect the character through constant trials. It is the task master and represents limitations and responsibilities. Its function is to test, limit, deepen, conserve, inhibit, delay, or restrict. Saturn signifies older, serious people, the father, and those in responsible positions.

Favorable aspects to Saturn give good business abilities, and the individual may become respected for his or her authority in some area. The sense of self-discipline is excellent. There is an ability to forego immediate pleasure in favor of persisting toward increased security later. Such an individual has good integrity and is cautious, loyal, and dependable. They seek perfection. A poorly aspected Saturn may exhibit bad health, a hard life, or the disfavor of authorities. Such people are sometimes depressed and gloomy and prefer to be alone. They may repel others with their attitude of being beaten down. They may be mean, stingy, or selfish, evaluating life in purely material terms. After many hardships and setbacks, they may become unable to take advantage of opportunities that do arise. However, many people with hard aspects to Saturn build character by overcoming obstacles.

When Saturn becomes prominent in the progressed chart, especially through an aspect to an angle, there are opportunities for advancement through hard work and responsibility. These aspects stimulate tendencies toward perseverance and endurance. There is a focus on business and those authorities who are older, respected, and who stand to aid the individual in his or her life direction. When the aspects are favorable, advancement may come as a result of steady efforts, common sense, frugality, and consolidation. One may begin a difficult or long-term project. Acquiring land or property is favored. There are great strides in achievement. With difficult aspects there may be a decline in status or prestige from an unwillingness to accept responsibility or due to a lack of self-discipline. Lost opportunities may result from excessive timidity, apprehension, or lack of confidence. There's a need to develop perseverance toward one constructive goal. Fears and inhibitions may result in low vitality or Saturn-related health issues. The adverse aspects present challenges in order to help the individual overcome a pessimistic or narrow outlook.

Saturn/Uranus Aspects

These aspects stimulate the constructive and organizational abilities. There are opportunities for advancement through determination and an energetic application of efforts. Favorable aspects promote constructive work, sometimes with the help of skilled or insightful associates. There is an ability to make plans carefully and then carry them out. Advanced ideas and imagination combines with discipline and determination. There is good insight and skill in diplomacy. It is easy to adapt to change. Adverse aspects incline toward stressful changes. Changes that break up established conditions produce emotional instability and insecurity that is apt to lead to further disadvantages. There may be an inability to grasp opportunities. Such a person may be disorganized, wastes efforts, or stubbornly sticks to faulty ideas. There may be a lack of self-control or a contradictory nature. A dictatorial attitude may be used in an attempt to overcome misfortune and reversals. Stress may react negatively on the health.

Saturn/Neptune Aspects

These aspects stimulate painstaking devotion to an ideal. The practical side of the nature combines with the idealistic side. Favorable aspects show good concentration and one who is able to bring ideals into reality, often because of superb foresight and the anticipation of forthcoming problems. The imagination is given concrete and practical expression. Intuition blends well with organizational skills. It is easy to feel inspired when doing commonplace tasks. There is joy in doing work for its own sake, and pleasure in serving others. Latent psychic faculties may develop. With hard aspects, lost opportunities may result from ignoring one's intuition. Or, complicated problems or involved circumstances may arise due to the neglect of everyday affairs. Errors in judgment or fanciful notions may override common sense. Sometimes connections are formed with deceptive individuals who may discredit the reputation. Loss of property (sometimes by flooding), or reduced circumstances entails unpleasant tasks. There may be a sense of foreboding. Health may be affected due to lowered resistance, sometimes as the result of pessimism.

Saturn/Pluto

These aspects stimulate the ambitions and encourage persistence. The favorable aspects give great powers of endurance and control. Opportunities come as a result of good inner fortitude, patience, and persistent efforts. The individual is capable of carrying out actions in a very deliberate and careful manner. Even with easy aspects, an individual often tends to frugality and self-denial, and there may be a lack of sympathy for others. Adverse aspects may bring setbacks as the result of a dictatorial attitude or harsh behavior to others. In some cases, an individual may become power hungry, inviting retaliation from others. Hardships may result from entanglements in complicated circumstances with unsavory people. There may be an accident or illness of an older relative.

Uranus

Uranus rules individualistic urges. The house position of Uranus shows the area in which one may behave eccentrically, or where there may be genius, depending on its condition and aspects. It represents originality, inventiveness, independence, and dynamic self-expression. It symbolizes the subconscious desires and that which one is magnetically attracted to. It is where total freedom is needed, so quite often its actions manifest in erratic, spasmodic, or unexpected ways.

The function of Uranus is to awaken, electrify, mobilize, and break down established conditions. It signifies unusual people, inventors, those who work in electronics or who have transcendental interests.

A well-aspected Uranus may show genius, intuitive awareness, and inventiveness. Those who naturally tinker with electronics and the latest technologies often have a prominent and well-aspected Uranus. There may be musical ability, and a lively personality that attracts others magnetically. If scientific areas pose difficulties or there is an aversion to learning the latest methods and techniques, chances are that Uranus is afflicted in the natal chart. Restlessness may lead to erratic actions and a rebellious nature, causing upsets to close friends and family. Sometimes the person is an unreliable, eccentric character.

When Uranus becomes prominent in the progressions, there is an accent on those people and things ruled by Uranus. These aspects stimulate originality and an ability to act in an independent, dynamic manner. With favorable aspects there are opportunities for recognition as a result of independent action and originality. Doors open that lead to new interests. It represents a new era or chapter in the life. Chance encounters or unusual or temporary relationships act as a catalyst to new experiences. Valuable ideas and insights come in a flash. Speedy progress often comes as a result of original ideas to save on time or labor. Opportunities come unexpectedly as Uranus acts suddenly, whether for good or ill. With adverse aspects, setbacks may come as a result of abrupt behavior, or due to stirring up the antagonism of others. Relationships may end, or there may be unexpected changes in circumstances. Restlessness and a craving for novelty may bring the desire to do something, anything, to relieve inner tension, a practice that leads to problems. Adverse aspects present tests to help overcome and control eccentric behavior and to encourage discrimination when it comes to enthusiasm for new ideas or in forming friendships.

Uranus/Neptune Aspects

These aspects stimulate inspiration and an appreciation for new experiences. The study of astrology or metaphysical topics may be taken up. There may be an interest in developing the intuitive faculties through meditation. Favorable aspects may show genius in scientific fields, and an advanced imagination. Opportunities for achievement may come as the result of an ability to combine inspired visions with purposeful action. The creative faculties are enhanced and artistic inspiration flows. Enjoyment may come from an involvement in music. Hard aspects might make one moody, nervous, and high-strung. Setbacks may come as a result of a desire for excitement or independence, leading to sudden ill-advised behavior in an attempt to satisfy cravings. This may cause the loss of friends or allies. Involvement in unhealthy indulgences might lead to reversals. Psychic confusion, with phobias, fears, or anxieties are sometimes problematic. A sense of doubt or apprehension may interfere with the ability to see projects through to a successful end. Anxiety may lead to health issues. In extreme cases, there may be neurotic complaints.

Uranus/Pluto Aspects

These aspects stimulate the inventive powers and the desire for independent action. The favorable aspects show discovery and genius in science. Extensive research leads to new discoveries. Advancement may come as the result of technical or inventive ability. There is an ability to grasp methods used by others and add a distinctive flair. There may be flashes of intuitive perception into the workings of the universe. These give great courage and an urge for independence. There are pioneering undertakings that win recognition. There may be a knack for acting swiftly at the most opportune time. Some may acquire unusual spiritual strength, developing insight. Adverse aspects may lead to problems as a result of an abuse of power. Setbacks may come for some from trying to take the law into their own hands. Others may resort to rage or become violent if things don't go their way. There is too great a need to control the way things go. In rare cases, there may be explosive disruptions in the life, sometimes through natural disasters.

Neptune

Neptune rules the utopian urges and inspiration. It is the planet of dreams and visions, imagination, subconscious thoughts, what one thinks about when not consciously directing thoughts. It represents intuition, illusion, idealism, sympathy, and compassion.

Neptune signifies those of an artistic, mystical, or highly sensitive nature. It signifies those in occupations having an element of unreality about them, such as pilots, actors, or photographers. Psychics and others with unusual talents of vision usually have a prominent Neptune. It also signifies those who care for the sick or institutionalized, whether physically ill, mentally disturbed, or incarcerated for crimes. Those whose work involves narcotics, alcohol, drugs, oils, or chemicals are under the rays of Neptune. Neptune's function is to dissolve or loosen boundaries, to greatly expand, to distort, inflate, refine, or sensitize.

When born strongly under the rays of Neptune, there is a certain charm and mysterious quality to the personality. These people are always a bit different or strange. Some are glamorous. If well aspected, Neptune gives good intuition and shows someone who is highly idealistic. There is inspiration and a highly advanced imagination. Such people may appear refined and fragile. They enjoy peace and tranquillity, which nourishes their psychic forces. Emotionally, they are receptive and have great powers of sympathy and compassion for others. Neptune badly aspected means the individual may be deceptive, wearing a mask to throw others off his or her true nature. Or, they may crave the unattainable, sometimes falsely glamorizing an unworthy person or object, becoming subject to abuse. There may be self-deception, disillusionment, treachery, deceit, or distorted views. Such a person might be messy and make no attempt to improve, choosing to escape reality through drugs, alcohol, fantasy, or even sleep. Perversions may be in evidence.

When Neptune becomes active in the progressions, the compassionate instincts are awakened and the artistic, idealistic, and visionary sensibilities are stimulated. These aspects expand the horizons and bring contacts with things and people ruled by Neptune. There is a loosening of old bonds leading to the forming of new ones. With easy aspects, there is inspiration and the fulfillment of dreams. Travel opportunities may arise, especially by air or water. Latent psychic faculties may awaken for development, or there may be profound mystical or spiritual experiences. In any aspect, sacrifices may be made for the sake of some ideal. With adverse aspects, disappointments may come as a result of striving after the unattainable. Setbacks may occur due to a lack of practicality or integrity. There may be connections with deceptive persons. Adverse aspects test the ability to distinguish between true and false, between the real and not real. Sensitivity to drugs, alcohol, and medications increase. Health may be affected by a lack of vitality or wasting diseases. Some tend to hypochondria.

Neptune/Pluto Aspects

These aspects stimulate a desire to transcend boundaries. There is a striving after some ideal. Favorable aspects incline to compassion and understanding of others. There is an ability to see others as they really are. Opportunities come through clear-sightedness and a highly developed intuition. There may be artistic endeavors, or mystical and spiritual interests. Efforts to develop the sensitivities may include the practice of meditation. There may be selfless service. Adverse aspects may bring setbacks due to instability or impracticality. Connections with unworthy companions may be the undoing. There may be obsessions or giving in to temptations. The individual may be the victim of deceptive or hostile characters. Or, his or her actions are misunderstood. Health may be affected by sensitivities to drugs, alcohol, or various contaminants. In some cases, there may be a deep-seated fearfulness that has no real basis.

Pluto

Pluto represents the urge to regenerate, eliminate, renew, and bring to the surface hidden conditions so that they may be transformed into a new source of power. Pluto signifies those who work beneath the surface in some way, from miners to psychologists, and those whose work deals with death or refuge. It rules underworld characters, uniformed workers, and scientists. Pluto's function is to isolate, intensify, purge, destroy, undermine, transmute, reinforce, or add a new dimension. Pluto is reputed to deal with karma, institutions, and police activity. Discovered at a time when organized crime and kidnappings were making headlines, Pluto stamped its significance with these issues upon its entry to our awareness.

Those who have Pluto prominent in the natal chart by an angular position and/or many aspects will be more responsive to its particular vibrations. With good aspects, the willpower is highly developed, and the person is able to stand on his or her own. There is an understanding of group psychology. These people may be leaders of reform movements that will affect the masses. Adversely aspected, Pluto may show jealousy and a forceful disposition. There may be strange compulsions or obsessive notions, sometimes leading to disastrous consequences.

When Pluto becomes prominent in the progressions, especially if an angle is involved, the urges represented by Pluto become prominent in life. These aspects stimulate the impulse to uncover and draw upon resources of all types including mental, physical, spiritual, emotional, and financial. There is a desire for regeneration, revival, and renewal. The urge to enter into a new phase of experience or to join in some group effort is strong. With favorable aspects, opportunities for advancement come through new enterprise, by leading a group, or through group involvement. In any aspect, there are connections or contacts with those ruled by Pluto. Adverse aspects may lead to coercion by a group, or the individual's own ruthless behavior may bring setbacks. A crisis in personal affairs might bring a complete alteration of character. Adverse aspects of Pluto bring challenges to test a person's ability to resist domination by mass opinion, sticking to his or her legitimate aims, to avoid obsessions, and to purify the self on all levels.

chapter fifteen

Eclipses & the Lunar Nodes

Throughout history, eclipses have been considered as very powerful phenomena. In early times astronomy and astrology were undivided, and because religious and other ceremonies were set to take place in accordance with the stars, priests were the acting astrologers. Only the influential were privy to these services, and leaders ruled their lands accordingly. Eclipses were noted to be of significance when preceding broad-scale events. When occurring within three degrees of the Sun, Moon, or Midheaven of a leader, they were regarded with much anticipation as reflecting upon destined events, often well into the future.

Little time is required to trace eclipses and monitor triggering transits, with results well worth the effort. This chapter examines eclipses and nodal activity occurring in the horoscope. A table of eclipses from 1900 through 2050 is provided at the end of the chapter for easy reference.

Eclipses

Eclipses occur when the New or Full Moon takes place within close proximity to one of the lunar nodes (within 18.5 degrees for a New Moon and within 12 degrees for a Full Moon). The first type is a Solar Eclipse, occurring at the conjunction of the Sun and Moon. Here, the Moon comes between the earth and the Sun. Depending on one's location, the Moon may cut off the light of the Sun. The second type is a Lunar Eclipse, taking place at the opposition of the Sun and Moon. During a Lunar Eclipse, the earth comes between the Sun and Moon and cuts off the light of the Sun to the Moon.

Usually, two Solar and two Lunar Eclipses occur each year as the Sun moves into the zodiacal sign occupied by either the North or South Lunar Node, although sometimes there are more. Each single eclipse belongs to a larger family series of eclipses. The family consists of up to seventy eclipses. Starting at the top or bottom of the globe, the family series spirals downward or upward until reaching the opposite pole. As one family series nears its demise, another takes over, resulting in an increase of yearly eclipses. That was the case in the year 2000. Eclipses also run in cycles, with the longest of these cycles lasting 1,260 years. Sequential years show eclipses within neighboring degrees and frequently in the same sign.

An eclipse is like a super New Moon or a super Full Moon, initializing the potential for important changes and transitions to occur in the matters signified by the position of the eclipse in the horoscope. The nodal influence magnifies the influence of the New or Full Moon and portends karmic experiences. We are evolving at a faster rate in the matters of the house where an eclipse falls.

When an eclipse falls on a significant point in the chart, such as on a natal or a progressed planet, dynamic events may be traced to the eclipse. Such an eclipse is a prelude to experiences and activities symbolized by the eclipsed planet. When falling within three degrees of a planet, it greatly sensitizes the planet to later transits. The eclipse starts a process that brings fresh invigoration and cleansing energy to areas of life represented by the planet.

The intensity of an eclipse is determined by how close it occurs to one of the nodes. The closer the Sun or Moon to the North or South Node, the more powerful the eclipse and the greater its potential effects. Initial activity usually begins shortly following an eclipse, often at the next New or Full Moon. Sometimes the initial activity stimulated by an eclipse can occur several days prior to the actual eclipse. The length of time the eclipse degree is prone to receiving stimulation is determined by the length of time the eclipse lasts. An eclipse degree is sensitive for at least a year and may be triggered by major transits for three to four years.

The transits of Mars and Saturn are most powerful as they cross an eclipsed degree. Mars will often stimulate and start dynamic events connected with an eclipse and Saturn will often bring the final conclusion. Mars frequently activates an eclipse, shortly following an eclipse, although Saturn's transit may come much later. When an eclipse falls on a planet, any of the outer planet transits across the eclipse degree may bring important happenings in connection with the nature of the planet.

The most significant eclipses are those that fall on the Sun, Moon, Ascendant, Midheaven, or the ruler of an individual's horoscope. An eclipse starts a process of transformation, and it shows where change is due. Eclipses sometimes point to imbalances in our personal lives and raise our consciousness to these. When an eclipse falls on one of these important personal significators, it usually means that noteworthy changes lie ahead. There may be a change of residence or a change of vocation, especially with an eclipse falling on an angle. Sometimes there are relationship changes or other personal changes. Angular eclipses are most notable for bringing substantial transformations, sometimes with a change in one area of life leading to many other changes in rapid succession, like a domino effect.

With an eclipse to the Sun, important decisions are made, and such an eclipse impacts the sense of personal power. When the Moon receives the rays of an eclipse, domestic and family changes are usually on the horizon. Each of the planets represents specific areas that are subject to change and transformation.

An eclipse calls individuals to their personal destinies, so when significant changes or karmic connections lie ahead, an eclipse will announce it ahead of time.

Sometimes the energy of an eclipse feels invigorating, like riding an ocean wave, or like being picked up by an incredible force and carried along. Positive developments happen with little effort. Other times, an eclipse may feel like an energy drain, when efforts are required to wrap up an old phase of experience. The process of transformation associated with an eclipse is always desirable in the long run. Eclipses help move us along our path and fulfill our purpose.

Even when an eclipse does not precisely spotlight a personal planet, a full set of eclipses sweeps slowly through all the various horoscope sectors approximately every nineteen years, invigorating and bringing cleansing energy to each department of life in a timely fashion. The horoscope houses each correspond with a specialized area of life experience. Eclipses show when transformations are coming and encourage us to take stock of each of these life areas on a regular basis. This is the first place to check for imbalances or needed changes. Often, we are aware of the need for change, but understanding a little about the people and affairs of a house can help jog our awareness.

From the following brief house descriptions, you can begin to assess the departments of life where current eclipses are falling for stagnant energy, a need for change, something you've been putting off, and so on. The house position of an eclipse shows where a more healthy state of affairs can evolve. If an eclipse falls on a personal planet, check the description of the house it naturally corresponds with to learn the likeliest events to follow. The eclipsed planet indicates the people and things that are highlighted and undergoing changes. These guidelines can be applied to the natal, progressed, or Solar Return charts.

The 1st house governs your personality, temperament, appearance, and physical health. Attributes of the 1st house show the color lens through which you view the world and the experiences you attract, based upon the first impression you make on others. Your attitude is changing, and you are apt to take everything more personally when an eclipse falls in this house. You become more health conscious, and you may initiate significant personal changes, even altering your appearance. The key phrase for this house is "I am," and it corresponds naturally with Mars. You may put forth great personal efforts and sometimes confrontations might result. It is a good time to guard the health.

The 2nd house governs your income-earning power, portable possessions and property, and general finances and resources. It indicates how you earn and spend your money. It also reveals your value system and how you set your priorities. There may be income changes, or you may make or spend big money with an eclipse falling in this house. The key phrase is "I have," and this house naturally corresponds with Venus. There is a reassessment of the finances, material assets, and creature comforts.

The 3rd house governs your mentality, communications, short trips, vehicles, immediate environment, relatives, neighbors, and siblings. It's the house of basic concepts, ideas, and written and spoken agreements. Communication and transportation are key issues. Life is busy with errands, contracts, and paperwork with an eclipse falling here. The key phrase is "I think," and this house naturally corresponds with Mercury. The mind becomes activated, and there may be an attachment to ideas.

The 4th house governs your home, family, parents, heritage, and real estate. It reveals the way you feel about yourself on the inside, based upon the degree of security and foundation provided to you from your heritage and background. Home and domestic and family matters are all important with an eclipse falling here. The key phrase is "I feel," and this house corresponds naturally with the Moon. Sensitivity is heightened. Getting along with others may be a key issue. Women's interests are in focus.

The 5th house governs love, children, romance, artistic expression, entertainment, sports, and speculation. This house corresponds to the urge to create something that will live on. Children, the pursuit of pleasure, friendships, and hobbies are highlighted with an eclipse falling here. Self-image may be at a high or low point. The key phrase for this house is "I will," and it corresponds naturally with the Sun. The sense of personal power is in focus.

The 6th house governs routine responsibilities, schedules, duties, service, occupation, co-workers, employees, health maintenance, and pets. Jobs, schedules, or new diet and exercise regimens are some of the things that come into focus with an eclipse falling here. The key phrase is "I analyze," and this house corresponds to Mercury. There may be changes in duties.

The 7th house governs "others" who attract your attention. This house rules marriage partners, business partners, adversaries, open enemies, counselors, and advisors. This is an important relationship house and multiple relationships are apt to be transformed with an eclipse falling here. The key phrase is "I balance," and this house corresponds naturally with Venus. There might be karmic attractions or separations.

The 8th house governs taxes, insurance, inheritance, shared property, and resources as opposed to the personal resources and earnings of the opposite house. It rules regenerative processes, sex, and death. You may take out a loan or have concerns about debts when an eclipse falls here. The key phrase is "I desire," and this house corresponds to Pluto. Permanent changes follow. Intense relationships may develop.

The 9th house governs higher learning and the abstract mind, long-range vision, philosophy, professors, religion, publishing, propaganda, and long journeys. It is an outer extension of the 3rd house. It rules in-laws and travelers. Education or travel may come into focus with an eclipse falling here. The key phrase is "I see," and this house corresponds to Jupiter. There's an urge to expand, and wisdom is tested.

The 10th house governs public reputation and status, profession, career, and authority figures. Whereas the 4th house is the most private area, the 10th house is the most public area and where you gain notice. You'll definitely get noticed with an eclipse falling here, so be prepared. The key phrase is "I use," and this house corresponds to Saturn. There may be a need to take on greater responsibility.

The 11th house governs friends, social groups, long-term hopes, wishes, and ideals. It is an outer extension of the 5th house; here creative goals are shared in common with a whole group. Changes in friendships, clubs, and affiliations are likely to follow an eclipse falling here. The key phrase is "I know," and this house corresponds with Uranus. There may be dynamic new associations. Sudden changes may occur.

The 12th house stores past deeds. It governs the subconscious mind, dreams, secrets, behind the scenes activities, recovery, confinement, or retreat. Introspection or the desire for solitude may follow an eclipse falling here. The key phrase is "I believe," and this house corresponds with Neptune. A period of transition is at hand. You might travel.

All together, the houses govern every single activity, association, interest, and so on.

As with any chart delineation, all factors should be taken into consideration when judging the possible outcome of an eclipse. If there are beneficial aspects to other planets in the chart, an eclipse to the Sun, Moon, Midheaven, or Ascendant may be a real blessing.

The Lunar Nodes

The nodes themselves, though nothing more than a point of intersection of orbital paths and not planetary bodies at all, show a point for potentially dynamic activity.

The names Dragon's Head and Dragon's Tail differentiate the North and South Nodes. The North Node is ascending and

of a positive nature. Both in the natal horoscope and in transit, it provides a positive influx of energy and power. It has been identified with Jupiter, and embodies a joining, expanding quality. In the natal chart it is related to dharma, or the direction we should be going this lifetime. The South Node is descending, and of a separating, limiting quality, akin to Saturn. It points to a place where we perform at a somewhat unconscious level, and it may indicate a point of self-dissipation. It shows where we might slip into unbecoming behavior. A planet in conjunction with one of the nodes in the birth chart may be influenced by the attending node to be either an innate source of fortune and honor or one of potential mishandling and self-undoing.

The transiting North Node appears to bestow special strength and a blessing, while the South Node reflects an area of potential vulnerability. The matters of the house of the North Node transit get the most attention, while the matters of the house of the South Node transit require the most caution.

Always opposite one another, the Lunar Nodes travel backward through the zodiac and take approximately nineteen years to complete a cycle. Showing the time and place of climax as they move slowly in transit to stimulate natal planets and points, the effects are as notable as outer planetary transits, sometimes coinciding with remarkable events. There is an up-beat tempo or increased focus on the matters governed by the houses of the nodal transit. We are evolving at a faster rate in those departments of life. We are having experiences that add to our wisdom in those areas. There are usually opportunities and an uplift in the affairs governed by the house of the North Node transit. There may be a drain, a downshift or sacrifices relating to the matters of the house of the South Node transit. Similarly, when a node passes over a personal planet, life lessons are at hand in the matters symbolized by the planet. The nodes represent a connection to time, space, and people.

Events related to the nodes often appear to be somewhat fated or karmic in nature. Traveling backward a little more than one degree per month, as they contact personal planets, they may show a time to correct imbalances that have built up in connection with the nature of the planet and with the issues signified by the area of the chart ruled by the planet. It often appears that an individual has very little control over events and is somewhat pulled into the current and swept along. The nodal transit times the result of past choices. The North Node contact is usually the more desirable transit, as it often brings expansion or growth relating to the planet contacted. With the South Node contact, there may be vulnerabilities or sacrifices attached

to the things ruled by the planet. Karmic debts and past obligations are attributed to the South Node, while the accruing of karmic rewards and favors are linked to the North Node.

Transiting nodal conjunctions with a natal planet, and conversely, the conjunction of a transiting planet with a natal node, place a great emphasis on the planet involved in the contact. These contacts can be relied on to forecast probable events in keeping with the nature of the planet and the particular node.

When it is a transiting planet passing over a natal node, the individual is encouraged (North Node) or forced (South Node) to take some action in the matters signified by the planet, utilizing the free will. There is an eye to the future (North Node) or an eye on the past (South Node). Other people, described by the planet making the contact to the node, are willing to lend their support when the planet crosses the North Node. Others, described by the planet, ask something of you when the planet contacts the South Node. Previously neglected problems are handled when a transiting planet contacts the South Node. The matters of the house ruled by this transiting planet will also experience uplift or a downshift, determined by which node is contacted. The same thing occurs when the nodes transit a natal or progressed planet—the node determines whether the matters of the house ruled by the planet will experience uplift or downshift.

The following are some guidelines for interpreting the nodes in combination with important planets or points. These will aid the interpretation of the nodes in any chart.

Nodes with the Sun— Natal/Progressed/Transit

With a nodal conjunction to the Sun in the birth chart, there are life lessons involving the right use of individuality and will. The node making the contact determines how much notice can be achieved and how much freedom of spirit opportunities will provide for. The North Node with the Sun brings personal elevation and recognition, although arrogance sometimes results. With South Node conjunct the Sun, there may be a lack of self-esteem, or it is hard to gain recognition. They may do best by using their inborn leadership skills on behalf of others. Some individuals suffer from a lack of physical vitality. Sun conjunct North Node is more auspicious for material growth and Sun conjunct South Node is more favorable for spiritual growth.

A North Node transit to the natal or progressed Sun brings changes in recognition of a positive sort, following some initial inner stress and tension. There are usually increased opportunities, elevation, and successes of a personal nature. There is newfound freedom. Important acquaintances are made, opening new doors. A South Node transit to the natal or progressed Sun brings changes in recognition, often with unexpected problems cropping up. The ego and identity are somewhat suppressed or forced into a downshift, and it is difficult to maintain status and position. There may be low self-esteem or feelings of despair.

When the Sun transits the natal North Node, there's a boost of energy, and helpful supporters extend opportunities. When the Sun transits the natal South Node, there's a need to make adjustments and serve others. Also, check the house ruled by the Sun to find the area influenced by the nodal contact.

Nodes with the Moon— Natal/Progressed/Transit

With a nodal conjunction to the Moon in the natal chart, there are life lessons involving the right use of the sympathies. The disposition and outlook is lighter with North Node conjunct the Moon, while a more serious tone is noted when South Node conjuncts the Moon. Themes surrounding motherhood or a mother figure are virtually always accented. There are often talents in vocations that cater to women. Frequently leading to popularity, many political figures have this aspect.

With South Node conjunct the Moon, there are difficult relationships with women and sometimes discomfort in a crowd. There might be anxieties.

A North Node transit to the Moon brings changes in mood and temperament, with increased sensitivity. There are new domestic conditions and changes involving family members. Women play a significant role in the life. A South Node transit to the Moon brings changes in mood and temperament. The emotions are blocked or melancholic. The imagination may work overtime, causing excessive fears or paranoia. Personal, domestic, or family changes may bring some upset.

When the Moon transits the natal North Node, there may be gains through a woman. Someone plays a positive, nurturing role in your life. This is a fleeting contact. When the Moon transits the natal South Node, women's interests and health issues are in focus, and you may be required to serve in a nurturing role. Check the house ruled by the Moon to find the department of life influenced by the nodal contact.

Nodes with Mercury— Natal/Progressed/Transit

With a nodal conjunction to Mercury in the birth chart, there are life lessons involving the right use of intellect and communication. North Node with Mercury indicates progressive thinkers, sometimes with a knack for promoting their bright ideas at just the right time to gain support. Anyone using a pen or the hands is favored. For some with South Node conjunct Mercury, there may be learning difficulties, memory problems, or ideas are out of sync with current trends. In extreme cases, the nodal influence on Mercury interferes with discretion, which can lead to severe setbacks.

A North Node transit to Mercury brings a busy time with desirable changes in job, environment, or communications. The mind is active and needs an outlet. Important discussions, plans, and decisions take place. Travel is highlighted. A South Node transit to Mercury brings job and other changes of a dismal nature. Areas of contracts, communication, and travel are likely to become complicated and unsatisfactory. Ideas may be challenged. There may be nerves and anxiety, or feelings of being unable to cope.

When Mercury transits the natal North Node, there is news and information of an uplifting sort, having a futuristic tone. There are favorable contacts with agents. When Mercury transits the natal South Node, news and information tend to present challenges, and it is time to wrap up previous obligations. Schedules, travel, or communication may experience snags. The house ruled by Mercury is impacted.

Nodes with Venus— Natal/Progressed/Transit

With a nodal conjunction to Venus in the natal chart, there are life lessons involving the right use of the affections. Social ease, a pleasing personality, and creature comforts are often indicated by this contact. These individuals are social creatures, moving in and out of social circles, distributing their personal charm to increase the joy and happiness of others. Potential for success lies in pursuits that cater to the happiness or entertainment of others. Those with South Node conjoined with Venus are born with exceptional artistic gifts and talents, but for some the love life and the social life suffer, leading to loneliness and isolation.

A North Node transit to Venus usually brings an increase in the social life. There is the need for a reassessment of the finances and/or affections. Sometimes a karmic attachment begins. There may be a financial increase. A South Node transit to Venus usually brings a low point when it comes to affections, romance, and feelings. One must watch for misdirected priorities when it comes to love and money. The finances may undergo a squeeze, and the social life is unsatisfactory.

When Venus transits the North Node, the social life picks up and there may be gifts or money coming in. It is an indulgent period, and there are connections with young women. When Venus transits the South Node, there is some general disharmony, often with relationship or financial problems. There may be extra expenses. Check the house ruled by Venus to find the area of life influenced by this nodal contact.

Nodes with Mars— Natal/Progressed/Transit

With a nodal conjunction to Mars in the birth chart, there are life lessons involving the right use of strength, passion, and drive. These people are endowed with stamina, intensely involved in life. Athletes, pioneers, and adventurers are in this group. Skills in science, engineering, or entrepreneurship may be present. The temper is sensitive and prone to misfire. When the South Node is conjunct Mars, excessive strain on the body may gradually weaken it. There may be difficult relationships with the opposite sex.

A North Node transit to Mars results in new enterprises: taking on large projects and a tendency to push the physical limits. Courage increases and the urge may come on suddenly to do big things that one would normally not consider. Significant experiences may revolve around a masculine figure. A South Node transit to Mars makes it easy to make mistakes in launching new projects or undertakings. Circumstances may block progress. Conflicts are common. Difficulties come through masculine figures. The energy is low, and the physical health may be vulnerable.

When Mars transits the North Node, the energy level is high and there is increased initiative. A large project may be undertaken. When Mars transits the South Node there may be conflicts or differences of opinion, often dealing with the unsatisfactory results of past actions. Effort is required to control impatience and anger. The matters of the house ruled by Mars are also influenced by the nodal contact.

Nodes with Jupiter— Natal/Progressed/Transit

With a nodal conjunction to Jupiter in the natal chart, there are life lessons involving the right use of wisdom and acquisition. There's a strong accent on philosophy. There are very definite belief systems, usually with an urge to spread the word and set standards. They may use their wisdom to contribute to the social morals in a positive way, or negatively if they are narrow and forceful, with social or religious philosophies that cross with society. Some are born into prominence and money.

A North Node transit to Jupiter brings expansion (sometimes weight gain). There is a reappraisal of the financial affairs. Extra money coming in may only cover an increased amount going out. Large expen-

ditures may bring gains of a spiritual or philosophical sort. A South Node transit to Jupiter brings unexpected expenditures, shortages or depletions of a financial sort. Over-expansion is a problem. One may take large risks that prove to be the undoing, seeing opportunities where there are actually drawbacks.

When Jupiter transits the North Node, it is a feel-good contact, tempting to take on too much and make big promises. There may be opportunities to travel or study. When Jupiter transits the South Node there is a re-evaluation of beliefs and philosophies. Travel or legal affairs may prove troublesome. The house affairs ruled by Jupiter are affected according to the influence of the node that Jupiter contacts.

Nodes with Saturn— Natal/Progressed/Transit

With a nodal conjunction to Saturn in the birth chart, there are life lessons involving the right use of ambition. Self-discipline and self-reliance are strong, along with patience and the ability to take on hefty responsibility. Achievements come from methodology and organization. There are usually conservative qualities. Some with South Node conjunct Saturn are bound to old mindsets and methods. Others are miserly, selfish, and ignore social duties.

A North Node transit to Saturn brings rewards for sustained efforts and hard work in the past. An older person may provide guidance. Relationships begun now or circumstances entered into have a good chance for long-term survival, especially if of a professional nature. A South Node transit to Saturn places considerable restrictions on the life efforts. There are obstacles and heavy responsibilities. Authority figures present problems or there may be disturbances, upsets, or losses that connect to older folks. There may be colds or Saturn-related health problems.

When Saturn transits the North Node, there may be material expansion. The outlook is mature and practical, and one enjoys increased recognition. When Saturn transits the South Node, efforts are required to deal with problems put off in the past. Restrictions crop up, and it is hard to find supporters. The matters of the house ruled by Saturn undergo uplift or downshift, determined by the influence of the node contacted.

Nodes with Uranus— Natal/Progressed/Transit

When there is a nodal conjunction to Uranus in the natal chart, there are life lessons involving the right use of creative flair and inventiveness. There is frequently a streak of brilliance or genius. Scientists, creative people, and those who introduce new techniques are in this group. Life comes at them in surprising ways; they meet with unusual or sudden situations. With the South Node contact, they may be nervous or eccentric. At worst they become weird and outlandish in the methods they use to solve problems.

A North Node transit to Uranus brings chance meetings or brief encounters that are significant, acting as a catalyst to new experiences. Unexpected developments tend to have a positive outcome. There are interests in Uranus-ruled fields such as astrology, computers, gadgetry, and technology. A South Node transit to Uranus brings unexpected developments from out of the blue. This is a disruptive and destructive vibration. Stability is lacking. It is a time to protect the reputation and avoid unwise risks, as there is increased vulnerability for scandals or black marks against one.

When Uranus transits the North Node, chance meetings may lead to positive developments. Unusual ideas or unconventional methods are entered into. Activities ruled by Uranus go well. When Uranus transits the South Node there may be very uncertain or surprising incidences. One may be thrown into forced changes when least expecting it. The matters of the house ruled by Uranus are impacted by the contact.

Nodes with Neptune—
Natal/Progressed/Transit

When there is a nodal conjunction to Neptune in the natal chart, there are life lessons involving the right use of vision and the psychic sensitivities. There may be visionary gifts and much artistic and creative potential. There is usually an attraction to the sea, and a love of travel. One pitfall of the conjunction is easy addiction to drugs or alcohol. Some prefer a reclusive life. Intrigue may touch the life in some way.

A North Node transit to Neptune stimulates the imagination—this is often a creative trend. Previously untapped artistic talents may reveal themselves. The intuition is stronger and more reliable, and spiritual or psychic experiences may occur. One may feel highly inspired, loving, and sympathetic toward others. Successful journeys are made. A South Node transit to Neptune brings a confusing or unsettled period. One's direction may be unclear. There may be intrigue or connections with deceptive people. The imagination is excessive, and sometimes there are fearful feelings that something is wrong. Travel is unsatisfactory.

When Neptune transits the North Node, it is often a spiritually enlightening period. One may feel very blessed—empathetic and giving to others. Life is divine. When Neptune transits the South Node one often prefers to avoid facing problems and pretends that all is well, sometimes using some method to escape reality such as sleep, drugs, or alcohol. The house affairs ruled by Neptune are impacted.

Nodes with Pluto—
Natal/Progressed/Transit

When there is a nodal conjunction to Pluto in the birth chart, there are life lessons involving the right use of power. Such a person may be good at strategy. In highly evolved individuals, it stimulates a deep interest in the meaning of life, a search for truth and illumination. Others use their power to manipulate, getting caught up in unrelenting power games and struggles. These conjunctions sometimes signal a brush with some form of violence at some point in the life.

A North Node transit to Pluto brings a change in consciousness with some significant and permanent change in the life. One is ready to confront obstacles, and there is increased power and inner strength to make changes that were previously put off. It is a constructive period with the power to greatly improve circumstances. A South Node transit to Pluto brings new conditions. There may be intense and complicated relationships, often with power struggles or confrontations. Some profound event may act as a catalyst to new experience and a change of consciousness. There may be closure of some significant issue.

When Pluto transits the North Node, it is a constructively regenerating period. One is able to work with situations, conditions, and resources to build up and improve various life areas. When Pluto transits the South Node there's a need to adapt to new conditions and circumstances. It is a transforming, regenerating influence, but it may tend to bring some disruption. The matters of the house ruled by Pluto are impacted.

Nodes with the Angles or Natal Nodes

Some of the most significant life developments take place when the Moon's nodes transit the angles of the chart. These transits often coincide with major events or turning points in life. A move, a marriage, a job change, or some other significant personal change may take place.

Since the nodes seem to show where something might happen, the nodes conjunct an angle bring this focus to a more personal level. A transit of the North Node to the Ascendant often brings an especially opportune time. An individual comes into a period of successful timing, in step with the universe. It is a coming-out phase. One tends to set the pace and special notice may be due. There may be mishaps when the South Node transits the Ascendant.

The self-confidence may be at a low point, or there may be concessions to make for others. Relationship changes occur with the transits of the nodes to the Ascendant. Transits of the nodes to the MC/IC axis often coincide with professional or home and family changes.

A major crossroad appears when the nodes realign with their natal position. This indicates karmic transitions as an old phase of growth and experience comes to an end and one enters into new experiences with new lessons to come.

Interpreting the Nodes in Return Charts

The above descriptions will help interpret the nodes in the return charts, whether it is a transiting node on a natal planet or a return planet conjoined with one of the natal nodes. Additionally, if the return chart contains a return planet in conjunction with one of the return nodes, the above descriptions can be applied to gain insights, especially according to the house location of the conjunction, which will be impacted by the influence. The nodes magnify the potential of any planet they contact. In conjunction with another transiting planet, they intensify the potential of the planet, according to the particular nodal influence.

Table of Eclipses

The following table provides eclipse data from the year 1900 through 2050. Rounded to the nearest degree, they are labeled with an S or an L to indicate a Solar or Lunar eclipse and are further defined as follows:

A = Annular: Refers to a Solar Eclipse in which the Moon is at such a distance from the Earth that the apex of its shadow falls short of the Earth's surface. In this case, the Moon's body will not entirely obliterate the Sun and a narrow rim of light will surround the dark body of the Moon.

T = Total: Refers to a Solar Eclipse in which the apex of the Moon's shadow approaches the equatorial regions. This and the Annular are Umbral Eclipses, meaning that the Moon's disc is fully contained within that of the Sun. Where there is an appreciable separation in latitude, the result is a partial eclipse. In the table, these partial eclipses have no further definition following the S.

U = Umbral: Refers to a Lunar Eclipse in which the Moon definitely enters the Earth's shadow.

P = Penumbral: Refers to eclipses of the Moon in which the Moon approaches closely enough to the Earth's shadow to cause an appreciable diminution of light, although it does not directly touch it. Not technically classified as eclipses, the conditions closely resemble those of an eclipse, and the phenomenon often produces effects similar to an actual eclipse.

Check eclipses occurring within a three-degree orb to the Sun, Moon, Midheaven, or Ascendant, as well as to other planets. Then track the subsequent transits of planets to this degree, especially those of the Sun, Mars, and Saturn. The Sun and Mars should show activity related to the planet that was initially involved in the eclipse, and Saturn may coincide with a wrap-up of the particular issue relating to the eclipse process. The other transiting planets may also bring their specific energy to an eclipsed degree on an important point, more so than if the natal planet had not been eclipsed.

For more on interpreting eclipses, please refer to the author's book *Eclipses: Predicting World Events & Personal Transformation*.

For more on interpreting the lunar nodes, please refer to the author's book *Lunar Nodes*.

Date	Degree/Sign	Eclipse Type	Date	Degree/Sign	Eclipse Type
05-28-1900	07 ♊	S - T	10-21-1911	28 ♎	S - A
06-12-1900	22 ♐	L - p	11-06-1911	13 ♉	L - p
11-22-1900	00 ♐	S - A	04-01-1912	12 ♎	L - U
12-06-1900	14 ♊	L - p	04-17-1912	27 ♈	S - T
05-03-1901	13 ♏	L - p	09-26-1912	03 ♈	L - U
05-18-1901	27 ♉	S - T	10-10-1912	17 ♎	S - T
10-27-1901	04 ♉	L - U	03-22-1913	01 ♎	L - U
11-11-1901	18 ♏	S - A	04-06-1913	16 ♈	S
04-08-1902	18 ♈	S	08-31-1913	08 ♍	S
04-22-1902	02 ♏	L - U	09-15-1913	22 ♓	L - U
05-07-1902	16 ♉	S	09-29-1913	06 ♎	S
10-16-1902	23 ♈	L - U	02-24-1914	06 ♓	S - A
10-31-1902	07 ♏	S	03-11-1914	21 ♍	L - U
03-28-1903	07 ♈	S - A	08-21-1914	28 ♌	S - T
04-11-1903	21 ♎	L - U	09-04-1914	11 ♓	L - U
09-20-1903	27 ♍	S - T	02-13-1915	24 ♒	S - A
10-06-1903	12 ♈	L - U	03-01-1915	10 ♍	L - p
03-01-1904	11 ♍	L - p	07-26-1915	02 ♒	L - p
03-16-1904	26 ♓	S - A	08-10-1915	17 ♌	S - A
03-31-1904	10 ♎	L - p	08-24-1915	00 ♓	L - p
09-09-1904	17 ♍	S - T	01-20-1916	29 ♋	L - U
09-24-1904	01 ♈	L - p	02-03-1916	14 ♒	S - T
02-19-1905	00 ♍	L - U	07-14-1916	22 ♑	L - U
03-05-1905	15 ♓	S - A	07-29-1916	07 ♌	S - A
08-14-1905	22 ♒	L - U	12-24-1916	03 ♑	S
08-30-1905	06 ♍	S - T	01-08-1917	18 ♋	L - U
02-09-1906	20 ♌	L - U	01-23-1917	22 ♑	S
02-23-1906	04 ♓	S	06-19-1917	28 ♊	S
07-21-1906	28 ♋	S	07-04-1917	12 ♑	L - U
08-04-1906	11 ♒	L - U	07-18-1917	26 ♋	S
08-19-1906	26 ♌	S	12-14-1917	22 ♐	S - A
01-13-1907	23 ♑	S - T	12-28-1917	06 ♋	L - U
01-29-1907	08 ♌	L - U	06-08-1918	17 ♊	S - T
07-10-1907	17 ♋	S - A	06-24-1918	02 ♑	L - U
07-24-1907	01 ♒	L - U	12-03-1918	11 ♐	S - A
01-03-1908	12 ♑	S - T	12-17-1918	25 ♊	L - p
01-18-1908	27 ♋	L - p	05-14-1919	23 ♏	L - p
06-14-1908	23 ♐	L - p	05-29-1919	07 ♊	S - T
06-28-1908	07 ♋	S - A	11-07-1919	14 ♊	L - U
07-13-1908	21 ♑	L - p	11-22-1919	29 ♏	S - A
12 07-1908	15 ♊	L - p	04-18-1920	28 ♈	S
12-23-1908	01 ♑	S - T	05-02-1920	12 ♏	L - U
06-03-1909	13 ♐	L - U	05-17-1920	27 ♉	S
06-17-1909	26 ♊	S - T	10-27-1920	04 ♉	L - U
11-27-1909	04 ♊	L - U	11-10-1920	18 ♏	S
12-12-1909	20 ♐	S	04-08-1921	18 ♈	S - A
05-08-1910	18 ♉	S - T	04-22-1921	02 ♏	L - U
05-23-1910	02 ♐	L - U	10-01-1921	08 ♎	S - T
11-01-1910	09 ♏	S	10-16-1921	23 ♈	L - U
11-16-1910	24 ♉	L - U	03-13-1922	22 ♍	L - p
04-28-1911	07 ♉	S - T	03-28-1922	07 ♈	S - A
05-12-1911	21 ♏	L - p	04-11-1922	21 ♎	L - p

Date	Degree/Sign	Eclipse Type	Date	Degree/Sign	Eclipse Type
09-20-1922	27 ♍	S - T	09-03-1933	11 ♓	L - p
10-05-1922	12 ♈	L - p	01-30-1934	10 ♌	L - U
03-02-1923	12 ♍	L - U	02-14-1934	25 ♒	S - T
03-17-1923	26 ♓	S - A	07-26-1934	03 ♒	L - U
08-26-1923	02 ♓	L - U	08-10-1934	17 ♌	S - A
09-10-1923	17 ♍	S - T	01-04-1935	14 ♑	S
02-20-1924	01 ♍	L - U	01-19-1935	29 ♋	L - U
03-05-1924	15 ♓	S	02-03-1935	14 ♒	S
07-31-1924	08 ♌	S	06-30-1935	08 ♋	S
08-14-1924	22 ♒	L - U	07-16-1935	23 ♑	L - U
08-30-1924	07 ♍	S	07-30-1935	07 ♌	S
01-24-1925	04 ♒	S - T	12-25-1935	03 ♑	S - A
02-08-1925	20 ♌	L -U	01-08-1936	18 ♋	L - U
07-20-1925	28 ♋	S - A	06-18-1936	28 ♊	S - T
08-04-1925	12 ♒	L - U	07-04-1936	12 ♑	L - U
01-13-1926	23 ♑	S - T	12-13-1936	22 ♐	S - A
01-28-1926	08 ♌	L - p	12-27-1936	06 ♋	L - p
06-25-1926	03 ♑	L - p	05-25 1937	04 ♐	L - p
07-09-1926	17 ♋	S - A	06-08-1937	18 ♊	S - T
07-24 1926	01 ♒	L - p	11-18-1937	26 ♉	L - U
12-18-1926	27 ♊	L - p	12-02-1937	10 ♐	S - A
01-03-1927	12 ♑	S - A	05-14-1938	23 ♏	L - U
06-15-1927	23 ♐	L - U	05-29-1938	08 ♊	S - T
06-28-1927	07 ♋	S - T	11-07-1938	15 ♉	L - U
12-08-1927	16 ♊	L - U	11-21-1938	29 ♏	S
12-23-1927	01 ♑	S	04-19-1939	29 ♈	S - A
05-19-1928	28 ♉	S - T	05-03-1939	12 ♏	L - U
06-03-1928	13 ♐	L - U	10-12-1939	19 ♎	S - T
06-17-1928	26 ♊	S	10-27-1939	04 ♉	L - U
11-12-1928	20 ♏	S	03-23-1940	03 ♎	L - p
11-27-1928	04 ♊	L - U	04-07-1940	18 ♈	S - A
05-08-1929	18 ♉	S - T	04-21-1940	02 ♏	L - p
05-23-1929	02 ♐	L - p	10-01-1940	08 ♎	S - T
11-01-1929	09 ♏	S - A	10-16-1940	23 ♈	L - p
11-16-1929	24 ♉	L - p	03-13-1941	22 ♍	L - U
04-12-1930	23 ♎	L - U	03-27-1941	07 ♈	S - A
04-28-1930	08 ♉	S - T	09-05-1941	13 ♓	L - U
10-07-1930	14 ♈	L - U	09-20-1941	28 ♍	S - T
10-21-1930	28 ♎	S - T	03-02-1942	12 ♍	L - U
04-02-1931	12 ♎	L - U	03-16-1942	26 ♓	S
04-17-1931	27 ♈	S	08-11-1942	19 ♌	S
09-11-1931	18 ♍	S	08-25-1942	02 ♓	L - U
09-26-1931	03 ♈	L - U	09-10-1942	17 ♍	S
10-11-1931	17 ♎	S	02-04-1943	15 ♒	S - T
03-07-1932	17 ♓	S - A	02-19-1943	01 ♍	L - U
03-22-1932	02 ♎	L - U	07-31-1943	08 ♌	S - A
08-31-1932	08 ♍	S - T	08-15-1943	22 ♒	L - U
09-14-1932	22 ♓	L - U	01-25-1944	05 ♒	S - T
02-24-1933	05 ♓	S - A	02-08-1944	19 ♌	L - p
03-11-1933	21 ♍	L - p	07-05-1944	14 ♑	L - p
08-05-1933	13 ♒	L - p	07-19-1944	28 ♋	S - A
08-20-1933	28 ♌	S - A	08-04-1944	12 ♒	L - p

Date	Degree/Sign	Eclipse Type	Date	Degree/Sign	Eclipse Type
12-29-1944	08 ♋	L - p	05-24-1956	03 ♐	L - U
01-13-1945	24 ♑	S - A	06-08-1956	18 ♊	S - T
06-25-1945	04 ♑	L - U	11-17-1956	26 ♉	L - U
07-09-1945	17 ♋	S - T	12-02-1956	10 ♐	S
12-18-1945	27 ♊	L - U	04-29-1957	09 ♉	S
01-03-1946	13 ♑	S	05-13-1957	23 ♏	L - U
05-30-1946	09 ♊	S	10-22-1957	00 ♏	S
06-14-1946	23 ♐	L - U	11-07-1957	15 ♉	L - U
06-28-1946	07 ♋	S	04-03-1958	14 ♎	L - p
11-23-1946	01 ♐	S	04-18-1958	29 ♈	S - A
12-08-1946	16 ♊	L - U	05-03-1958	13 ♏	L - U
05-20-1947	29 ♉	S - T	10-12-1958	19 ♎	S - T
06-03-1947	12 ♐	L - U	10-27-1958	04 ♉	L - p
11-12-1947	20 ♏	S - A	03-24-1959	03 ♎	L - U
11-28-1947	05 ♊	L - p	04-07-1959	18 ♈	S - A
04-23-1948	03 ♏	L - U	09-16-1959	23 ♓	L - p
05-08-1948	18 ♉	S - T	10-02-1959	09 ♎	S - T
10-17-1948	25 ♈	L - p	03-13-1960	23 ♍	L - U
10-31-1948	09 ♏	S - T	03-27-1960	07 ♈	S
04-12-1949	23 ♎	L - U	09-05-1960	13 ♓	L - U
04-28-1949	08 ♉	S	09-20-1960	28 ♍	S
10-06-1949	14 ♈	L - U	02-15-1961	27 ♒	S - T
10-21-1949	28 ♎	S	03-02-1961	12 ♍	L - U
03-18-1950	28 ♓	S - A	08-11-1961	19 ♌	S - A
04-02-1950	13 ♎	L - U	08-25-1961	03 ♓	L - U
09-11-1950	19 ♍	S - T	02-04-1962	16 ♒	S - T
09-25-1950	03 ♈	L - U	02-19-1962	00 ♍	L - p
03-07-1951	17 ♓	S - A	07-17-1962	24 ♑	L - p
03-23 1951	02 ♎	L - p	07-31-1962	08 ♌	S - A
08-16-1951	23 ♒	L - p	08-15-1962	22 ♒	L - p
09-01-1951	08 ♍	S - A	01-09-1963	19 ♋	L - p
09-15 1951	22 ♓	L - p	01-25-1963	05 ♒	S - A
02-10-1952	21 ♌	L - U	07-06-1963	14 ♑	L - U
02-25-1952	06 ♓	S - T	07-20-1963	28 ♋	S - T
08-05-1952	13 ♒	L - U	12-30-1963	08 ♋	L - U
08-20-1952	28 ♌	S - A	01-14-1964	24 ♑	S
01-15-1953	25 ♑	S	06-09-1964	19 ♊	S
01-29-1953	10 ♌	L - U	06-24-1964	04 ♑	L - U
02-13-1953	25 ♒	S	07-09-1964	17 ♋	S
07-10-1953	18 ♋	S	12-03-1964	12 ♐	S
07-26-1953	03 ♒	L - U	12-18-1964	27 ♊	L - U
08-09-1953	17 ♌	S	05-30-1965	09 ♊	S - T
01-04-1954	14 ♑	S - A	06-13-1965	23 ♐	L - U
01-18-1954	28 ♋	L - U	11-22-1965	01 ♐	S - A
06-30-1954	08 ♋	S - T	12-08-1965	16 ♊	L - p
07-15-1954	23 ♑	L - U	05-04-1966	14 ♏	L - p
12-25-1954	03 ♑	S - A	05-20-1966	29 ♉	S - A
01-08-1955	17 ♋	L - p	10-29-1966	06 ♉	L - p
06-05-1955	14 ♐	L - p	11-12-1966	20 ♏	S - T
06-19-1955	28 ♊	S - T	04-24-1967	04 ♏	L - U
11-29-1955	07 ♊	L - U	05-09-1967	18 ♉	S
12-14-1955	22 ♐	S - A	10-18-1967	24 ♈	L - U

Date	Degree/Sign	Eclipse Type	Date	Degree/Sign	Eclipse Type
11-01-1967	09 ♏	S - T	03-13-1979	23 ♍	L - U
03-28-1968	08 ♈	S	08-22-1979	29 ♌	S - A
04-12-1968	23 ♎	L - U	09-06-1979	13 ♓	L - U
09-22-1968	00 ♎	S - T	02-16-1980	27 ♒	S - T
10-06-1968	13 ♈	L - U	03-01-1980	11 ♍	L - p
03-17-1969	27 ♓	S - A	07-27-1980	05 ♒	L - p
04-02-1969	13 ♎	L - p	08-10-1980	18 ♌	S - A
08-27-1969	04 ♓	L - p	08-25-1980	03 ♓	L - p
09-11-1969	19 ♍	S - A	01-20-1981	00 ♌	L - p
09-25-1969	03 ♈	L - p	02-04-1981	16 ♒	S - A
02-21-1970	02 ♍	L - U	07-16-1981	25 ♑	L - U
03-07-1970	17 ♓	S - T	07-30-1981	08 ♌	S - T
08-16-1970	24 ♒	L - U	01-09-1982	19 ♋	L - U
08-31-1970	08 ♍	S - A	01-24-1982	05 ♒	S
01-29-1971	06 ♒	S	06-21-1982	00 ♋	S
02-10-1971	21 ♌	L - U	07-06-1982	14 ♑	L - U
02-25-1971	06 ♓	S	07-20-1982	28 ♋	S
07-22-1971	29 ♋	S	12-15-1982	23 ♐	S
08-06-1971	14 ♒	L - U	12-30-1982	08 ♋	L - U
08-20-1971	27 ♌	S	06-10-1983	20 ♊	S - T
01-16-1972	25 ♑	S - A	06-25-1983	04 ♑	L - U
01-30-1972	10 ♌	L - U	12-04-1983	12 ♐	S - A
07-10-1972	19 ♋	S - T	12-19-1983	28 ♊	L - p
07-26-1972	03 ♒	L - U	05-14-1984	24 ♏	L - p
01-04-1973	14 ♑	S - A	05-30-1984	09 ♊	S - A
01-18-1973	29 ♋	L - p	06-13-1984	23 ♐	L - p
06-15-1973	25 ♐	L - p	11-08-1984	16 ♉	L - p
06-30-1973	08 ♋	S - T	11-22-1984	01 ♐	S - T
07-15-1973	23 ♑	L - p	05-04-1985	14 ♏	L - U
12-09-1973	18 ♊	L - U	05-19-1985	28 ♉	S
12-24-1973	03 ♑	S - A	10-28-1985	05 ♉	L - U
06-04-1974	14 ♐	L - U	11-12-1985	20 ♏	S - T
06-19-1974	28 ♊	S - T	04-08-1986	19 ♈	S
11-29-1974	07 ♊	L - U	04-24-1986	04 ♏	L - U
12-13-1974	21 ♐	S	10-03-1986	10 ♎	S - T
05-11-1975	20 ♉	S	10-17-1986	24 ♈	L - U
05-24-1975	03 ♐	L - U	03-29-1987	08 ♈	S - T
11-03-1975	10 ♏	S	04-13-1987	24 ♎	L - p
11-18-1975	26 ♉	L - U	09-22-1987	00 ♎	S - A
04-29-1976	09 ♉	S - A	10-06-1987	13 ♈	L - U
05-13-1976	23 ♏	L - U	03-03-1988	13 ♍	L - p
10-22-1976	00 ♏	S - T	03-17-1988	28 ♓	S - T
11-06-1976	15 ♉	L - p	08-27-1988	04 ♓	L - U
04-03-1977	14 ♎	L - U	09-10-1988	19 ♍	S - A
04-18-1977	28 ♈	S - A	02-20-1989	02 ♍	L - U
09-27-1977	04 ♈	L - p	03-07-1989	17 ♓	S
10-12-1977	19 ♎	S - T	08-16-1989	24 ♒	L - U
03-24-1978	04 ♎	L - U	08-30-1989	08 ♍	S
04-07-1978	17 ♈	S	01-26-1990	07 ♒	S - A
09-16-1978	24 ♓	L - U	02-09-1990	21 ♌	L - U
10-01-1978	09 ♎	S	07-21-1990	29 ♋	S - T
02-26-1979	07 ♓	S	08-06-1990	14 ♒	L - U

Date	Degree/Sign	Eclipse Type	Date	Degree/Sign	Eclipse Type
01-15-1991	25 ♑	S - A	06-10-2002	20 ♊	S - A
01-29-1991	10 ♌	L - p	06-24-2002	03 ♑	L - p
06-26-1991	05 ♑	L - p	11-19-2002	28 ♉	L - p
07-11-1991	19 ♋	S - T	12-04-2002	12 ♐	S - T
07-26-1991	03 ♒	L - p	05-15-2003	25 ♏	L - U
12-21-1991	29 ♊	L - U	05-30-2003	09 ♊	S - A
01-04-1992	14 ♑	S - A	11-08-2003	16 ♉	L - U
06-14-1992	24 ♐	L - U	11-23-2003	01 ♐	S - T
06-30-1992	09 ♋	S - T	04-19-2004	30 ♈	S
12-09-1992	18 ♊	L - U	05-04-2004	15 ♏	L - U
12-23-1992	02 ♑	S	10-13-2004	21 ♎	S
05-21-1993	01 ♊	S	10-27-2004	05 ♉	L - U
06-04-1993	14 ♐	L - U	04-08-2005	19 ♈	S - T
11-13-1993	21 ♏	S	04-24-2005	04 ♏	L - p
11-29-1993	07 ♊	L - U	10-03-2005	10 ♎	S - A
05-10-1994	20 ♉	S - A	10-17-2005	24 ♈	L - U
05-25-1994	04 ♐	L - U	03-14-2006	24 ♍	L - p
11-03-1994	11 ♏	S - T	03-29-2006	09 ♈	S - T
11-17-1994	26 ♉	L - p	09-07-2006	15 ♓	L - U
04-15-1995	25 ♎	L - U	09-22-2006	29 ♍	S - A
04-29-1995	09 ♉	S - A	03-03-2007	13 ♍	L - U
10-08-1995	15 ♈	L - p	03-18-2007	28 ♓	S
10-23-1995	00 ♏	S - T	08-28-2007	05 ♓	L - U
04-03-1996	15 ♎	L - U	09-11-2007	18 ♍	S
04-17-1996	28 ♈	S	02-06-2008	18 ♒	S - A
09-26-1996	04 ♈	L - U	02-20-2008	02 ♍	L - U
10-12-1996	20 ♎	S	08-01-2008	10 ♌	S - T
03-09-1997	19 ♓	S - T	08-16-2008	24 ♒	L - U
03-23-1997	04 ♎	L - U	01-26-2009	06 ♒	S - A
09-01-1997	10 ♍	S	02-09-2009	21 ♌	L - p
09-16-1997	24 ♓	L - U	07-07-2009	15 ♑	L - p
02-26-1998	08 ♓	S - T	07-21-2009	29 ♋	S - T
03-12-1998	22 ♍	L - p	08-05-2009	14 ♒	L - p
08-07-1998	15 ♒	L - p	12-31-2009	10 ♋	L - U
08-21-1998	29 ♌	S - A	01-15-2010	25 ♑	S - A
09-06-1998	14 ♓	L - p	06-26-2010	05 ♑	L - U
01-31-1999	11 ♌	L - p	07-11-2010	19 ♋	S - T
02-15-1999	27 ♒	S - A	12-21-2010	29 ♊	L - U
07-28-1999	05 ♒	L - U	01-04-2011	14 ♑	S
08-11-1999	18 ♌	S - T	06-01-2011	11 ♊	S
01-20-2000	01 ♌	L - U	06-15-2011	24 ♐	L - U
02-05-2000	16 ♒	S	07-01-2011	09 ♋	S
07-01-2000	10 ♋	S	11-24-2011	03 ♐	S
07-16-2000	24 ♑	L - U	12-10-2011	18 ♊	L - U
07-30-2000	08 ♌	S	05-20-2012	00 ♊	S - A
12-25-2000	04 ♑	S	06-04-2012	14 ♐	L - U
01-09-2001	20 ♋	L - U	11-13-2012	22 ♏	S - T
06-21-2001	00 ♋	S - T	11-28-2012	07 ♊	L - p
07-05-2001	14 ♑	L - U	04-25-2013	06 ♏	L - U
12-14-2001	23 ♐	S - A	05-09-2013	20 ♉	S - A
12-30-2001	09 ♋	L - p	05-24-2013	04 ♐	L - p
05-26-2002	05 ♐	L - p	10-18-2013	26 ♈	L - p

Date	Degree/Sign	Eclipse Type	Date	Degree/Sign	Eclipse Type
11-03-2013	11 ♏	S - T	09-07-2025	15 ♓	L - U
04-15-2014	25 ♎	L - U	09-21-2025	29 ♍	S
04-28-2014	09 ♉	S - A	02-17-2026	29 ♒	S - A
10-08-2014	15 ♈	L - U	03-03-2026	13 ♍	L - U
10-23-2014	00 ♏	S	08-12-2026	20 ♌	S - T
03-20-2015	29 ♓	S - T	08-27-2026	05 ♓	L - U
04-04-2015	14 ♎	L - U	02-06-2027	18 ♒	S - A
09-12-2015	20 ♍	S	02-20-2027	02 ♍	L - p
09-27-2015	05 ♈	L - U	08-02-2027	10 ♌	S - T
03-08-2016	19 ♓	S - T	08-17-2027	24 ♒	L - p
03-23-2016	03 ♎	L - p	01-11-2028	21 ♋	L - U
08-18-2016	25 ♒	L - p	01-26-2028	06 ♒	S - A
09-01-2016	09 ♍	S - A	07-06-2028	15 ♑	L - U
09-16-2016	24 ♓	L - p	07-21-2028	30 ♋	S - T
02-10-2017	22 ♌	L - p	12-31-2028	11 ♋	L - U
02-26-2017	08 ♓	S - A	01-14-2029	25 ♑	S
08-07-2017	15 ♒	L - U	06-11-2029	21 ♊	S
08-21-2017	29 ♌	S - T	06-25-2029	05 ♑	L - U
01-31-2018	11 ♌	L - U	07-11-2029	20 ♋	S
02-15-2018	27 ♒	S	12-05-2029	14 ♐	S
07-12-2018	21 ♋	S	12-20-2029	29 ♊	L - U
07-27-2018	05 ♒	L - U	05-31-2030	11 ♊	S - A
08-11-2018	19 ♌	S	06-15-2030	25 ♐	L - U
01-05-2019	15 ♑	S	11-24-2030	03 ♐	S - T
01-20-2019	01 ♌	L - U	12-09-2030	18 ♊	L - p
07-02-2019	11 ♋	S - T	05-06-2031	16 ♏	L - p
07-16-2019	24 ♑	L - U	05-21-2031	00 ♊	S - A
12-25-2019	04 ♑	S - A	06-05-2031	14 ♐	L - p
01-10-2020	20 ♋	L - p	10-30-2031	07 ♉	L - p
06-05-2020	16 ♐	L - p	11-14-2031	22 ♏	S - T
06-20-2020	00 ♋	S - A	04-25-2032	06 ♏	L - U
07-04-2020	14 ♑	L - p	05-09-2032	19 ♉	S - A
11-30-2020	09 ♊	L - p	10-18-2032	26 ♈	L - U
12-14-2020	23 ♐	S - T	11-02-2032	11 ♏	S
05-26-2021	05 ♐	L - U	03-30-2033	10 ♈	S - T
06-10-2021	20 ♊	S - A	04-14-2033	25 ♎	L - U
11-19-2021	27 ♉	L - U	09-23-2033	01 ♎	S
12-04-2021	12 ♐	S - T	10-08-2033	15 ♈	L - U
04-30-2022	10 ♉	S	03-20-2034	30 ♓	S - T
05-15-2022	25 ♏	L - U	04-03-2034	14 ♎	L - p
10-25-2022	02 ♏	S	09-12-2034	20 ♍	S - A
11-08-2022	16 ♉	L - U	09-27-2034	05 ♈	L - U
04-19-2023	30 ♈	S - T	02-22-2035	04 ♍	L - p
05-05-2023	15 ♏	L - p	03-09-2035	19 ♓	S - A
10-14-2023	21 ♎	S - A	08-18-2035	26 ♒	L - U
10-28-2023	05 ♉	L - U	09-01-2035	09 ♍	S - T
03-25-2024	05 ♎	L - p	02-11-2036	23 ♌	L - U
04-08-2024	19 ♈	S - T	02-26-2036	08 ♓	S
09-17-2024	26 ♓	L - U	07-23-2036	01 ♌	S
10-02-2024	10 ♎	S - A	08-06-2036	15 ♒	L - U
03-13-2025	24 ♍	L - U	08-21-2036	29 ♌	S
03-29-2025	09 ♈	S	01-16-2037	27 ♑	S

Date	Degree/Sign	Eclipse Type	Date	Degree/Sign	Eclipse Type
01-31-2037	12 ♌	L - U	03-13-2044	24 ♍	L - U
07-12-2037	21 ♋	S - T	08-22-2044	01 ♍	S - T
07-26-2037	04 ♒	L - U	09-07-2044	15 ♓	L - U
01-05-2038	15 ♑	S - A	02-16-2045	29 ♒	S - A
01-20-2038	01 ♌	L - p	03-03-2045	13 ♍	L - p
06-16-2038	26 ♐	L - p	08-12-2045	20 ♌	S - T
07-02-2038	11 ♋	S - A	08-27-2045	05 ♓	L - p
07-16-2038	24 ♑	L - p	01-22-2046	03 ♌	L - U
12-11-2038	20 ♊	L - p	02-05-2046	17 ♒	S - A
12-25-2038	04 ♑	S - T	07-17-2046	26 ♑	L - U
06-06-2039	16 ♐	L - U	08-02-2046	10 ♌	S - T
06-21-2039	00 ♋	S - A	01-11-2047	22 ♋	L - U
11-30-2039	08 ♊	L - U	01-25-2047	06 ♒	S
12-15-2039	24 ♐	S - T	06-23-2047	02 ♋	S
05-10-2040	21 ♉	S	07-07-2047	15 ♑	L - U
05-26-2040	06 ♐	L - U	07-22-2047	00 ♌	S
11-04-2040	13 ♏	S	12-16-2047	25 ♐	S
11-18-2040	27 ♉	L - U	12-31-2047	11 ♋	L - U
04-30-2041	10 ♉	S - T	06-11-2048	21 ♊	S - A
05-15-2041	26 ♏	L - U	06-25-2048	05 ♑	L - U
10-24-2041	02 ♏	S - A	12-05-2048	14 ♐	S - T
11-07-2041	16 ♉	L - U	12-19-2048	29 ♊	L - p
04-05-2042	16 ♎	L - p	05-17-2049	27 ♏	L - p
04-19-2042	00 ♉	S - T	05-31-2049	11 ♊	S - A
09-29-2042	06 ♈	L - p	06-15-2049	25 ♐	L - p
10-13-2042	21 ♎	S - A	11-09-2049	18 ♉	L - p
10-28-2042	06 ♉	L - p	11-24-2049	03 ♐	S - T
03-25-2043	05 ♎	L - U	05-06-2050	17 ♏	L - U
04-09-2043	20 ♈	S	05-20-2050	00 ♊	S - T
09-18-2043	26 ♓	L - U	10-29-2050	07 ♉	L - U
10-02-2043	10 ♎	S	11-14-2050	22 ♏	S
02-28-2044	10 ♓	S			

chapter sixteen

Special Points

The following special points can be used in conjunction with other prediction techniques. These points offer specialized information when, on occasion, they become highlighted or prominent in the chart. The special points are the Pleiades, the Aries Point, Saturn Chasing the Moon, and the Vertex. The symbolism of each of these special points is discussed in this chapter.

The Pleiades

A fixed star cluster known as the Pleiades is located in the last degree of Taurus. It is also called Alcyone. Fixed stars were routinely used in the earlier days of astrological chart delineation. The cluster known as the Pleiades consists of seven stars. The leading star, Alcyone is the first of seven sisters, one of which is lost and invisible. Besides Alcyone, the stars are named Maia, Electra, Merope, Taygete, Celaeno, and Sterope.[1] The group is often referred to as the "weeping sisters," for when this degree falls in conjunction with the rising degree, the Midheaven, or another significant point, tragedies ranging from blindness to disgrace and ruin, or even violent death have been associated with these stars. Accidents to the face are noted and this fixed star group has a Moon/Mars connotation. The Pleiades often bring something to weep about.

The Pleiades are mentioned in *Planets in Composites*, by Robert Hand, as a rather extreme point of affliction if on the MC or otherwise emphasized. As it is traditionally associated with a violent death, Hand uses the word "tragedy" in connection with this point.[2]

In the *Encyclopedia of Medical Astrology*, Dr. Howard Cornell refers to the influence of the Pleiades as connected to many of the evils that befall humanity if they rise with the Lights or are directed to the Ascendant. If rising in a nativity, the Pleiades are associated with blindness. If, at the same time, the Sun opposes the Ascendant or Mars, a tragic or violent death may occur.[3]

As a brief example, David A. Paterson, who began serving as New York Governor in 2008, was born on May 20, 1954. This places his Sun in the degree of the Pleiades. Pluto squares his Sun, and, although a time of birth is not available, his Sun may very well be rising. At the age of three months, he contracted an ear infection that spread to his optic nerve, leaving him with no sight in his left eye and severely limited sight in his right. He is the first legally blind governor of any state. Another interesting point is that after he was sworn into office, March 17, 2008, on his next birthday he was admitted to the hospital, complaining about migraine headaches. He was diagnosed with acute glaucoma. With the Sun again in the degree of the Pleiades, a Full Moon in Scorpio may have been what triggered the migraines.

The degree of the Pleiades has been found to be quite revealing when occupied by a planet in any kind of chart. There is remarkable evidence of its particular significance. Much depends on the type of chart it is found in, as well as the planet occupying the point. While not always an indication of violent death or tragedy to follow, it has been found to be associated with misfortune of various kinds and is frequently linked to the health, well-being, or safety of the individual. These results have been found in both progressed and return charts.

A planet in this degree appears to be somewhat debilitated. A planet in opposition to the Pleiades, or from any other angle, is not affected unless there is also a planet or significant point conjunct the Pleiades. It does hold more significance if on an angle, and even more if also conjunct a planet. Following are some illustrative notes regarding the point.

A troubled young woman has her natal Moon within a conjunction to the Pleiades and several planets afflict it. The Moon is her ruler with Cancer rising. With her Moon closely opposing Mercury and Venus, while in a close square to Mars, there are themes of mental confusion and instability. She seems to attract unfortunate events and questionable acquaintances that border on the corrupt. Highly rebellious, she puts herself into unwise and dangerous situations. Later she seems unable to recognize that she has brought about the very conditions in which she finds herself. Many of her family and friends have given up on helping her, and she is unpopular even with them (afflicted Moon). Motherhood is strongly tied to the Moon, and abortion followed two unwanted pregnancies with her 5th house rule, Venus, opposing her Moon, while she lost custody of her other children. This may be most significant as it relates to the degree of the Pleiades. The term "tragic" does seem to apply. Although the condition of the Moon reflects many of these things, her Moon conjoined with the Pleiades may reflect the extent of the troubles.

Angie, an astrology hobbyist, noticed that her progressed Moon was approaching the degree of the Pleiades. She wondered what it would bring. She was struggling as it was: finishing a novel, teaching, writing a critical essay, and trying to get her son into college. She was having a tough time financially. Angie looked back to see what had happened the previous time her progressed Moon passed through the degree of the Pleiades some twenty-nine years earlier. She was thirteen at the time, and her mother, who was putting herself through graduate school, had to send Angie and her three siblings to live with their grandmother for a while because she was unable to afford a home large enough for all of them near her school. It was not until right after Angie moved, during the month of the Moon's passage through the degree of the Pleiades, that she realized

a similar scenario had repeated. Due to limited finances, her son was to stay with his grandmother until he got his dorm room, while Angie stayed in a small family-owned studio to complete her work. In each case there had been the loss of a family home and some tears from the pain of a separation, but with a degree of gains as a result. The Moon relates to family and domestic themes.

During a Solar Return period that showed Mercury conjunct the Pleiades and Pluto in opposition, this male individual sustained a fall at work, injuring his knee. The result was a later operation on his knee. Mercury went retrograde shortly following the return, and upon its return to the degree of the Pleiades, the operation took place. At the time of the surgery, the Moon, Mars, and returning Mercury were transiting within a conjunction of the Pleiades. Obviously, his Solar Return Mercury on the point was associated with misfortune involving movement or transport; in this case, injury to one of the body's pairs, his knee. The opposition to Pluto suggested the need for the knee surgery.

More evidence comes from another Solar Return chart in which the Moon was exactly conjunct the Pleiades. During that year, this female individual came down with a bad case of the flu. She never fully recovered from the flu and was eventually diagnosed with fibromyalgia. This illness continues to plague her.

Similarly, a woman diagnosed with breast cancer had the Moon on the Midheaven and in the degree of the Pleiades in her Solar Return prior to her diagnosis. She eventually made a complete recovery.

In another female case, the Solar Return Moon was conjunct the Pleiades, near Saturn, and forming a Full Moon, with Mars conjunct the Sun. The first major event at the onset of the Solar Return was a spousal separation, the ramifications of which led to the separation from a group as well. The Full Moon is operating true to form in this instance. Later, during the same year, the individual's back went out, requiring her to wear a brace. Later a root canal was needed. There were other minor accidents and upsets, but the main theme for the year was one of domestic disharmony. A couple of years later, the Pleiades fell on the cusp of her Solar Return 7th house, opposite the Sun and Mercury on the Ascendant. During this return period, the woman's shaky marriage ended in divorce.

Though not in every case, in several of these examples, the term tragic is descriptive. While the rest of the chart indications should provide sufficient information to read the chart without considering the Pleiades, it does appear to hold particular significance in giving something to weep about.

Near the beginning of the new millennium, the Pleiades began to move into the sign of Gemini, so at this point the seven sisters are straddling the cusp between the signs Taurus and Gemini. Alcyone has just entered Gemini. We'll be three-quarters into the century before Alcyone reaches one degree of Gemini.

The Aries Point

Zero-degree Aries is a point of spectacular outrushing energy. It is called the Aries Point and is representative of all four of the cardinal signs and the most dynamic activities associated with each.

The degree is associated with fame, new undertakings, and coming before the world in a very public way. While it does not always guarantee fame, it is an extremely dynamic point and does guarantee that events surrounding the individual will receive special interest from the public, who often become caught up in the affairs of the individual without previous desire or inclination to do so.

The first degree of the remaining cardinal signs works similarly, automatically inferring activities and events associated with their particular signs, and any time a planet or significant point is found in one of these dynamic degrees, certain particulars can be counted on to take place. There is some interaction with the world at large if a planet occupies 0° Aries, 0° Cancer, 0° Libra, or 0° Capricorn.

Having one of these degrees become active by virtue of holding a planet signifies that personal issues are about to arise, represented by the first cardinal sign, Aries. Private issues are activated, as indicated by the second cardinal sign, Cancer. The way one relates to others is activated as represented by the third cardinal sign, Libra. Finally, the way the public perceives the individual is due some attention as indicated by the last cardinal sign, Capricorn. Having just one planet in one of these degrees signifies all of these things. It is as if there is simultaneous stimulation to the four angles of the chart. An event that begins to transpire in association with one area quickly escalates to cause a domino effect, bringing activity and changes to each of these personal areas in turn.

Whether found in a natal, progressed, or return chart, outside experts will be involved or some publicity will occur involving the planet and sign in which it is found. Events associated with the placement and planet will extend outward and beyond an individual's usual surroundings. Other people are often quite compelled to become involved in the affairs of the individual.

There is some difference in the magnitude of the events associated with these degrees depending on the type of chart in which they are found to be prominent.

The natal chart would show potential events occurring over a lifetime at times of stimulation. With a natal planet in one of the Aries point degrees, the individual may have the opportunity to make a big impact in the world and become famous as a result, like Walt Disney who had Neptune at 0° of Cancer. Neptune signifies his talents involving illusion and fantasy, and the sign indicates family themes. His particular talent has had a positive impact in the lives of families for generations. For those people who have one of these degrees occupied by a planet in the natal chart, the progressions and transits to it work very dynamically, and it seems they are constantly involved in major changes and eventful situations. John McCain has his natal North Node at 0° Capricorn, and he has led a dynamic life, having quite a profound impact on the masses from his career in government and politics.

The Aries point becoming prominent in the progressed chart also appears to be quite dynamic. It may be a significant factor, showing a time of climax for the current trends. A situation has developed to a point of maturation, and new beginnings will follow whatever transpires now.

The nature of the particular planet positioned in the degree indicates the type of activity or event that will follow. For example, if the sign is Aries or the planet is Mars that is tenanting the degree, the outsiders who are called in might be of a masculine nature or connected to affairs ruled by Mars. In chapter 2, a couple of examples are illustrated in the progressed chart. One is when Annie was kidnapped, calling for police intervention. When her house burned, Mars was a factor in the formula, calling for firefighters. In both cases, the initial event had a ripple effect, impacting all of the most personal areas as indicated by the first degree of each cardinal sign. The first effects surrounded her personal physical safety, followed by new developments in the areas of home and family, relationships, and status.

If 0° Capricorn holds a planet, or if Saturn is the planet occupying an Aries point, then an issue of authority is indicated. In Annie's kidnapping there were also planets at 0° Capricorn, reflecting the involvement of authority figures. Saturn signifies the father, usually the most authoritative parent. And, in this case, Saturn symbolized the judge who decided who should have custody of Annie.

With 0° Cancer holding the planet or the Moon in one of the Aries point degrees, it is a family issue or events surrounding the home that will be taking place. The Moon is also symbolic of the mother. If 0° Libra is occupied by a planet or if Venus is the planet occupying one of the Aries degrees, relationships are a point of dynamic activity. This might indicate

events impacting a close partner or loved one.

There will always be a personal matter that becomes a point of interest, often calling for the help or interference from those who would not normally get involved. The rest of the chart should help to clarify the matter at hand.

The location by house where the stimulated Aries Point is found is significant as well. The planet, sign, and house must be blended. For instance, when his mother drowned him in 1994, little three-year-old Michael Smith had his progressed Moon at 0° Capricorn in the Midheaven. The Moon signifies both the mother and the drowning that made headlines. Capricorn signifies the need for authority figures to get involved. The public reputation of the mother was under scrutiny and her affairs were made public. The Moon in an Aries point degree in the Midheaven showed the overwhelming publicity and interest into the whole family situation, as well as Michael's publicity.

If this point is found to be prominent in the return chart, the events are of a more temporary nature, but still quite significant in the life of the individual. Similar as before, the sign, the planet, and the house are significant in the interpretation and must be blended. Having an Aries degree on a house cusp in a return chart is also informative about the matters of the particular house. There may be more dynamic activity, always involving interaction with people outside the usual circle, and regarding the matters of the house. For instance, research has shown that an Aries point degree on the cusp of the 9th house has been related to legal matters on many occasions. In a few cases, it was divorce. On the 7th house cusp, it has corresponded with both marriage and divorce. On the 11th house cusp, it corresponded with some spectacular events involving a friend. On the cusp of the 5th house, it has coincided with pregnancy and childbirth, and on the 10th house cusp with new careers. By considering the aspects to the house cusp, the condition and aspects of the house ruler, and the remaining chart factors, it can be determined whether the event to come is one that will be desirable.

The Aries point never fails to provide an exciting treasure of information in chart readings.

Saturn Chasing the Moon

One of the first things to suspect when an individual appears to be going through an especially long and difficult time period is that there is an affliction of long duration from transiting Saturn to the progressed Moon. This is a condition called "Saturn Chasing the Moon."

Saturn/Moon afflictions are serious and depressing times. They nearly always coincide with some hardship(s) for an individual. Since the progressed Moon reflects personal and domestic fluctuations and Saturn represents restrictions and limitations, these combinations often indicate times of emotional lows and sad experiences of a personal nature.

Saturn's rate of travel in transit very nearly matches that of the progressing Moon, depending on how fast the Moon was traveling at birth. It takes each of them about twenty-nine years to make a complete circuit of the horoscope. There may be occasions when the transit of Saturn comes to an afflicting point of contact with the progressed Moon, showing a short-term trend of difficulties, a longer and more difficult series of experiences occurs when the movement of the progressing Moon continues to match that of Saturn's transit.

The most unfortunate aspect in the natal chart is a close square or opposition between Saturn and the Moon, if the Moon is slow in motion. In such cases the Moon progresses slowly, matching Saturn's transiting speed, and the adverse aspect can continue for years, even for a lifetime in rare cases.

While transiting Saturn may appear to be moving away from the progressed Moon while in its retrograde movement, the following direct transit brings it back into the afflicting aspect. Saturn may also appear to be moving away while in direct motion, but then during its retrograde motion returns to make an exact conjunction, square, or opposition to the progressed Moon. Thus the two get caught in a continuous conflicting aspect, and the individual gets no relief. While the term "Saturn Chasing the Moon" is most often applied to the conjunction, the same or more serious effects result when the two become linked in a continuous square or opposition. These aspects have also been termed "Saturn Hunting the Moon."

This can become a serious matter for some individuals, who may become despondent, preferring in some cases to just give up. These are very sad cases. The individual may be unable to take full advantage of opportunities that do present themselves, as shown by positive directions of the other planets during the time period. It is as though a black cloud hangs overhead, and any small achievement may be overshadowed by setbacks, disappointments, and limitations. Depression can become serious, and some individuals may even entertain the idea of suicide. One individual comes to mind who took an escape into drugs and alcohol. By the time the Saturn/Moon aspect was over, the problem of addiction had taken root, and presented its own problems.

On the positive side, the aspect may indicate a period of concentrated soul development and personal growth. If Saturn was prominent in the natal chart, it may be reflective of an older soul whose progress this life stems from situations that appear harsh to those unequipped for such a reality. The period when this aspect comes into play reflects a time of testing through trial.

Some individuals handle the aspect very well once they have adjusted to the limitations set forth. Patience and discipline are necessary. Problems might be presented for handling once and for all. With careful handling, the individual can make progressive strides similar to those associated with the more flowing Saturn/Moon aspects, such as professional recognition or a more stable domestic environment.

The configuration is an interesting one, especially when Saturn's reputation as a karmic planet is taken into consideration. The possibility for one of these extended aspects is totally dependent on the Moon's rate of speed at birth, along with the position of Saturn. So, these things are determined at birth, and the soul had a hand in the plan, even if he or she doesn't consciously remember it. If the lingering aspect does form, the choice left is in how the individual will handle it. Some come to appreciate the wisdom and growth achieved as a result of the contact, especially once it is over. At that point there may be a notice-able feeling of a weight being lifted, mixed with an appreciation for all that has been learned. It is an aspect that makes a person stronger if it doesn't do them in.

On a more auspicious note, there are also times when the progressed Moon and transiting Saturn come together in a trine or sextile. These would be very profit-able times in relation to achievement and reaching goals. When they get locked into one of these beneficial aspects, it may in-dicate an extended period of rewards. It is easy to make advancements and prog-ress in personal and professional affairs. Maybe these aspects should be called Sat-urn Shining on the Moon. Does this mean that these individuals have karmic rewards coming for past good deeds? It is pos-sible. This progressed aspect was found in the chart of Dan in chapter 8. He had the transiting Saturn and progressed Moon locked in a trine for several years up to and including the time he was given an award for bravery. It does seem that he had some elements of protection extended to him at the time he was wounded. Even more noteworthy is that the harmful situation soon turned out to bring him increased professional status and public recognition.

As always, the rest of the progressed aspects will help determine how challeng-ing or how profitable the Moon/Saturn aspect will be. If the remaining progressed

aspects are quite favorable, the condition of Saturn Chasing the Moon will likely only entail professional delays and minor personal setbacks along with mild depres-sion. The condition will be more serious if the remaining progressed aspects are chal-lenging. The natal chart must also be con-sidered. Nothing can come to pass that is not suggested in the natal chart.

The Vertex

The Vertex, which is the west end of the true east-west axis through the birthplace, is associated with experiences and encoun-ters with others over which one has little or no control. Astrology programs calcu-late the Vertex for you.

The significance of the Vertex is some-what comparable to the Descendant. This is where we attract others to fill in missing parts of ourselves, or to play those parts of ourselves that we disown.

The degree opposite the Vertex is called the Anti-vertex. It is like an auxiliary As-cendant, where we personally identify. Ed-ward Johndro pioneered research to these points, noting the quality of destiny asso-ciated with each. Similar to the Ascendant, Johndro called the Anti-vertex the Electric Ascendant, and observed that while the Ascendant shows free choice and voli-tional life, the Electric Ascendant showed no choice and involuntary actions.

Later, Charles Jayne convinced Johndro that the Vertex showed the greater emphasis as a point of fate. Not only encounters with others, but also experiential encounters are noted with the Vertex. It represents appointments with destiny. Besides the lunar nodes, the Vertex is a most "fateful" indicator.

The Vertex appears to be a point of fated meetings and karmic interactions. It is often active in ties between individuals who seem to have a relationship of a fateful quality, or who feel they may have known one another in a previous incarnation. To illustrate, a middle-aged couple met and immediately felt that they had known one another forever. Their relationship developed as if they had, and did not much surprise those who knew them by the speed in which it progressed. Those around them commented on how they acted like an old married couple right from the start, and that it would seem strange if they were not together. In this case, his Sun is closely conjunct her Vertex. The woman says that it felt as if their souls had always been holding hands, and that they had just finally met in the flesh. The man says he felt as if he already knew everything about her from the moment they met. They were engaged within two weeks, and when they married five months later, the transiting North Node was exactly conjunct her Vertex and his Sun. This further reflects a re-

lationship where the couple is destined to experience major life events together due to the common ground of his Sun and her Vertex.

The relationship between Lee and Trish (see chapter 3) shows that his natal Venus was conjunct her Vertex, a powerful connection to draw them together. In this case, even though other planetary configurations indicated problems, they still wanted to be together. This may be a revealing factor in relationships between couples who have otherwise incompatible backgrounds, beliefs, ages, and so on.

While the Vertex seems to be very significant in terms of relationships, it also appears to be a point of destiny or karma for the individual in more personal terms as well.

In several instances the Solar or Lunar Return chart prior to death contains the Vertex of the individual on an important point. It appears frequently that the Vertex is rising in these returns.

Grant Lewi, a famous and inspiring astrologer and author, had his natal Vertex rising in both his Solar and Lunar Return prior to his death. Evangeline Adams had her natal Vertex appearing on the Ascendant of her converse Lunar Return prior to her death. The South Node was conjunct her natal Vertex in her Solar Return prior to her death. The natal Vertex was rising in President Kennedy's Solar Return chart prior to his assassination, and several planets were transiting his Vertex in the Lunar Return before the event. In Elvis Presley's Solar Return prior to his death, Pluto conjoined his natal Vertex. The nodes were transiting his Vertex axis at the time of his death. Of course there were also other disturbing indicators in each of these cases, and the significance of the Vertex must be considered alongside remaining features.

If the Solar Return Vertex is conjoined with a natal planet, it suggests destined experiences of personal significance. If conjoined with the Moon, for example, there may be destined events impacting the family. If Pluto is joined with the Vertex in the Solar Return, there may be fateful experiences connecting to debts, mortgages, or tax concerns. If the Vertex falls on Neptune ,there may be the need for hospitalization or some intrigue might touch the life. Falling on Mercury, a job change may be destined.

Reverse aspects also work. A Solar Return planet falling on the natal Vertex is meaningful. With Solar Return Mars conjoined with natal Vertex, there may be a conflict with someone. If the return node is conjoined with the natal Vertex this might signify very fateful events. Always check for verification from other chart features to refine your interpretation. For any one event, many aspects will show it.

This point is also revealing when the Solar or Lunar Return Vertex is conjoined with another return planet. In that case, note the symbolism of the planet that is conjunct the Vertex, which may represent a destined appointment of a specific nature. There may be a destined partnership if the planet is Venus, an appointment with an agent if the planet is Mercury, with a publisher if the planet is Jupiter, with an unusual individual if Uranus, or with an authority figure if the planet is Saturn.

Check for any combination. Then watch for the transit of the Moon or any other planet over the pair, which may bring important developments. The Vertex is a fascinating point, worthy of attention.

1. Nicholas DeVore. *Encyclopedia of Astrology* (New York: Philosophical Library, 1947), p 95.

2. Robert Hand, *Planets in Composite* (Westchester, PA: Para Research Inc. 1975), p 59.

3. Howard L. Cornell, *Encyclopedia of Medical Astrology* (Third Revised Edition published jointly by Llewellyn Publications, St. Paul, MN. and Samuel Weiser, Inc. New York, n.d.).

Bibliography

Adams, Evangeline. *The Bowl of Heaven*. New York: Dodd, Mead and Company, Inc. 1926. Santa Fe, NM: Sun Books, 1995. An inspirational history of Evangeline Adams. Techniques and predictions are shared.

Davison, Ronald C. *Cycles of Destiny*. Dartford, Kent, UK: Aquarian Press, 1990. Solar and Lunar Returns are detailed. Usage of the precessed and non-precessed methods, as well as both forward motion and converse motion of chart erection.

———. *The Technique of Prediction*. Romford,Essex, UK: 1990. The progressed chart is detailed.

DeVore, Nicholas. *Encyclopedia of Astrology*. New York: Philosophical Library, 1947. Information on eclipses, on fixed points in the zodiac, Horary techniques, and much more. An excellent reference.

Hand, Robert. *Horoscope Symbols*. Westchester, PA: Whitford Press, 1981. Good all-around astrological basics are provided. An informative reference.

———. *Planets in Composite: Analyzing Human Relationships*. Atglen, PA: Schiffer Publishin, 1980.

Koparkar, Mohan, Ph.D. *Lunar Nodes*. Rochester, NY: Mohan Enterprises, 1977. Interpretations of the nodes as they are combined with other planets by aspect, both natal and transiting.

Milburn, Leigh Hope. *Progressed Horoscope Simplified*. First printing 1928. Tempe, AZ: AFA, 1989. Good basic, cookbook-style descriptions of the progressed combinations and aspects.

Shea, Mary. *Planets in Solar Returns*. San Diego, CA: ACS Publications, 1992. Basic meaning of the planets as they appear in particular houses of the Solar Returns.

Teal, Celeste. *Eclipses, Predicting World Events & Personal Transformation*. Woodbury, MN: Llewellyn Worldwide, 2006. Discusses the many various features of eclipses and what they mean: Solar, Lunar, sign, ruler, North or South Node influence, house position, and more.

———. *Identifying Planetary Triggers*. Woodbury, MN: Llewellyn Worldwide, 2000. Predictive techniques using planetary return charts. Discusses Solar and Lunar returns as well as the Mercury, Venus, Mars, Jupiter, and Saturn returns.

———. *Lunar Nodes, Discover Your Soul's Karmic Mission*. Woodbury, MN: Llewellyn Worldwide, 2008. Learn to interpret your nodes' positions and each of their aspects. Provides descriptions for nodal contacts in the natal, progressed, return charts, and from transits. Provides nodal connections in synastry and more. A comprehensive reference on the Lunar Nodes.

Glossary

Afflicted: A stressful aspect, such as the square or opposition. Mars or Saturn with another planet in conjunction is sometimes an afflicted aspect, depending on their placement and aspects made to the pair. Associated with challenging or harmful conditions.

Angles: Houses 1, 4, 7, and 10 are the angular houses. The cusps of these form the angles of the chart. These are high points of energy manifestation. Conditions are ideal at these points for planetary energy to manifest.

Angular: A planet on an angle is said to be angular.

Aries Point: The first degree of the zodiac, 0º Aries. It is a point of extreme outrushing energy and representative of one's relationship with the world at large. See Chapter 16.

Ascendant: The start of the 1st house; rules the demeanor and physical body.

Aspect: The relationships of the planets to one another; easy or difficult.

Benefic: Jupiter and Venus are planets of fortune and benefits, therefore called benefic. The Sun can usually be deemed a benefic as well.

Cadent: Houses 3, 6, 9, and 12 are called cadent houses. A subordinate position or condition of obscurity is associated with the cadent houses. They are often linked with transitional periods.

Cardinal: Aries, Cancer, Libra, Capricorn, the signs that correspond with the seasons, are called Cardinal. These are signs of high energy, initiative, and activity, similar to the angles of the chart.

Common: The mutable signs are also called common. Gemini, Virgo, Sagittarius, and Pisces are the common signs.

Conjunction: Two or more planets within eight to ten degrees of one another in the natal chart. In the progressed chart, this orb must be reduced to one degree, unless the Sun or Moon is involved, in which case the aspect extends to one and a half degrees. The conjunction is a major aspect that joins the energetic forces of two planets, either harmoniously or inharmoniously, according to the natures of the planets involved. The closer the two planets are to one another, the stronger the aspect. Aspects to the conjunction from other bodies must also be considered to interpret the aspect.

Converse: A point in time prior to birth. Converse calculations are done identically to direct or forward motion calculations, except they correspond with the same amount of time in reverse direction or prior to birth.

Critical degree: The first degree of Aries, Cancer, Libra, and Capricorn are critical degrees. These are also called Aries Point degrees. See chapter 16.

Decan: A subdivision of a sign. See chapter 6.

Delineation: An explanation or discussion of aspects and planetary configurations in a natal chart or any type of chart.

Descendant: The 7th house cusp. A relational point associated with marriage, partnerships, and other people.

Eastern: Houses 10 through 3 inclusive. The left side of the horoscope wheel.

Ephemeris: A book, table, or list that gives the daily positions of the planets for long increments.

Fated: Events that take place of either a positive or negative nature that appear to be brought about by a series of events having little to do with actions taken by the individual.

Fixed: The fixed signs are Taurus, Leo, Scorpio, or Aquarius.

Hemisphere: Half of the horoscope wheel. Either the eastern (left) or western (right) half of the horoscope or above or below the horizon.

Horary: Meaning "of the hour," the yes or no answer to a question can be found by drawing a chart of the heavens at the moment of a sincere question and a great need to know the answer. A specialized branch of astrology, there are specific rules to apply when working with Horary charts. In this work, one of the principles of Horary is used to determine the type of experience most likely to manifest in the life of the individual in the immediate future. See chapter 2.

Horizon: The division of the horoscope through the 1st and 7th houses. The 1st house cusp is the eastern horizon, and the 7th house cusp is the western horizon.

Karma: The rewards for past deeds, whether positive or negative. Karma is an objective, impersonal balancing mechanism existing in the universal spirit.

Lights: The Sun and Moon. The Lights are commonly referred to as planets in astrology.

Luminaries: The Sun and Moon.

Malefic: Planets that are associated with trouble are termed malefic. Mars and Saturn frequently correspond with stressful or harmful conditions, therefore they are called malefics. Mars and Saturn are the traditional malefics although Pluto and Uranus may also manifest as malefic at certain times.

Mutable: The mutable signs are Gemini, Virgo, Sagittarius, and Pisces. They are changeable, versatile signs.

Mutual reception: When two planets occupy the sign ruled by the other. For example, Sun in Aries and Mars in Leo. There can also be mutual reception by house. If Pluto is in Leo in the 11th house and the Sun in a Pluto ruled 2nd house, this forms a mutual reception by house. Mutual receptions often function as if the two planets are in a conjunction—they have similar interests and goals.

Nativity: The birth chart or natal horoscope. The planetary configurations at the moment of birth.

Nodes: The Moon's nodes are not tangible bodies, but a point of intersection in space. The intersection of the Moon's path with the plane of the ecliptic creates the opposite points of the North and South Nodes. Shows where something might happen at certain times.

Non-precessed: Precession of the equinoxes has not been taken into consideration in calculations. In a Solar Return, the Sun would be at exactly the same degree and minute as in the natal chart. See Part Two.

Opposition: A one-hundred-eighty-degree angle between two planets is an opposition aspect. It is a major aspect that is challenging and inharmonious, often representing separations or stressful encounters with others.

Orb: The allowance of space between two bodies that are forming an aspect. The standard orb for natal aspects is from seven to ten degrees for the conjunction, square, trine, and opposition. The Sun and Moon are given slightly more of an allowance than the other planets. If within orb, the aspect is influential.

The orb of allowance for progressed aspects is greatly reduced, with only one to one and a half degrees permitted, either applying or separating. Again, the Sun and Moon are allowed the greater orb.

Pleiades: A fixed star cluster in the last degree of Taurus. Associated with weeping and misfortune. See chapter 16.

Polarities: Opposing houses share a polarity or relationship. For example, the 2nd house rules the individual's personal income and earning potential, while the 8th house represents the partner's income and resources shared with another. Both are financial houses or houses of resource. The 3rd house and 9th house both correspond to ideas and travel. The 3rd house rules elementary studies, while the 9th house rules advanced education. Travel is close to home in the 3rd house, while longer journeys are associated with the 9th house.

Precessed: Chart calculations have taken the precession of the equinoxes into consideration. Some astrologers prefer this method when running return charts; astrology programs offer this method for calculating return charts. When the Solar Return is calculated this way, the Sun will advance very slightly from the exact degree and minute it held in the birth chart.

Predominance: Several planets in one sign or house. This puts a predominate focus on the matters of the house and sign. Many planets in fire signs would also reflect a predominance of fire, and be very dynamic in action.

Progressed: Secondary progressions are the configurations of the nativity recalculated for any time following birth based on a day of ephemeral time for each year of life. Thus, the Sun will progress forward one degree for each year of the individual's life. The rest of the planets also progress, as does the Ascendant and Midheaven. Aspects formed between progressed and natal planets are informative of the trends and likely events for any point in time. See chapter 1.

Radical: The natal or birth chart, and the condition of the planets at birth.

Radix: The natal chart or birth chart, and the condition of the planets at birth.

Rising: The sign as well as any planet near the 1st house cusp or on the eastern horizon may be said to be rising.

Saturn Chasing the Moon: When transiting Saturn comes into a conflicting aspect with the progressing Moon and the two remain in the aspect for an extended period of time it is called Saturn Chasing the Moon, often bringing hardships. See chapter 16 for details.

Sextile: A sixty-degree angle between two planets is a sextile. The sextile is an easy, flowing aspect, representing opportunities.

Square: A ninety-degree angle between two planets. A major aspect that is challenging, inharmonious, and stressful. These are the most destabilizing and demanding aspects, requiring attention. Some squares are more stressful than others. Malefic planets in square represent much greater challenges and tension than squares involving the benefic planets.

Stellium: A grouping of four or more planets in which each planet is within orb of conjunction to one or more of the other planets in the group. A Stellium is a multiple conjunction that usually falls in one sign or one house, bringing an immense emphasis to the matters signified.

Succeedant: Houses 2, 5, 8, and 11 are termed the Succeedant houses. They are financial houses.

Trine: A one-hundred-and-twenty-degree angle between two points. The trine is a major aspect, representing harmony, ease, and sometimes fortune, but it is undemanding of action.

Vertex: A point in the western hemisphere created by the intersection of the prime vertical with the ecliptic. Appears in many cases to be associated with encounters of a fateful nature, either with people or circumstances. Researched originally by L. Edward Johndro. See chapter 16.

Western: Houses 4 through 9, inclusive. The right side of a horoscope wheel.

Index

Lunar Nodes
Discover Your Soul's Karmic Mission
Celeste Teal

Are you an old soul or a young soul? Will this life be filled with cosmic blessings or karmic sacrifices? The story of your evolving soul—through the past, present, and future—can be read in your lunar nodes.

No other book on the market offers such in-depth information on the lunar nodes—the points where the moon's orbit crosses the sun's path. Natioally renowned astrologer Celeste Teal explores numerous ways to interpret the north and south nodes—in relation to houses, ruling planets, aspects, signs, the Part of Fortune, the Vertex, and more—in the natal chart. As your karmic path is revealed, you'll learn which personality traits to leave behind, where spiritual growth is needed, and where opportunity for rewards may be found. This comprehensive guide will also help you gain insights into relationships, make predictions, and understand how fate may be impacting your life.

978-0-7387-1337-3, 240 pp., 7½ x 9⅛ $24.99

To order, call 1-877-NEW-WRLD
Prices subject to change without notice
Order at Llewellyn.com 24 hours a day, 7 days a week!

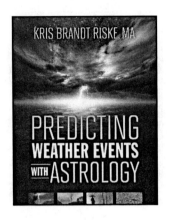

Predicting Weather Events with Astrology
Kris Brandt Riske, MA

Discover how to predict large weather events, from hurricanes and tornadoes to droughts and floods, with astrology as your guide. Using past examples of what was in the stars when major events occurred and sample calculations for the future, Llewellyn's bestselling astrology author explains how you can chart weather events.

Predicting Weather Events with Astrology features an extensive collection of techniques for forecasting weather that will occur weeks, months, or years in advance. By studying the planets and their aspects, solar ingresses and lunar phases, and latitude and longitude, you can generate predictions for large weather events happening at any time, any place. Ideal for intermediate astrologers and weather enthusiasts, this book is a valuable guide to astrometeorology.

978-0-7387-4158-1, 240 pp., 7½ x 9⅛ $18.99

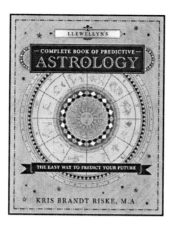

Llewellyn's Complete Book of Predictive Astrology
The Easy Way to Predict Your Future
Kris Brandt Riske, MA

Being able to forecast your future gives you a remarkable edge. Whether it's taking advantage of approaching opportunities or preparing for challenges that are heading your way, predictive astrology helps you maximize your innate potential—and make choices that will lead to a more satisfying life.

The perfect companion to *Llewellyn's Complete Book of Astrology*, popular astrologer Kris Brandt Riske lends her signature easy-to-understand style to this definitive guide to predictive astrology. Step by step, she lays out clear instructions for performing each major predictive technique, including solar arcs, progressions, transits, lunar cycles, and planetary returns. She also provides a basic introduction to horary astrology, the method used to obtain answers to specific questions.

Discover how to read all elements of a predictive chart and pinpoint when changes in your career, relationships, finances, and other important areas of life are on the horizon. To make learning even easier, this astrology book includes examples that illustrate major events in the lives of the author's clients as well as celebrities such as Marilyn Monroe, Jimmy Carter, Martha Stewart, and Pamela Anderson.

978-0-7387-2755-4, 288 pp., 8 x 10 $16.95

To order, call 1-877-NEW-WRLD
Prices subject to change without notice
Order at Llewellyn.com 24 hours a day, 7 days a week!

Saturn Cycles
Mapping Changes in Your Life
Wendell C. Perry

Would you like to get a clear picture of the changes and challenges in every area of your life, today and in the future? Now you can predict and prepare for significant life events, make positive choices, and enjoy a journey of self-discovery—simply by mapping Saturn's movement through your natal chart.

Written in a down-to-earth style with a primer for beginners, this book makes an invaluable astrological tool accessible and interesting to all levels of astrologers. Learn how to piece together the ups and downs of every stage of life, from childhood to adulthood. See how Saturn influences your life as it makes aspects to specific points in your natal chart, such as the Midheaven, Ascendant, Imum Coeli, and Descendant.

The easy-to-follow methods of charting Saturn transits are brought to life through fascinating historical and biographical case studies of two dozen famous people, such as Oprah Winfrey, Bill Clinton, and Britney Spears.

978-0-7387-1493-6, 336 pp., 6 x 9 $27.95

Sun Signs & Soul Mates
An Astrological Guide to Relationships
Linda George

Understanding your relationships through astrology is a way to reach deeply and insightfully into the territory of your soul.

Today's overly materialistic and ego-centered world makes it difficult to recognize our inner selves, let alone connect on a spiritual level with another person. Thankfully, astrology reveals the true patterns in ourselves and in others.

Evolutionary astrologer Linda George looks at the nature of the soul and relationships through the lens of astrology, exploring the lighter and darker sides of the twelve Sun signs of the zodiac. She reveals the compatibility potential for each pairing and offers entertaining and insightful relationship clues to help you better relate to your partner. Learn about each Sun sign's strengths, challenges, and behavioral quirks. From deciding whether to date that flirtatious Gemini to identifying your soul's fundamental needs, *Sun Signs & Soul Mates* will help you understand yourself—and your partner—more completely.

978-0-7387-1558-2, 240 pp., 6 x 9 $17.95

Astrology for Beginners
A Simple Way to Read Your Chart
Joann Hampar

Getting a glimpse of your own astrological chart isn't a challenge these days. The tough part is finding meaning in this complex diagram of symbols.

In *Astrology for Beginners*, Joann Hampar shows that interpreting your birth chart is actually easy. Emphasizing a practical approach, this step-by-step guide takes you effortlessly through the language of astrological symbols. As each chapter unfolds, a new realm of your horoscope will be revealed, including chart patterns, zodiac signs, houses, planets, and aspects. By the last lesson, you'll be able to read and interpret your chart—what originally looked like a jumble of symbols—and gain valuable insight into yourself and others.

978-0-7387-1106-5, 240 pp., 6 x 9 $14.95

Aspects

A New Approach to Understanding the Planetary Relationships in Your Chart

ROBIN ANTEPARA

Planetary aspects—the dynamic relationships and energy exchanges between planets—can influence birth charts in profound ways. Picking up where sun sign astrology leaves off, aspects open up new dimensions in understanding how the stars affect us.

This innovative guide challenges the conventional notion that certain planetary relationships (squares, oppositions, and conjunctions) are "bad," while harmonious ones (sextiles and trines) are "good." Using plain language, Robin Antepara explores both types and explains how each is important. Her down-to-earth, lively approach includes many case histories of famous people, ranging from historical figures to celebrities. Readers will learn how Princess Diana alchemized a square between Venus and Uranus, and about Martha Stewart's problematic trine between the Sun and Mars.

978-0-7387-0928-4, 192 pp., 7½ x 9⅛ $16.95

CPSIA information can be obtained
at www.ICGtesting.com
Printed in the USA
FFOW05n1613220817